招商局文库·文献丛刊

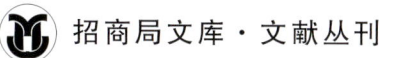

SHIPS OF CHINA MERCHANTS

招商局船谱

主 编：胡 政

CHIEF EDITOR: HU ZHENG

社会科学文献出版社
SOCIAL SCIENCES ACADEMIC PRESS (CHINA)

《招商局船谱》编委会

主　编

胡　政

副主编

谢春林　　罗志奇　　李亚东

编　委

樊　勇　　孙　波　　贺晨曦　　曲春燕　　曹　群

张建省　　涂　瑞　　肖　斌　　曾　智　　陈丹丹

EDITORIAL BOARD OF SHIPS OF CHINA MERCHANTS

Chief Editor

Hu Zheng

Deputy Chief Editor

Xie Chunlin, Luo Zhiqi, Li Yadong

Editors

Fan Yong, Sun Bo, He Chenxi

Qu Chunyan, Cao Qun, Zhang Jiansheng

Tu Rui, Xiao Bin, Zeng Zhi, Chen Dandan

航程、船与历史

招商局的公司歌开头一句就是:"问我航程有多远,一八七二到今天。"

招商局历史博物馆一进门就有一副对联:"藉洋务创于晚清擎一代商旗,始航运历经百年奠千秋基业。"

招商局是从航运起家的,因此它的第一个名字就是"轮船招商公局"。

招商局是从船起家的。在中国航海博物馆有一个船模十分突出,那便是招商局在1872年创立时购置的第一艘客货两用蒸汽动力船——"伊敦"轮,它也是中国民族航运业的第一艘现代商轮。

招商局把自己的百年历史常比作历史航程。招商局这艘轮船已走过了140余年的不平凡航程。

因此,航运业是招商局的祖业。招商局的船队是招商局最具历史意义的代表。而招商局的每一艘船又是招商局历史的承载。

从第一艘"伊敦"轮,到今天的 VLCC 超大型油轮,连接起了一条百年历史航程。

招商局史研究会搜集整理了曾在招商局历史上奋斗过的每一艘船,把它们留在历史的铭记中,把威武雄壮的招商局船队展现给人们,以船记史,以船叙史,可称得上是一种写史的创新。

因此我祝贺《招商局船谱》出版!

招商局集团董事长

二〇一四年十二月

Voyage, Ships and History

The first sentence of the song of China Merchants was "You ask me how far the voyage sails, it set sail from 1872".

Stepping into the historic museum of China Merchants, you will see a pair of couplets, saying "Established in the Self-strengthening Movement of late Qing Dynasty,China Merchants is the pioneer as well as the leader in national enterprises , starting with shipping business and now has become a century-old comprehensive enterprise with a solid foundation".

Starting with shipping business, China Merchants was originally named as "China Merchants Steam Navigation Company".

China Merchants began with ships. A remarkable ship model in China Maritime Museum was "Aden", it was the 1st ship of China Merchants bought in 1872 , the 1st steel-made steam ship for both passenger and freight transportation,as well as the 1st modernized commercial ship in China.

The century-old history was metaphorically referred as "a voyage" by China Merchants. China Merchants,as a ship, has been sailing more than 140 year-long extraordinary voyage.

Therefore, shipping is an ancestral business for China Merchants. The fleet of China Merchants is the most historical representative of China Merchants, and every ship of China Merchants is the witness of the history of China Merchants.

From the 1st ship Aden to today's VLCC(very large crude carrier), the ships of China Merchants link up the century-old voyage.

China Merchants Historical Research Institute has searched and collected information and materials of every ship ever existed in the century-old voyage, graving those ships into history,and unfolding the magnificent fleet of China Merchants to the readers. To record and narrate the history through ships could be a new way to write history.

Congratulate the publication of *Ships of China Merchants*!

Chairman of China Merchants Group

Li Jianhong

2014.12

目 录

第一章　晚清时期　　　　　　　　　　　　　　　**011**

　　第一节　商局初创 组建船队（1872—1876）　　013
　　第二节　并购旗昌 局势壮大（1877—1911）　　026

第二章　民国时期　　　　　　　　　　　　　　　**057**

　　第一节　时局动荡 艰难前行（1912—1936）　　059
　　第二节　沉船御敌 江轮入川（1937—1945）　　067
　　第三节　战后复员 航产剧增（1946—1949）　　073

第三章　新中国成立后　　　　　　　　　　　　　**169**

　　第一节　投向光明 航业新生（1950—1979）　　171
　　第二节　改革开放 轮运复苏（1980—2000）　　173
　　第三节　跨越世纪 振兴崛起（2001年至今）　　252

附录　招商局船舶汇总表　　　　　　　　　　　　**287**

编印说明　　　　　　　　　　　　　　　　　　　**307**

CONTENTS

CHAPTER ONE   IN THE LATE QING DYNASTY 011

Section One   Newly Establishment of
China Merchants and Construction of Fleet (1872-1876) 013

Section Two   The Acquisition of Shanghai Steam Navigation Company of
U.S. Russell & Co and Expansion of Business (1877-1911) 026

CHAPTER TWO   IN THE ERA OF THE REPUBLIC OF CHINA 057

Section One   Arduous Growth in Chaotic Situation (1912-1936) 059

Section Two   Shipwreck against Enemy with River Steamers into
Sichuan (1937-1945) 067

Section Three   Post War Recovery & Dramatic Growth (1946-1949) 073

**CHAPTER THREE   AFTER THE FOUNDATION OF
THE PEOPLE'S REPUBLIC OF CHINA** 169

Section One   Return to Mainland China and
New Birth of Shipping Industry (1950-1979) 171

Section Two   The Reform and Opening-up &
Recovery of Shipping (1980-2000) 173

Section Three   Rapid Rise in the New Century (2001 till Now) 252

APPENDIX   THE SUMMARY OF CHINA MERCHANTS' SHIPS 287

STATEMENT 307

第 一 章
晚清时期

CHAPTER ONE
IN THE LATE QING DYNASTY

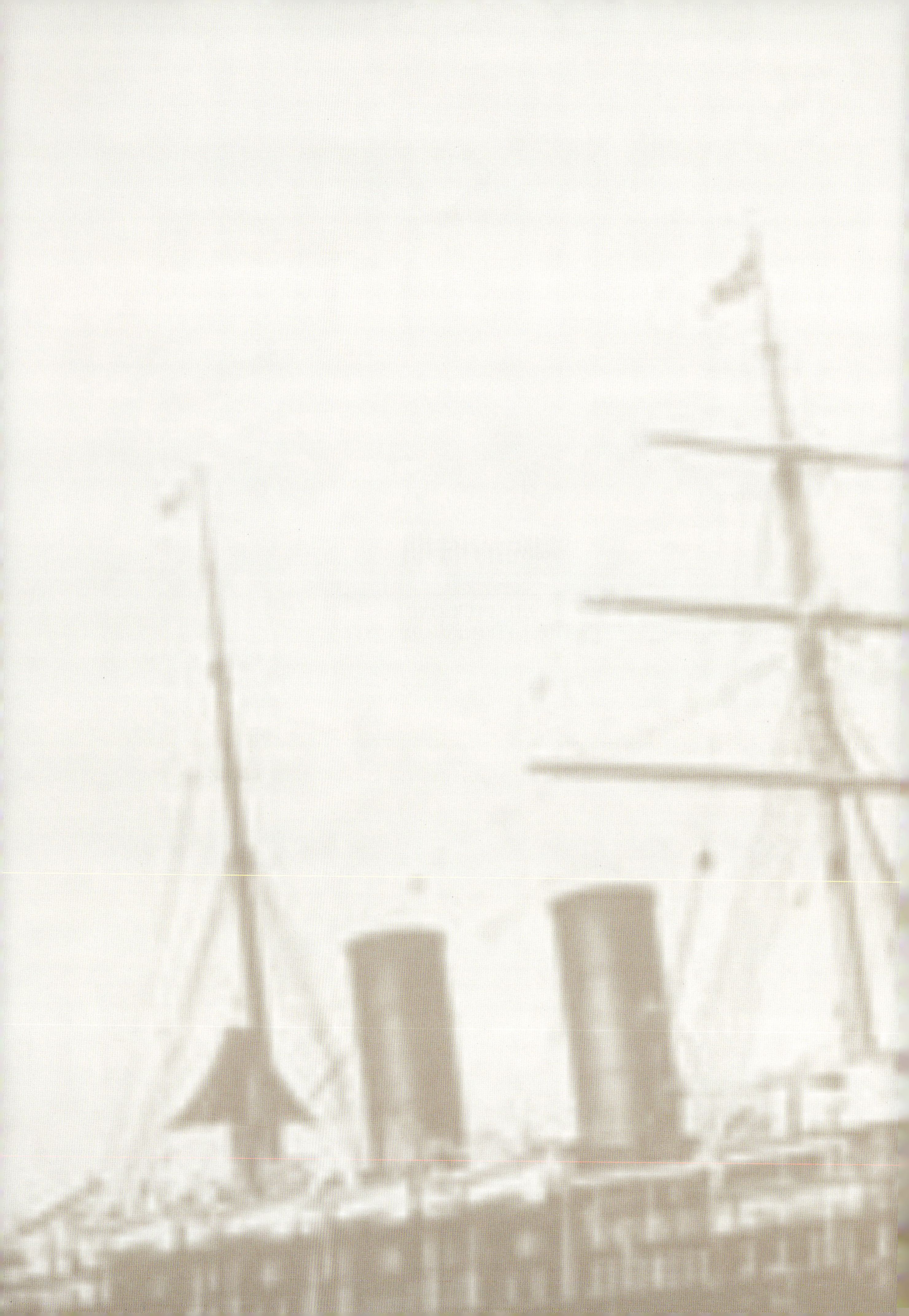

第一节　商局初创　组建船队（1872—1876）

SECTION ONE
Newly Establishment of China Merchants and Construction of Fleet (1872-1876)

19世纪中叶的两次鸦片战争，使中国的国门洞开，外国的新式轮船航运企业不断涌入，逐渐垄断了中国的江海航运。以旧式木帆船为主的中国传统航运业面临前所未有的危局。为了挽救民族航权、解决"国之大政"的漕粮运输难题，晚清洋务派官员李鸿章等人开始筹设轮船招商局。1872年11月，招商局在开局之前即购买了第一艘局轮"伊敦"号，并于该月30日首航汕头，这是中国商船第一次行驶南洋航线。1873年，招商局开局之后又陆续购进"永清"号、"利运"号、"福星"号，并从浙江省调拨"伏波"号轮船，组建了中国近代第一支商船队。1874年，招商局因轮运业务扩大，添购"和众"、"富有"、"利航"（驳船）等轮。1875年至1876年，招商局又购买了"日新"、"厚生"、"保大"、"丰顺"、"江宽"、"江永"等轮，至此招商局的航运实力日渐壮大。到1876年底，招商局航运船只达11艘，总吨位超过万吨。这时期招商局又开辟了北至天津、营口的北洋航线和南至汕头、香港的南洋航线，并积极拓展远洋航线，其轮船到达日本神户、长崎，吕宋（今菲律宾），新加坡等地。招商局商船队的成立、远洋航线的开辟，标志着中国近代民族航运业的诞生。

The two Opium Wars[1] in the mid-19th century forced China to be opened to the world. By this opportunity, the shipping enterprises with new-style ships flowed into China and monopolized China's shipping industry in both rivers and seas gradually. China's traditional shipping industry, with wooden junks as its main transportation tools, was faced with unprecedented crisis. To control traffic rights in China and solve the problem of official grain transportation, Li Hongzhang[2] together with other self-strengthening[3]

1　Opium Wars: The First Opium War was from 1839 to 1842, also known as the Anglo-Chinese War, was fought between Great Britain and China starting by the control of opium in China. The Second Opium War was from 1856 to 1860 and fought over similar issues.
2　Li Hongzhang: Or Li Hungchang (1823 –1901), was a politician, general and diplomat of the late Qing Dynasty.
3　The Self-Strengthening Movement: It was from 1861 to 1895, was a period of institutional reforms initiated during the late Qing Dynasty following a series of military defeats and concessions to foreign powers.

officials began to prepare for the establishment of China Merchants. In November 1872 before the opening of China Merchants, it bought the first vessel named Aden. Aden made its maiden voyage to Shantou on November 30 in the same year, which was the first sailing to Nanyang[1]. Later in 1873, China Merchants bought Yong Qing, Li Yun and Fu Xing successively and established the first merchant fleet with these ships as well as Fu Bo from Zhejiang Province. In 1874, with the expansion of shipping business of China Merchants, He Zhong, Fu You and Li Hang (a barge) were purchased. From 1875 to 1876, China Merchants bought some more ships, including Ri Xin, Hou Sheng, Bao Da, Feng Shun, Jiang Kuan and Jiang Yong, etc. and further grew its shipping business. By the end of 1876, China Merchants owned 11 ships with a gross tonnage over 10,000 tons. During the same period, China Merchants opened more routes, including the Beiyang[2] routes to Tianjin and Yingkou in the north, the Nanyang routes to Shantou and Hong Kong in the south, and explored ocean routes to Kobe and Nagasaki of Japan, Luzon (today's Philippine) and Singapore, etc. The establishment of China Merchants' fleet and exploration of ocean routes marked the birth of national shipping business in modern China.

⚓ 伊敦　Aden

"伊敦"轮，英文船名 Aden，船舶呼号 MBGV，下水时曾命名为 Delta，是招商局正式成立前夕从大英轮船公司购进的客货船，船价 50397 两，507 总吨，954 马力，长 78.49 米，宽 9.08 米，航速每小时 11 海里，1856 年 5 月 21 日由英国南安普敦船厂建造。

Aden, with MBGV as its call sign and Delta as its former name when it was laid down, was a China Merchants passenger and cargo ship bought before the establishment of China Merchants from the Peninsular and Oriental Steam Navigation Company. It was built by the shipyard in Northam, Southampton on May 21, 1856 at a cost of 50,397 liang[3]. It was 78.49 meters in length, at a beam of 9.08 meters and with a gross tonnage of 507 tons. With its engine power at 954 HP, it could sail at a speed of 11 kn.

1　Nanyang: In the late Qing Dynasty, Nanyang refers to the coastal areas in the southern part to Jiangsu Province.
2　Beiyang: The north coastal areas to Jiangsu Province.
3　Liang or tael in European is the basis of the silver currency in Imperial China period. During Qing Dynasty, a nominal liang or tael equals to 36 grammes of silver. Modern studies suggest that, on purchasing power parity basis, one tael of silver was worth about 4,130 RMB (modern Chinese yuan) in the early Tang Dynasty, 2,065 RMB in the late Tang Dynasty, 660.8 RMB in the mid Ming Dynasty and about 150 to 220 RMB in late Qing Dynasty.

1872年11月30日，"伊敦"轮载货开往汕头，开辟中国商船行驶的南洋航线，也是中国商船首次在中国近海航行。1873年1月19日，"伊敦"轮由上海港装货开往香港。1873年8月，首航日本的神户、长崎，成为近代中国商船在国际航线上的第一次航行。1875年"伊敦"轮因耗煤多、装载货物少而停航。1877年5月拆卸改装后，成为一艘趸船泊在天津大沽口外。1879年3月31日，因操作不慎，"伊敦"趸船在天津大沽口倾覆沉没。

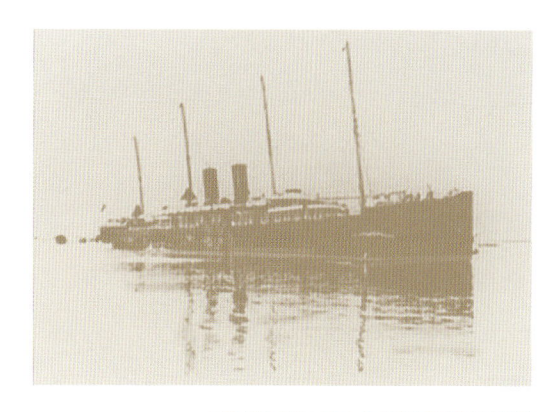

"伊敦"轮1873年初抵琉球时所摄
Photo shot when Aden just arrived at Ryukyu in 1873

Aden sailed to Shantou loaded with cargo on November 30, 1872, which opened up the route for Chinese merchant ships to Nanyang and was also the first offshore navigation by a Chinese merchant ship. Aden sailed to Hong Kong from Shanghai Port loaded with cargo on January 19, 1873, and to Kobe and Nagasaki of Japan for the first time in August 1873, which was also the first voyage of Chinese merchant ships in international routes in modern China. For large consumption of coal and less load of cargo, Aden was suspended its service in 1875, and then disassembled and converted into a pontoon berthing at Dagu Port of Tianjin in May in the same year. It sunk there caused by an ill operation on March 31, 1879.

永清　Yong Qing

"永清"轮，原名"代勃来开"，为第一艘行驶北洋航线的中国商轮，载货1.8万石（核装漕米1万石），航速每小时10海里，一昼夜烧煤12吨。经英商信洋行之手，以10万两银，从英国买回。同治十二年（1873）二月到沪，改名"永清"轮。"永清"轮抵沪后第三天，即承运漕米9000石首航天津。在招商局早期船舶中，其质量堪称上乘。枯水季节，"永清"轮首次由大沽水浅处，驶至天津紫竹林码头，需4小时25分钟，时速近40里。时有报刊赞曰："向来大沽至天津虽划船货艇，从无如此之速，盖其路有一百六十五里之遥，而水道迂回殊不易行驶，真可谓神速之矣。"该轮一直承担漕运任务，每月来回沪津两次。清光绪二十八年（1902）改作趸船。

Yong Qing, originally named as Dai Bo Lai Kai, was the first Chinese merchant ship that sailed on Beiyang routes with a capacity of 18,000 dan[1] (tribute grain 10,000 dan), with a cruising speed at 10 kn and a

---

1　Dan: A unit of dry measure for grain in Chinese units of measurement and equals to 100 L.

第一章 晚清时期　CHAPTER ONE　IN THE LATE QING DYNASTY

伊敦 Aden

daily coal consumption of 12 tons. The ship was bought by China Merchants through Glover and Company, a British one at a cost of 100,000 liang from Britain and renamed as Yong Qing after arriving at Shanghai in February in the 12th year of the reign of Emperor Tongzhi[1] in Qing Dynasty (1873). Three days after its arrival, Yong Qing made its maiden voyage to Tianjin with 9,000 dan tribute grain loaded. Among the ships of China Merchants at the early stage, Yong Qing was one of the ships with excellent quality. During the dry season, Yong Qing took 4 hours and 25 mins for its first sailing from shallow area of Dagu wharf to Zizhulin wharf, Tianjin at a speed of nearly 40 li[2] per hour. Therefore, the local newspaper commented with compliment to Yong Qing as follows: "Although ships had been used for cargo transportation from Dagu wharf to Tianjin in the past, it had never taken such a short time to finish this long-distance route of 165 li with roundabouts and corners. It's really an amazing speed!" Since then, Yong Qing was used for transportation of tribute grain and traveled between Shanghai and Tianjin twice a month until it was changed into a pontoon in 28th year of the reign of Emperor Guangxu[3] in Qing Dynasty (1902).

⚓ 利运 Li Yun

"利运"轮是招商局通过德商载生洋行在英国采购的海轮，价值8.3万两，排水量734总吨，船长231尺，宽29尺，深14尺9寸，载货1032吨至1500吨（可用压载水调节），载客300余人。据《申报》介绍，"系当时最新之制"。舱内有装水铁箱以代压载石，如货物多时，可将箱内之水放去，仍可装货。该船若载货1032吨，则吃水12尺7寸；若载货1500吨，则吃水13尺6寸。航速每小时9海里，用煤每12小时10吨。"船舯面系铁所成，可居客300余人"。

Li Yun was an ocean vessel bought through a German trading house at a cost of 83,000 liang from Britain. Its displacement was 734 tons, with a length overall of 231 chi[4], a beam of 29 chi and a height of 14.9 chi. It could be loaded with cargo from 1,032 to 1,500 tons (adjusted by ballast water) and over 300 passengers. According to the report of *Shun Pao*[5], Li Yun was the most advanced ship at that time. Inside the cabin, the ballast stone was replaced by water tank where water could be released so that more cargo could be loaded if needed. When the ship was loaded with cargo of 1,032 tons, the draught was 12.7 chi while the

---

1 Emperor Tongzhi: Or Tung-chih Emperor (1856–1875), was the tenth emperor of the Qing Dynasty from 1861 to 1875.
2 Li: A unit of length in traditional measurement of China and equals to 500 meters.
3 Emperor Guangxu: Or Kuang-hsu Emperor (1871–1908), was the eleventh emperor of the Qing Dynasty from 1875 to 1908.
4 Chi: A unit of length in traditional measurement of China and equals to 1/3 meter.
5 *Shun Pao*: A Newspaper that was founded by Ernest Major on April 30, 1872 and was suspended on May 27, 1949, lasting for 77 years.

draught was 13.6 chi when the ship was loaded with cargo of 1,500 tons. The vessel could sail at a speed of 9 kn with a coal consumption of 10 tons every 12 hours. "With the amidship made of iron, the vessel had a capacity of more than 300 passengers".

清同治十二年（1873），轮船招商局在厦门设分局。"利运"轮由上海行驶厦门、汕头航线。光绪七年，"利运"与"永清"、"日新"、"镇东"、"拱北"等轮春夏协运漕米兼客，秋冬行驶北洋线的牛庄（今营口）及南洋线的汕头、香港、广州等埠。1904年"利运"轮拆改镇江趸船，后售予北洋水师做兵驳。

China Merchants Steam Navigation Company set up a branch in Xiamen in the 12th year of the reign of Emperor Tongzhi in Qing Dynasty (1873). Li Yun sailed along the routes from Shanghai to Xiamen and Shantou. In the 7th year of the reign of Emperor Guangxu in Qing Dynasty, Li Yun, together with other vessels, including Yong Qing, Ri Xin, Zhen Dong and Gong Bei, served for transportation of tribute grain and passengers during Spring and Summer and sailed along the Beiyang routes to Niuzhuang (today's Yingkou) as well as the Nanyang routes to ports of Shantou, Hong Kong and Guangzhou. In 1904, Li Yun was disassembled and converted to a pontoon at Zhenjiang, and later sold to Beiyang Fleet[1] used as a barge for soldiers.

福星　Fu Xing

"福星"轮原名"其波利克有利"号，532总吨，由信洋行经手从苏格兰购进，航速10海里/小时，其舱容甚小，载重1.7万石，船价高达7.4万两。1875年"福星"轮由沪驶津途中在僚木洋被怡和公司之"澳顺"轮撞沉，溺亡63人，损失漕米7200余石。

Fu Xing, originally named as Qi Bo Li Ke You Li, was an ocean vessel bought through Glover and Company at a cost as high as 74,000 liang from Scotland. Its gross tonnage was 532 tons and loading capacity was 17,000 dan, but its cabin capacity was quite small. It could sail at a speed of 10 kn. In 1875, Fu Xing was run down by Ao Shun ship from Jardine Matheson and sunk at Liaomuyang when sailing from Shanghai to Tianjin, causing 63 deaths and a loss of tribute grain for more than 7,200 dan.

1　The Beiyang Fleet or Northern Seas Fleet was one of the four modernized Chinese navies in the late Qing Dynasty and sponsored by Li Hongzhang.

和众 He Zhong

"和众"轮，849 总吨，1874 年 3 月自马尾船政局接收，1878 年开辟汕头、厦门航线。1881 年"和众"轮由汕头回上海途中在福建乌丘屿被英国军舰撞沉。损失船本 9 万两，货物 5203 件，值银 58120 元。

He Zhong, with a gross tonnage of 849 tons, was taken over from Mawei Arsenal[1] in March 1874 and sailed along the newly opened Shanghai-Shantou route and Shanghai-Xiamen route in 1878. It was run down by a British warship in 1881 and sunk near Wuqiuyu Island while sailing from Shantou to Shanghai, causing the loss of the ship worthy of 90,000 liang and cargo of 5,203 pieces costing about 58,120 silver dollars.

富有 Fu You

"富有"轮，920 总吨，1874 年 10 月自马尾船政局接收，1883 年行驶香港、广州，1890 年 6 月 6 日"富有"轮由上海开往烟台途中在山东成山洋面触礁搁浅而沉没。

Fu You, with a gross tonnage of 920 tons, was taken over from Mawei Arsenal in October 1874 and sailed along the routes to Hong Kong and Guangzhou in 1883. It was stranded after hitting the reef near Chengshan, Shandong during its trip from Shanghai to Yantai on June 6, 1890 and sunk later.

利航 Li Hang

"利航"轮，属于驳船，920 总吨，1874 年 10 月自马尾船政局接收，抵达上海参加漕米运输。

Li Hang, with a gross tonnage of 920 tons, was a barge taken over from Mawei Arsenal in October 1874 and used for tribute grain transportation after arriving at Shanghai.

日新 Ri Xin

"日新"轮，900 总吨，1876 年 3 月自马尾船政局接收，抵达上海参加漕米运输。1893 年"日新"轮与"江平"轮拆卸作为驳船。

Ri Xin, with a gross tonnage of 900 tons, was taken over from Mawei Arsenal in March 1876 and used

---

1 Mawei Arsenal: Also Foochow Arsenal, was one of several shipyards in China built under orders from Li Hongzhang and Zuo Zongtang, leaders of the Qing government's Self-Strengthening Movement during the mid to late 19th century.

for tribute grain transportation after arriving at Shanghai. In 1893, Ri Xin and Jiang Ping were disassembled and used as barges.

厚生　Hou Sheng

"厚生"轮，595总吨，1876年4月自马尾船政局接收，抵达上海参加漕米运输。1878年1月31日，"厚生"轮由汕头回上海途中在厦门附近的答屿山触礁沉没，失踪大副一人，损失货物6200余件。

Hou Sheng, with a gross tonnage of 595 tons, was taken over from Mawei Arsenal in April 1876 and used for tribute grain transportation after arriving at Shanghai. It sunk after hitting the reef near Dayushan Island near Xiamen when returning from Shantou to Shanghai on January 1, 1878, causing one mate missing and a loss of more than 6,200 pieces of cargo.

保大　Bao Da

"保大"轮，870总吨，1876年8月自马尾船政局接收，抵达上海参加漕米运输。1887年"保大"轮由上海驶天津途中在山东荣成青山头遇雾触礁，人员货物被救起，船身被风浪击碎。

Bao Da, with a gross tonnage of 870 tons, was taken over from Mawei Arsenal in August 1876 and used for tribute grain transportation after arriving at Shanghai. It hit the reef at Qingshantou near Rongcheng, Shandong when sailing from Shanghai to Tianjin in 1887. The crew and cargo were saved but the ship was crashed into pieces in the stormy waves.

丰顺　Feng Shun

"丰顺"轮，900总吨，1875年10月从马尾船政局接收，抵达上海参加漕米运输，1894年甲午战争时，该轮与其他招商局轮船共9艘被征为运兵船开往朝鲜。

Feng Shun, with a gross tonnage of 900 tons, was taken over from Mawei Arsenal in October 1875 and used for tribute grain transportation after arriving at Shanghai. Together with other 8 ships, Feng Shun was requisitioned for army transportation and sailed to Korea when the First Sino-Japanese War[1] broke out in 1894.

1　The First Sino-Japanese War: Also known as the War of Jiawu, was fought between Qing Dynasty China and Meiji Japan, primarily over control of Korea from 1894 to 1895.

⚓ 成大　Cheng Da

1875年11月下旬，"成大"夹板船前往长崎运输煤炭。

Cheng Da was an old-style double-board sailing ship used for coal transportation to Nagasaki, Japan in late November, 1875.

⚓ 伏波　Fu Bo

1873年初，招商局拨借浙江省"伏波"轮，以供漕运之用，后该轮又调出。

At the beginning of 1873, China Merchants borrowed Fu Bo from Zhejiang Province for tribute grain transportation and it was returned later.

⚓ 汉广　Han Guang

"汉广"轮由湖北省购买，1876年交招商局使用，1881年失事，船身于6月11日被风浪击碎，损失漕米5842石，货物4800余件。该轮系湖广总督李瀚章为筹办江防于1876年购买的"兵商并用"的轮船，是年6月19日从英国开抵上海，7月13日租给招商局营运，招商局付给价银3.45万两。

Han Guang, a ship for both military and merchant use, was bought by Li Hanzhang, Viceroy of Hukwang Provinces for the purpose of defense works along the Yangtze River in 1876. It arrived at Shanghai from Britain on June 19. Han Guang was rent to China Merchants for operations at a cost of 34,500 liang on July 13, 1876. It wrecked on July 11, 1881 and was broken into pieces by stormy waves, causing a loss of tribute grain 5,842 dan and cargo over 4,800 pieces.

⚓ 江宽　Jiang Kuan

"江宽"为招商局江轮，1000总吨，与"江永"轮同在英国订造，总价365000两，属明轮结构，1877年9月完工抵沪启用。

Jiang Kuan, a China Merchants river steamer with a gross tonnage of 1,000 tons and propelled by paddle wheels, was bought from Britain together with Jiang Yong, at a cost of 365,000 liang in total. It arrived at Shanghai and was put into use in September 1877.

1918年4月25日夜，段祺瑞从汉口乘"楚泰"舰赴九江，由"楚材"舰护航，在长江丹水池附近，"江宽"轮被"楚材"舰撞沉，船上乘客及船员共1200人，溺毙900人。事发后，

"楚材"舰不但不停下救援，舰上士兵反以刺刀将攀附舰旁之落水者一一驱离。事后罹难家属上告法院，法院屡传"楚材"舰长赵进锐，但赵进锐拒到，北京政府官官相护，最后官司不了了之。

At night of April 25, 1918, Duan Qirui[1] travelled by warship Chu Tai from Hankou to Jiujiang and was escorted by warship Chu Cai. Chu Cai ran into Jiang Kuan near Danshuichi in the Yangtze River, causing the sinking of Jiang Kuan and 900 deaths of 1,200 passengers and crew. After the crash, soldiers on Chu Cai neither stopped the ship nor rescued the people, and even drove away those who tried to climb up to Chu Cai via bayonets. After that, the relatives of the dead people sued to the court later. However, Zhao Jinrui, Captain of Chu Cai refused to appear on the court after being summoned for many times. The case ended with no result because of the shielding of the government.

⚓ 江永 Jiang Yong

"江永"轮为招商局江轮，与"江宽"轮同在英国订造，两船总价 365000 两，1876 年在英国格拉斯哥（Glasgow）船厂建造，船长 91.4 米，船宽 12.2 米，船深 3.7 米，吃水 2.9—3.1 米，空船吃水 1.3—2.2 米，注册吨位 1451 吨，毛吨位 1921 吨，净吨位 1451 吨，功率 780 马力，航速每小时 10 海里，日煤耗 23 吨，载客数 1409 人次，排水量约 5000 吨，属明轮结

1　Duan Qirui (1865-1936), was a Chinese warlord and politician, commander in the Beiyang Army, and the Provisional Chief Executive of Republic of China (in Beijing) from 1924 to 1926 and the Premier from 1916 to 1918.

构，1877 年 9 月完工抵沪启用。

Jiang Yong, built by Glasgow Shipyard of Britain in 1876, was a China Merchants river steamer at a cost of 365,000 liang together with Jiang Kuan in total. It was 91.4 meters in length, at a beam of 12.2 meters and a depth of 3.7 meters ,with a draught of 2.9 m to 3.1m (1.3 m to 2.2 m if unloaded). The steamer measured 1,451 registered tons, 1,921 gross tons and 1,451 net tons. With its engine power at 780 HP, it could sail at a speed of 10 kn with a daily coal consumption of 23 tons and passenger capacity of 1,409. The steamer, with a displacement of about 5,000 tons, was propelled by paddle wheel, and was put into use after arriving at Shanghai in September, 1877.

1926 年 10 月 16 日，该轮被军阀孙传芳征用，自上海满载军火与士兵于清晨五点半抵达九江，锚于招商局趸船西侧江心，至六时许该轮被潜入的国民革命军地下工作人员纵火爆炸，经燃烧一昼夜而沉没，船员仅 25 人生还，船长及以下高级船员共死亡 88 人，兵士民夫死亡约 1000 人，仅 300 余人获救，是民国以来最大的船难。

江永　Jiang Yong

On October 16, 1926, the steamer, requisitioned by the warlord Sun Chuanfang[1] and fully loaded with munitions and soldiers from Shanghai, arrived at Jiujiang at half past five in the morning and dropped the anchor at the center of the river to the west of China Merchants's pontoon. Half an hour later, Jiang Yong was put on fire by National Revolution Army[2] who slipt into the steamer and exploded. After burning on for one day and night, the steamer sunk with only 25 crew members and 300-odd soldiers and workers survived,

---

1　Sun Chuanfang (1885-1935), was called the "Nanking Warlord" or leader of the "League of Five Provinces" was a Zhili clique warlord.
2　The National Revolutionary Army: The military arm of the Kuomintang from 1925 until 1947 in the Republic of China.

while 88 senior crew members and about 1,000 soldiers and workers were killed. This was the biggest shipwreck during the Republic of China period.

⚓ 永宁　Yong Ning

"永宁"轮，240总吨。1873年7月，招商局附局轮船"永宁"号从上海开航镇江、九江、汉口，同年走上海、宁波线。1877年开辟上海、温州线，1887年"永宁"轮大修改为"海昌"，1895年"海昌"轮改作趸船。

Yong Ning, with a gross tonnage of 240 tons, was a ship belonging to China Merchants affiliates. It began sailing along the routes from Shanghai to Zhenjiang, Jiujiang and Hankou in July 1873 and Shanghai-Ningbo route in the same year. In 1877, the route between Shanghai and Wenzhou was ushered in. The name of the ship was changed from Yong Ning into Hai Chang in 1887 and the ship was converted into a pontoon in 1895.

⚓ 洞庭　Dong Ting

1873年招商局附局轮船"洞庭"号投入长江营业，转运川、汉、津、粤各货。1878年开辟省、澳线。1879年开辟广东新河线。1881年开辟海口、海防线。

Dong Ting, a ship belonging to China Merchants affiliates, began its sailing along the Yangtze River in 1873 and was used for transportation of cargos from Sichuan, Hankou, Tianjin and Guangdong. In 1878, routes across-province and routes to Macau were explored. It also began to sail along Xinhe route in Guangdong in 1879, Haikou route and Haiphong route in 1881.

第二节 并购旗昌 局势壮大（1877—1911）

SECTION TWO
The Acquisition of Shanghai Steam Navigation Company of U.S. Russell & Co and Expansion of Business (1877-1911)

招商局是在外国航运势力垄断中国江海航权的背景下产生的。面对艰难的时局，承载维护民族航权使命的招商局，不断与在华的西方航运企业抗衡、竞争。1877年，招商局以222万两白银一举并购了外国在华最大的轮船公司——美国旗昌轮船公司，开中资企业收购外资企业之先河。并购美国旗昌轮船公司之后，招商局的船舶数量和船舶总吨位急剧增长，新增大小船舶18艘，招商局的轮船数量达29艘，总吨位30526吨，达到了招商局在晚清时期航运数量的最高点。

China Merchants was born during the period when the foreign shipping powers monopolized traffic rights of rivers and seas in China. Facing the hardships, China Merchants, with the mission to protect China's national shipping rights, contended and competed with foreign shipping enterprises with continuous endeavors. In 1877, China Merchants acquired Shanghai Steam Navigation Company of U.S. Russell & Co, the largest foreign shipping company in China at a price of 2.22 million liang, which was the first acquisition of foreign enterprise by a Chinese one. After the acquisition, China Merchants grew very fast in both numbers and gross tonnage of the ships. By then, with another 18 ships being brought into the fleet after acquisition, China Merchants owned 29 ships with a gross tonnage of 30,526 tons and reached its peak in terms of ship numbers in the late Qing Dynasty.

1879年招商局派"和众"轮试航檀香山。1880年，招商局又派"美富"轮、"和众"轮抵达美国旧金山。同年，招商局的"海琛"轮载北洋水师员弁前往英国实习。1881年，招商局派"美富"轮运载茶叶抵达伦敦。招商局开辟的远洋航线进一步延伸至日本、南洋诸岛、欧美等国。

China Merchants sent He Zhong ship to Honolulu for trial voyage in 1879, Mei Fu and He Zhong to San Francisco, U.S.A in 1880 and Mei Fu to London for tea transportation in 1881. Besides, members of Beiyang Fleet were sent to Britain by Hai Chen for practice in 1880. With all these efforts, the ocean routes explored by China Merchants were expanded to Japan, islands in Southeast Asia, Europe and the United States.

海晏 Hai Yan

"海晏"原为美商旗昌公司海轮，原名"盛京"，1877年招商局购并旗昌时纳入船队。1873年该船在英国格拉斯哥（Glasgow）船厂建造，船长74.7米，船宽10米，船深5.5米，吃水4.1米，空船2.8米，注册吨位1033吨，毛吨位1344吨，净吨位837吨，功率880马力，航速每小时11.5—12海里，日煤耗22吨，载客281人。

海晏 Hai Yan

Hai Yan, originally named as Sheng Jing and belonged to Shanghai Steam Navigation Company of U.S. Russell & Co, became a China Merchants ocean vessel when China Merchants acquired Shanghai Steam Navigation Company of U.S. Russell & Co in 1877. It was built by Glasgow Shipyard of Britain in 1873. Its length overall was 74.7 meters, with a beam of 10 meters, depth of 5.5 meters and a draught of 4.1 meters (2.8 meters if unloaded). The vessel measured 1,033 registered tons, 1,344 gross tons and 837 net tons. With its engine power at 880 HP, Hai Yan could sail at a speed of 11.5 to 12 kn with a daily coal consumption of 22 tons and passenger capacity of 281.

该轮与中国近代史关系密切，1884年7月14日刘铭传在中法战争期间自上海秘密搭乘该轮突破法舰队封锁来台上任，法国军舰自后追杀，幸海上大风雨未得手。

Hai Yan was an important witness of China's modern history. It was the ship that broke through the block of French fleet and took Mr. Liu Mingchuan[1] secretly to Taiwan to take office on July 14, 1884 during the Sino-French War[2]. After being discovered by the French fleet, it was chased but successfully escaped with the help of big storm on the sea.

1886年北洋舰队成军初操，"海晏"轮作为大阅官奕譞座舰，甲午战争时该轮被征为运兵船载叶志超部登陆朝鲜仁川。

1　Liu Mingchuan (1836-1896): A Chinese official in Qing Dynasty. In the aftermath of the Sino-French War, he was appointed the first governor of the newly established province of Taiwan.
2　The Sino-French War: A limited conflict fought from August 1884 through April 1885, to decide whether France would supplant China's control of Tonkin (northern Vietnam).

In 1886 when Beiyang Fleet was established, Hai Yan was the ship that took Yi Xuan[1], the inspecting officer to review the first drill of the fleet. During the First Sino-Japanese War, it was requisitioned as a troopship, by which Ye Zhichao[2] and his army landed on Inchon, North Korea.

1895年《马关条约》签订，李经方奉父亲李鸿章命搭乘"海晏"轮来台交割，李经方畏惧台湾士绅唾骂不敢下船，在船上与日本代表签字后匆匆逃回大陆。康有为在戊戌变法失败后亦先来天津藏身该轮，后因迟未开船，只好改乘英国太古公司的"重庆"轮逃往日本。

In 1895 after the Treaty of Shimonoseki[3] was signed between China and Japan, Li Jingfang, under the order of his father Li Hongzhang, came to Taiwan by Hai Yan for delivery. Fearing the spurns from the local patriots, Li Jingfang was afraid to get off the ship, just signed with Japanese representative and fled back to Mainland China. When the Hundred Days' Reform[4] failed, Kang Youwei[5] came to Tianjin and hided himself in Hai Yan at first. However, when he found he needed to wait for a long time before Hai Yan set sail, he had to change his plan and traveled by Chong Qing, a vessel of Swire from Britain, and escaped to Japan.

该轮于1937年8月13日战争爆发时奉命在上海十里铺自沉阻塞航道，阻挡日本军舰沿江西进。

On August 13, 1937 when the Second Sino-Japanese War broke out, Hai Yan was ordered to sink itself at Shilipu, Shanghai to block the fairway to prevent Japanese warship from going west along the river.

⚓ 美富 Mei Fu

"美富"轮为1879年建造，原为一铁甲板船，1880年底由招商局与耶松洋行合购后改造为二层甲板，航速每小时9海里，载货2440吨，载客889人。1883年"美富"轮行驶香港、广州。

Built in 1879, Mei Fu was originally an iron-deck ship and was converted into a double-deck ship after

---

1 Yi Xuan (1840 - 1891): A Manchu prince and statesman of the late Qing dynasty. He was the father of the dynasty's second-to-last emperor, the Guang Xu emperor, and the paternal grandfather of China's last emperor Pu Yi.
2 Ye Zhichao (1838-1899): A disputable leader of Huai Army.
3 The Treaty of Shimonoseki: It was signed in Japan on April 17, 1895, between the Empire of Japan and the Qing Empire, ending the First Sino-Japanese War.
4 The Hundred Days' Reform: A failed 104-day national cultural, political and educational reform movement from 11 June to 21 September 1898 in the late Qing dynasty China. It was undertaken by the young Guang Xu Emperor and his reform-minded supporters. The movement proved to be short-lived, ending in a coup d'état by powerful conservative opponents led by Empress Dowager Ci Xi.
5 Kang Youwei (1858-1927): A Chinese scholar. He led movements to establish a constitutional monarchy and was an ardent Chinese nationalist and internationalist. His ideas inspired a reformation movement that was supported by the Guang Xu Emperor but loathed by Empress Dowager Ci Xi.

being jointly purchased by China Merchants and Farnham & Company at the end of 1880. It could sail at a speed of 9 kn and had a cargo capacity of 2,440 tons and passenger capacity of 889. In 1883, Mei Fu sailed along the routes to Hong Kong and Guangzhou.

美富　Mei Fu

1885年招商局为解决经济困难，将该轮售予福建省。1911年3月25日该轮自厦门返上海途中在爱尔加岛附近被招商局的"广利"轮撞沉，40余人失踪。

To solve the financial problems, China Merchants sold Mei Fu to Fujian Province in 1885. On March 25, 1911, it was ran down by Guang Li of China Merchants when returning from Xiamen to Shanghai and sunk near Ai'erjia Island, causing over 40 people missing.

⚓ 江天 Jiang Tian

"江天"轮原为美商旗昌轮船公司江轮，原名"其宁"号及"湖北"轮，1877年招商局购并旗昌时纳入船队。该轮为英国格拉斯哥（Glasgow）船厂1870年建造，铁质船壳，长88.2米，宽12.3米，吃水3米，空船吃水2米，注册吨位1368吨，毛吨位2012吨，净吨位1737吨，功率900马力，航速每小时9.5海里，日耗煤28吨，载客1256人。主机为单汽缸滚动条蒸汽机，属明轮结构，用于行驶上海至杭州与普陀山航线。

Jiang Tian, originally named as Qi Ning and Hu Bei, was a river steamer belonging to Shanghai Steam Navigation Company of U.S. Russell & Co and was brought into China Merchants' fleet when China Merchants acquired Shanghai Steam Navigation Company of U.S. Russell & Co in 1877. It was built by Glasgow Shipyard of Britain in 1870 with iron hull. It was 88.2 meters in length and at a beam of 12.3 meters, with a draught of 3 meters (2 meters if unloaded). The vessel measured 1,368 registered tons, 2,012 gross tons and 1,737 net tons. With its engine power at 900 HP, Jiang Tian could sail at a speed of 9.5 kn with a daily

江天　Jiang Tian

coal consumption of 28 tons and passenger capacity of 1,256. Jiang Tian, with a single-cylinder steam engine with scroll bars and propelled by paddle wheel, sailed along the Shanghai-Hangzhou route and Shanghai-Putuoshan route.

1937年8月13日,"江天"轮随南京城一起陷入敌手,12月8日被炸沉没。

On August 13, 1937, with Nanjing being occupied, Jiang Tian was caught by the enemy on a military mission and sunk after being exploded on December 8 in the same year.

⚓ 江孚、江长 Jiang Fu & Jiang Chang

"江孚"与"江长"皆为原美商旗昌公司江轮,总吨806吨,1877年招商局购并旗昌时纳入船队,"江孚"轮为1873年江南制造局建造,属明轮结构,有特殊的并排双烟囱外形,用于行驶上海至武汉航线。1937年中日战争爆发时本轮已无记录,可能已报废。

Jiang Fu and Jiang Chang, with a gross tonnage of 806 tons each, were both river steamers belonging to Shanghai Steam Navigation Company of U.S. Russell & Co, and brought into China Merchants' fleet when China Merchants acquired Shanghai Steam Navigation Company of U.S. Russell & Co in 1877. Built in Kiangnan Arsenal in 1873, Jiang Fu was propelled by paddle wheel with a special exterior of double chimneys side by side. Jiang Fu sailed along the Shanghai-Wuhan route and might be left obsolete when the second Sino-Japanese War broke out in 1937, because no records were found since then.

江孚 Jiang Fu

"江长"轮于1878年正月初三由汉口驶回上海途中在离汉口90里之猴子矶触礁沉没。

Jiang Chang sunk on the third day of the first month of the Chinese lunar calendar in 1878 after striking the reef at Houziji, 90 li from Hankou when returning to Shanghai from Hankou.

江裕 Jiang Yu

"江裕"轮为招商局江轮，1883年在上海建造，属明轮结构，用于行驶上海至武汉航线。船长91.4米，船宽12.9米，船深4.2米，吃水3米，空船吃水2米，注册吨位2207吨，毛吨位3090吨，净吨位1490吨，功率1750马力，航速每小时10海里，日耗煤34吨，载客1536人。1938年4月，为阻挡日本军舰沿长江西进，该轮奉命与"新丰"轮一同自沉于马当阻塞航道。

江裕 Jiang Yu

Jiang Yu, built in Shanghai in 1883, was a China Merchants river steamer propelled by paddle wheel and sailed along the Shanghai-Wuhan route. It was 91.4 meters in length, at a beam of 12.9 meters and a depth of 4.2 meters, with a draught of 3 meters (2 meters if unloaded). The vessel measured 2,207 registered tons, 3,090 gross tons and 1,490 net tons. With its engine power at 1,750 HP, Jiang Yu could sail at a speed of 10 kn with a daily coal consumption of 34 tons and passenger capacity of 1,536. In April 1938, Jiang Yu was ordered to sink itself at Madang together with Xin Feng to block the fairway so as to prevent Japanese warships from going west along the Yangtze River.

海定 Hai Ding

"海定"轮于1874年建造，曾用船名"保定"，原为美商旗昌公司海轮，1877年招商局购并旗昌时纳入船队。1894年甲午战争时该轮与"海晏"等同被征为运兵船载叶志超部登陆朝鲜仁川。该轮在1907年改做趸船。

Hai Ding, originally named as Bao Ding and built in 1874, was an ocean vessel belonging to Shanghai Steam Navigation Company of U.S. Russell & Co and was brought into China Merchants' fleet when China Merchants acquired Shanghai Steam Navigation

海定 Hai Ding

Company of U.S. Russell & Co in 1877. Together with Hai Yan, it was requisitioned as a troopship, by which Ye Zhichao and his army landed on Inchon, North Korea during the First Sino-Japanese War in 1894. In 1907, it was converted into a pontoon.

图南、拱北 Tu Nan & Gong Bei

"图南"轮于1881年与"拱北"轮同批在英国纽格梭（New Castle）建造。"图南"原名"鲁理"，单层甲板，铁质船壳，暗轮结构，船身长77.1米，宽11米，深9.1米，吃水5.5米，空船吃水2.5米，注册吨位1404吨，毛吨位1537吨，净吨位942吨，功率840马力，航速每小时10.5海里，日耗煤23吨，载货1261吨，载客596人。"图南"轮是1894年甲午战争时被征调运兵朝鲜的九艘招商局轮船之一，曾载运聂士成军910人自大沽前往牙山。该轮于1933年6月25日在山东成山附近被日商大连汽船会社的"长春丸"拦腰撞沉，溺亡104人并损失银行托运的财物甚多，由于管辖的大连海事法庭被日人控制，最后没有获得任何赔偿。

图南　Tu Nan

Tu Nan, originally named as Lu Li, was built in New Castle in 1881 together with Gong Bei. It was of single deck, iron hull and propelled by paddle wheel. It was 77.1 meters in length, at a beam of 11 meters and a height of 9.1 meters, with a draught of 5.5 meters (2.5 meters if unloaded). The vessel measured 1,404 registered tons, 1,537 gross tons and 942 net tons. With its engine power at 840 HP, Tu Nan could sail at a speed of 10.5 kn with a daily coal consumption of 23 tons, cargo capacity of 1,261 tons and passenger capacity of 596. Tu Nan was one of the nine China Merchants vessels requisitioned to ship troops to North Korea during the First Sino-Japanese War in 1894 and had shipped 910 soldiers led by Nie Shicheng[1] from Dagu to Yashan. On June 25, 1933, Tu Nan was ran down in the middle by Changchun Maru of Dairen Kisen Kaisha[2] and sunk near Chengshan, Shandong, causing the 104 deaths and a big loss of cargos. However,

---

1　Nie Shicheng (1836-1900), was a Chinese general who served the Imperial government during the Boxer Rebellion. In April 1894, Nie was recalled from Manchuria due to the worsening situation in Korea.
2　Dairen Kisen Kaisha: A Japanese steamboat company built in Dalian in 1915.

nothing was compensated because Admiralty Court of Dalian in charge of this crash was manipulated by Japanese at that time.

"拱北"轮为铁壳海轮，注册吨位620吨，航速每小时28海里，吃水4米，船价6.5万两，1895年10月14日应军差在辽东锦州湾因所装载弹药爆炸而沉没，死亡200余人，包括船员57人。

Gong Bei was an iron-hull ocean vessel with a registered tonnage of 620 tons, draught 4 meters and cost 65,000 liang. It could sail at a speed of 28 Li per hour. On October 14, 1895, Gong Bei sunk at Jinzhou Gulf, Liaoning during a military mission, caused by the explosion of ammunition loaded on the ship. More than 200 people died in this accident, including 57 crew members.

⚓ 致远、怀远 Zhi Yuan & Huai Yuan

"致远"为招商局海轮，1881年向英国订造，同批订造的还有"普济"轮。"致远"轮是远洋轮船，长86.9米，宽10.4米，深7.9米，功率200马力，航速每小时22海里，日烧煤18吨，总吨2300吨，"系铁壳三枝桅大船"，定价32300磅（合规银13万两），于1918年11月6日在仰光失火，全船焚毁。

Built in 1881 together with Pu Ji in Britain, Zhi Yuan was a China Merchants ocean vessel. It was 86.9 meters in length, at a beam of 10.4 meters and a depth of 7.9 meters. With its engine power at 200 HP, Zhi Yuan could sail at a speed of 22 li per hour with a daily coal consumption of 18 tons. As a vessel with iron hull and three masts, Zhi Yuan was priced at 32,300 pounds (equivalent to silver of 130,000 liang) and had a gross tonnage of 2,300 tons. It was caught on fire in Rangoon on November 6, 1918 and was burnt out.

致远 Zhi Yuan

"怀远"轮原为美商旗昌洋行海轮，原名"飞似海马"（或译"富士"），排水量1215吨。1877年招商局购并旗昌轮船公司时并入船队，行驶上海至广州线。"怀远"轮于1883年12月1日由上海开往香港途中在浙江石浦海面触小鱼山暗礁而沉，因风浪大及海水冰冷，只有5人搭救生舢板登小鱼山岛，其余169人死亡。

Huai Yuan, originally named as Fusi Yama ("Fusi" by translation), was an ocean vessel with a displacement of 1,215 tons. It belonged to Shanghai Steam Navigation Company of U.S. Russell&Co and was brought into China Merchants' fleet when China Merchants acquired Shanghai Steam Navigation Company of U.S. Russell & Co in 1877, sailing along the Shanghai-Guangzhou route. Huai Yuan sunk on December 1, 1883 after striking the submerged reef of Xiaoyu Mount at Shipu, Zhejiang on its way to Hong Kong from Shanghai. Due to the big storm and cold water in the sea, only 5 people survived with the help of the lifeboat and climbed onto the island of Xiaoyu Mount while the other 169 people died in the accident.

⚓ 普济 Pu Ji

"普济"轮为招商局海轮，钢壳船，载重吨880，长64米，宽10.7米，深4.4米，吃水2.6米，航速每小时34海里，日烧煤14吨，定价18500磅（合规银7.4万两），1882年建造，是1894年甲午战争时九艘被征调运兵朝鲜的招商局轮船之一。

普济 Pu Ji

Pu Ji was a China Merchants ocean vessel with steel hull plates, measuring 880 tons. It was 64 meters in length, at a beam of 10.7 meters and a depth of 4.4 meters, with a draught of 2.6 meters. Pu Ji could sail at a speed of 34 li per hour with a daily coal consumption of 14 tons. Built in 1882 and priced at 18,500 pounds (equivalent to silver of 74,000 liang), Pu Ji was one of the nine China Merchants' vessels requisitioned to ship troops to North Korea during the First Sino-Japanese War.

该轮于1918年1月5日满载乘客由上海驶向温州，在吴淞口被违反航行规则的英国"新丰"轮撞沉，船上300余名乘客中生还者仅数人，其余都遇难。

The vessel was hit at Wusong estuary by Xin Feng, a British vessel sailing against the maritime safety regulations on January 5, 1918 when heading from Shanghai to Wenzhou fully loaded with over 300 passengers. Puji sunk with only a few passengers survived.

⚓ 飞鲸 Fei Jing

"飞鲸"轮为1883年建造的海轮，该轮原为英商鸿安轮船公司（实为华商向英国登记的公司）所有，排水量1539吨，长77.1米，宽11米，深4.9米，吃水5米，空船吃水2.1—2.9米，净吨位968吨，注册吨位960吨，蒸汽主机功率790马力，航速每小时9.5海里，日耗煤26吨，载客532人。

飞鲸 Fei Jing

Fei Jing was built in 1883 and owned by a British company named Hong An Steamship (a company in fact registered in Britain by a Chinese merchant). It was 77.1 meters in length, at a beam of 11 meters and a depth of 4.9 meters, with a draught of 5 meters (2.1 meters to 2.9 meters if unloaded). It displaced 1,539 tons. The vessel measured 968 net tons and 960 registered tons. With its main steam engine powered at 790 HP, it could sail at a speed of 9.5kn with a daily coal consumption of 26 tons and passenger capacity of 532.

该轮由招商局承租参与了1894年中日甲午战争的运兵任务，该次运兵行动中另一艘招商局向英商怡和租用的"高升"轮于7月25日在"济远"舰护航下于丰岛被日舰击沉，871名清兵及62名船员罹难，同役清军还有"广乙"舰焚毁及"操江"舰被俘虏，是为中日甲午战争海上战斗的开始。

China Merchants leased Fei Jing for troop transportation in the First Sino-Japanese War in 1894. During the transportations, Gao Sheng, another vessel China Merchants leased from a British company Jardine Matheson, was struck at Feng Island by a Japanese ship when shipping troops escorted by Ji Yuan Convoy. The vessel sunk along with 871 soldiers and 62 crew members died. In the same battle, Guang Yi was burnt and Cao Jiang was captured. This event marked the beginning of maritime battlefield of the First Sino-Japanese War in 1894.

"飞鲸"轮于 1923 年 11 月 17 日搁浅于厦门、汕头交会处的古雷湾而报废。

Fei Jing was stranded at Gu Lei gulf, the cross section between Xiamen and Shantou on November 17, 1923 and was later left obsolete.

⚓ 广大（富顺） Guang Da (Fu Shun)

"广大"轮原名"富顺",于 1883 年在英国格拉斯哥（Glasgow）船厂建造,1902 年改装并重新命名为"广大"。船长 85.3 米,船宽 12.1 米,船深 7.7 米,吃水 5.2—5.3 米,空船吃水 2.7 米,注册吨位 2166 吨,毛吨位 2474 吨,净吨位 1536 吨,功率 1015 马力,航速每小时 10.5 海里,日耗煤 33 吨,载客 846 人。

广大（富顺） Guang Da (Fu Shun)

Guang Da, originally named as Fu Shun, was built in 1883 by Glasgow Shipyard of Britain, and was modified and renamed as Guang Da in 1902. It was 85.3 meters in length, at a beam of 12.1 meters and a depth of 7.7 meters, with a draught of 5.2 meters to 5.3 meters (2.7 meters if unloaded). It measured 2,474 gross tons, 2,166 registered tons and 1,536 net tons. With its engine power at 1,015 HP, it could sail at a speed of 10.5 kn with a daily coal consumption of 33 tons and passenger capacity of 846.

⚓ 广利 Guang Li

"广利"轮为招商局于 1883 年在英国格拉斯哥（Glasgow）船厂建造的海轮,船长 85.3 米,船宽 12.1 米,船深 7.7 米,吃水 5.2—5.3 米,空船吃水 2.7 米,注册吨位 2092 吨,毛吨位 2359 吨,净吨位 1468 吨,功率 1100 马力,航速每小时 10.5 海里,日耗煤 33 吨,载客 905 人。

Guang Li was built in 1883 by Glasgow Shipyard of Britain. It was 85.3 meters in length, at a beam of

12.1 meters and a depth of 7.7 meters ,with a draught of 5.2 meters to 5.3 meters (2.7 meters if unloaded). It measured 2,092 registered tons, 2,359 gross tons and 1,468 net tons. With its engine power at 1,100 HP, it could sail at a speed of 10.5 kn with a daily coal consumption of 33 tons and passenger capacity of 905.

广利　Guang Li

该轮于 1935 年因老旧标售待拆。1937 年抗日战争爆发后该轮被征用，于 8 月 12 日起随同 12 艘老旧军舰、185 艘被征用的民船沉塞在长江江阴航道以阻绝日军向首都南京进犯，并拦捕在长江上游未及撤出的日本船舰。

The vessel was prepared for disassembly due to long-time service, and was later requisitioned after the Sino-Japanese War started in 1937. It was put in the Jiangyin part of the Yangtze River along with another 12 old warships and 185 civil boats on August 12 of that year to prevent the Japanese army's aggression to the capital Nanjing and hold up the Japanese ships in the upstream of the Yangtze River which failed to make a successful retreat.

⚓ 固陵　Gu Ling

"固陵"轮，船长 48.8 米，宽 8.2 米，深 2.1 米，吃水 1.5—1.6 米，空船吃水 0.5—1.1 米，注册吨位 304 吨，毛吨位 458 吨，功率 175 马力，航速每小时 8.5 海里，日耗煤 16 吨，载客 502 人。原为英国人立德乐所开设的川江轮船公司于 1887 年在英国订造，在上海装配，计划作为专门行驶川江航线的江轮。

Gu Ling was 48.8 meters in length, at a beam of 8.2 meters and a depth of 2.1 meters, with a draught of 1.5 meters to 1.6 meters (0.5 meters

固陵　Gu Ling

to 1.1 meters if unloaded). The vessel measured 304 registered tons and 458 gross tons. With its engine power at 175 HP, it could sail at a speed of 8.5 kn with a daily coal consumption of 16 tons and passenger capacity of 502. The vessel was ordered in 1887 in Britain by Chuan Jiang Ships owned by a British named Ridler and was assembled in Shanghai. It was designed for sailing on Chuanjiang River route, i.e.the upstream section of the Yangtze River from Yibin, Sichuan to Yichang, Hubei.

该轮装配完成后在宜昌待命准备驶进四川时，却为川江百姓激烈反对而暂缓，中英双方经多次商谈于1889年初达成协议，英轮十年内不驶入川江，清政府则责成招商局以白银12万两的高价收购立德乐的"固陵"轮和在宜昌的码头、栈房，并同意开重庆为通商口岸。1926年该船报废拆解。

When the vessel was assembled and ready in Yichang for the direction to pull into Sichuan, the trip was suspended due to the strong opposition from local people in Chuan Jiang section. Later in early 1889 after many rounds of negotiations between Chinese and British governments, they made an agreement that British ships were not allowed to sail on Chuanjiang River within 10 years. The Qing government then pointed China Merchants to purchase Gu Ling along with the wharfs and warehouses in Yichang from Ridler with 120,000 liang and agreed to open Chongqing as a trade port. Gu Ling was scraped and disassembled in 1926.

⚓ 广济 Guang Ji

"广济"轮1887年在上海建造，铆接钢壳。排水量505吨，净重313吨，船身长56.4米，宽8.2米，深3.4米，满载吃水4.5米，空载吃水2.3米，蒸汽主机功率540马力，航速每小时9海里，日耗煤16吨，载客257人。

Guang Ji was built in Shanghai in 1887. Hull plates were steel and joined with rivets. The vessel displaced 505 tons and measured 313 net tons. It was

广济 Guang Ji

56.4 meters in length, at a beam of 8.2 meters and a depth of 3.4 meters, with a draught of 4.5 meters fully loaded (2.3 meters if unloaded). With its main steam engine power at 540 HP, it could sail at a speed of 9kn with a daily coal consumption of 16 tons and passenger capacity of 257.

"广济"轮是1894年甲午战争时九艘被征调运兵朝鲜的招商局轮船之一，该轮后来的服役历史暂缺。

Guang Ji was one of the nine China Merchants' vessels requisitioned to transport troops in the First Sino-Japanese War in 1894. There was no record for its subsequent services.

新裕 Xin Yu

"新裕"轮为招商局客货海轮，1889年在英国建造，排水量1629吨，长250尺，宽36尺，吃水8尺，蒸汽主机单轴推进。

Xin Yu was a passenger and cargo ocean vessel of China Merchants. It was built in 1889 in Britain, with a displacement of 1,629 tons and a draught of 8 chi. It was 250 chi in length, at a beam of 36 chi and propelled by a single-shaft steam engine.

新裕 Xin Yu

1916年袁世凯为了镇压南方反帝制的叛乱，征调"新裕"轮为运兵船搭载步兵第十三团自天津开往福建。4月22日"新裕"轮在浙江温州刀鱼山附近海面大雾中被护航的"海容"号巡洋舰撞击，锅炉震裂引发火药爆炸，船迅即沉没，溺死陆军官兵及海军部员达700多人，仅船长和两名电工获救。

In 1916, to oppress the southern uprising against monarchy in China, Yuan Shikai[1] requisitioned Xin Yu to transport the 13th infantry from Tianjin to Fujian. On April 22, the vessel was hit by the convoying

---

1 Yuan Shikai (1859-1916), was a Chinese general and politician during the late Qing Dynasty. He had been the first President of the Republic of China and tried to restore monarchy in China, with himself as the Emperor for 83 days.

Hai Rong Cruiser due to the heavy fog on the sea near a hill named Dao Yu in Wenzhou of Zhejiang. The hit broke the boiler which resulted in the explosion of the gunpowder loaded. The vessel sunk shortly, along with all the land and naval army of over 700 people died, and only the captain and two electricians were rescued.

⚓ 爱仁 Ai Ren

"爱仁"轮为1890年建造的海轮,1894年参与了中日甲午战争运兵任务。此外"爱仁"轮还参与了1916年"新裕"轮被"海容"舰撞沉的那次运兵任务。该轮后来作为行驶于香港、汕头、上海之间的客轮。1927年间20多名水匪化装为乘客在香港登船,在出海后挟持驶往大鹏湾,结果被英国皇家海军"L4"号潜艇发现,水匪拒绝降服,潜艇发射两枚鱼雷击沉了"爱仁"号,大半乘客溺亡,10余名水匪被捕后处以死刑。

爱仁 Ai Ren

Ai Ren was an ocean vessel built in 1890 and was also in service for troop transportation during the First Sino-Japanese War in 1894. Ai Ren was also in the assignment in 1916 where Xin Yu was ran down by Hai Rong Cruiser . The vessel later was used as a passenger ship along the routes among Hong Kong, Shantou and Shanghai. In 1927, over 20 bandits disguised as passengers boarded the ship in Hong Kong and hijacked it toward Da Peng gulf. The hijack was found by the British Royal Navy submarine L4 and it launched two torpedoes after the bandits refused to surrender. The torpedoes hit down Ai Ren. The majority of the passengers were drowned. A dozen of the bandits were captured and sentenced to death.

⚓ 新济、新丰 Xin Ji & Xin Feng

"新济"与"新丰"两轮为1891年招商局向英国格拉斯哥船厂订造的海轮,钢质船壳,两层船舱,排水量1864吨,长79.3米,宽11.3米,深6.7米,吃水4.4米,注册吨位1707吨,毛吨位1846吨,净吨位1062吨,蒸汽主机900马力,暗轮结构,载客562人,装货量1300吨,日耗煤22.5吨。同批订造的还有"新丰"轮(1891年交船,"新济"为1892年交船),造价

新济　Xin Ji

53500 英镑。

Xin Ji and Xin Feng were ocean vessels ordered by China Merchants in 1891 from Glasgow Shipyard of Britain. Xin Ji had steel hull plates with two floors of cabins. The vessel was screw propelled. It was 79.3 meters in length, at a beam of 11.3 meters and a depth of 6.7 meters, with a draught of 4.4 meters. It measured 1,707 registered tons, 1,846 gross tons and 1,062 net tons. It displaced 1,864 tons. The main steam engine power was 900 HP with a daily coal consumption of 22.5 tons. The passenger and cargo capacity were 562 and 1,300 tons respectively. Another ship that was on the same order was Xin Feng (turned over to China Merchants in 1891 and Xin Ji in 1892). Total cost for the two ships was 53,500 pounds.

"新济"轮服役后经营北洋至上海航线，该轮于 1928 年 11 月 8 日在福建富阳山外触礁遇海盗被焚毁。

Xin Ji sailed along the route between Beiyang and Shanghai after the military service. It hit a rock near the hill of Fuyang in Fujian on November 8, 1928, and then was robbed and burnt by pirates.

"新丰"轮经营青岛至北洋航线，抗战爆发后的 1938 年 4 月该轮奉命与"江裕"轮及安庆地区的趸船一同自沉于马当阻塞航道。

Xin Feng was used as a commercial vessel along the Qingdao-Beiyang Route.

新丰　Xin Feng

In April of 1938, after the Second Sino-Japanese War broke out, Xin Feng sunk with Jiang Yu and other pontoons from Anqing at Madang to block the fairway.

快利 Kuai Li

"快利"为招商局 1893 年建造的江轮，行驶上海至重庆航线。船长 76.2 米，宽 12.2 米，深 3.1 米，吃水 2.3 米，空船吃水 1.3 米，毛吨位 1293 吨，净吨位 879 吨，功率 700 马力，速率每小时 8.5 海里，日耗煤 23 吨，载客 665 人。

快利 Kuai Li

Kuai Li was a river steamer built in 1893 and sailed along the route between Shanghai and Chongqing. It was 76.2 meters in length, at a beam of 12.2 meters and a depth of 3.1 meters, with a draught of 2.3 meters (1.3 meters if unloaded). It measured 1,293 gross tons and 879 net tons. With its engine power at 700 HP, it could sail at a speed of 8.5 kn with a daily coal consumption of 23 tons and passenger capacity of 665.

1923 年 11 月孙中山派戴季陶自上海搭"快利"轮入川计划说服川军将领合作，戴季陶在本轮行经宜昌、沙市之间竟跳水自杀，后获救（戴季陶战后仍以自杀身亡）。

In November, 1923, Dai Jitao, sent by Sun Yat-sen[1] from Shanghai, was taking Kuai Li to negotiate with Sichuan warlords for cooperation. While the vessel was between Yichang and Shashi, Dai attempted to commit suicide by jumping off the ship and was unsuccessful (Dai committed suicide after the war ended).

该轮于抗战爆发后载运复旦大学师生和物资迁入四川，后脱离招商局管辖归长江业务管理处统筹调度。1940 年 9 月 7 日，在秭归被炸沉。

After the Second Sino-Japanese War began, Kuai Li transported students and faculties of Fudan

---

1 Sun Yat-sen (1866-1925): A Chinese revolutionary, first president and founding father of the Republic of China.

University, together with goods and facilities to Sichuan. Later the vessel was converted under the control of Changjiang Business Administration office from China Merchants. On September 7, 1940, the vessel was bombed and sunk in Zigui.

⚓ 公平、安平、泰顺、遇顺 Gong Ping, An Ping, Tai Shun and Yu Shun

"公平"轮为招商局1894年在英国格拉斯哥船厂建造的海轮,长97.5米,宽14米,深6.9米,吃水4.6米,空船吃水2.1米,排水量2705吨(毛重),净吨位1724吨,注册吨位2472吨,蒸汽主机功率1600马力,航速每小时9.5海里,日耗煤28吨,载客796人,用于行驶上海至青岛航线。1937年8月12日,沉于江阴。

Gong Ping is an ocean vessel built by Glasgow Shipyard of Britain on the purchase order of China Merchants. It was 97.5 meters in length, at a beam of 14 meters and a depth of 6.9 meters, with a draught of 4.6 meters(2.1 meters if unloaded). It displaced 2,705 tons (gross weight). The vessel measured 1,724 net tons and 2,472 registered tons. With its main steam engine power at 1,600 HP, it could sail at a speed of 9.5kn with a daily coal consumption of 28 tons and passenger capacity of 796. The vessel sailed along the route between Shanghai and Qingdao. On August 12, 1937, the vessel sunk in Jiangyin.

公平 Gong Ping

"安平"轮于1896年在英国格拉斯哥船厂建造,毛吨位1857吨,净吨位1159吨,注册吨位1159吨,同"泰顺"轮一批制造,两船总造价418000两,孙中山先生曾在

安平 An Ping

1912年8月搭"安平"轮自烟台赴天津。1917年5月14日"安平"轮自天津返回上海的途中在山东威海卫附近遇雾触礁沉没，34人失踪。

An Ping was built in 1896 by Glasgow Shipyard of Britain. It measured 1,857 gross tons, 1,159 net tons and 1,159 registered tons. An Ping was fabricated in the same batch with Tai Shun. The two vessels cost a total silver of 418,000 liang. Sun Yat-sen once took An Ping in August, 1912 from Yantai to Tianjin. On May 14, 1917, An Ping hit a rock and sunk due to the heavy fog near Weihai, Shandong on its trip back to Shanghai from Tianjin. 34 passengers were missing.

"泰顺"为招商局1896年建造的海轮，主要行驶上海至北洋航线。该轮排水量1962吨，长80.8米，宽11.6米，深6.9米，吃水5米，空船吃水2.2米，毛吨位1962吨，净吨位1216吨，注册吨位1216吨，蒸汽机功率860马力，航速每小时9.5海里，日耗煤23吨，载客600人。1937年8月12日，该轮沉没于江阴。

泰顺　Tai Shun

Tai Shun was a China Merchants ocean vessel built in 1896 and sailed between Beiyang and Shanghai. The vessel displaced 1,962 tons. It was 80.8 meters in length, at a beam of 11.6 meters and a depth of 6.9 meters, with a draught of 5 meters (2.2 meters if unloaded). The vessel measured 1,962 gross tons, 1,216 net tons and 1,216 registered tons. With its steam engine power at 860 HP, it could sail at a speed of 9.5kn with a daily coal consumption of 23 tons and passenger capacity of 600. Tai Shun sunk in Jiangyin on August 12, 1937.

遇顺　Yu Shun

"遇顺"为招商局1900年在谷兰哥摩司（Grangemouth）建造的海轮，排水量1696吨，长79.3米，宽12.2米，深5.9米，吃水4.6米，蒸汽主机功率950马力，航速每小时7海里，日耗煤26吨，载客456人，完

工后主要行驶上海至青岛航线。

Yu Shun was a China Merchants ocean vessel built in 1900 in Grangemouth. The vessel displaced 1,696 tons. It was 79.3 meters in length, at a beam of 12.2 meters and a depth of 5.9 meters, with a draught of 4.6 meters. With its steam engine power at 950 HP, it could sail at a speed of 7 kn with a daily coal consumption of 26 tons and passenger capacity of 456. Yu Shun was mainly used for the route between Shanghai and Qingdao after it was completed.

"公平"轮与"泰顺"、"遇顺"轮于1937年抗日战争爆发后被征用，于8月12日起随同12艘老旧军舰、185艘被征用的民船沉塞在长江江阴航道以阻绝日军向首都南京进犯，并拦捕在长江上游未及撤出的日本船舰。

After the Second Sino-Japanese War broke out, Gong Ping, Tai Shun and Yu Shun were requisitioned on August 12 along with 12 old warships and 185 civil boats to block the Jiangyin fairway of the Yangtze River to prevent Japanese army's aggression to the capital Nanjing and hold up the Japanese ships in the upstream of the Yangtze River which failed to make a successful retreat.

新昌、新康、新铭（新捷） Xin Chang, Xin Kang and Xin Ming (Xin Jie)

"新昌"轮为招商局1905年在英国格拉斯哥船厂建造的海轮，造价244000两，排水量2000吨，长82.3米，宽12.2米，深6.6米，吃水4.9米，空船吃水2.1米，毛吨位2000吨，净吨位1258吨，注册吨位2000吨，功率987马力，航速每小时10海里，日耗煤27吨，载客491人，用以行驶上海、青岛航线，本轮于1930年因事故沉没。

Xin Chang was a China Merchants ocean vessel built by Glasgow Shipyard of Britain in 1905 at a cost of 224,000 liang. Xin Chang displaced 2,000 tons. It was 82.3 meters in length, at a beam of 12.2 meters and a depth of 6.6 meters, with a draught of 4.9 meters (2.1 meters if unloaded). The vessel measured 2,000 gross tons, 1,258 net tons and 2,000 registered tons.

新昌 Xin Chang

With its engine power at 987 HP, it could sail at a speed of 10 kn with a daily coal consumption of 27 tons and passenger capacity of 491. Xin Chang sailed along the route between Shanghai and Qingdao. It sunk in an accident in 1930.

"新康"轮为招商局1906年在上海建造的海轮，造价243000两，船长82.3米，宽12.2米，深6.6米，吃水5.1—5.2米，空船吃水1.8—2.4米，净吨位1262吨，注册吨位2100吨，功率1300马力，航速每小时10海里，日耗煤30吨，载客494人，排水量2149吨，主要用以行驶上海至青岛航线，曾参加了1916年"新裕"轮被"海容"舰撞沉那次的运兵任务。

Xin Kang was a China Merchants ocean vessel built in Shanghai in 1906 at a cost of 243,000 liang. It was 82.3 meters in length, at a beam of 12.2 meters and a depth of 6.6 meters, with a draught of 5.1 meters to 5.2 meters (1.8 meters to 2.4 meters if unloaded). The vessel measured 1,262 net tons and 2,100 registered tons. With its engine power at 1,300 HP, it could sail at a speed of 10 kn with a daily coal consumption of 30 tons and passenger capacity of 494. Xin Kang displaced 2,149 tons. The vessel mainly sailed along the route between Shanghai and Qingdao. It was also on the assignment when Xin Yu was run down by Hai Rong.

新康　Xin Kang

"新康"轮于1929年7月21日中午在山东角成山头被日本邮船会社"龙野丸"撞入右舵楼后倒车退出致使当场沉没，溺死57人，日轮肇事后逃往神户，事后调查并作伪证拒绝理赔。

On July 21, 1929, Xin Kang was hit on the right rudder by a Japanese ship named Tatsuno Maru from Nippon Yusen Kabushiki Kaisha and sunk while trying to exit backward. 57 passengers were drowned. The Japanese fled to Kobe and refused to pay compensation with perjury in post-event investigation.

"新铭"轮为招商局1907年在英国格拉斯哥船厂建造的海轮，造价348000两，原定名"新捷"，后改"新铭"；排水量2133吨，长82.3米，宽12.6米，深6.6米，吃水4.4米，空船吃水2.6米，毛吨位2133吨，净吨位1428吨，注册吨位1603吨，功率1600马力，航速每小时12海里，日耗煤36吨，载客639人。该轮建成后用于行驶上海至青岛航线。1931年1月10日该轮在汕头附近的红海湾曾被海盗抢劫。

新铭　Xin Ming

Xin Ming was a China Merchants ocean vessel built in 1907 by Glasgow Shipyard of Britain at a cost of 348,000 liang. The first name of the vessel before Xin Ming was Xin Jie. The vessel displaced 2,133 tons and it was 82.3 meters in length, at a beam of 12.6 meters and a depth of 6.6 meters, with a draught of 4.4 meters (2.6 meters if unloaded). The vessel measured 2,133 gross tons, 1,428 net tons and 1,603 registered tons. With its engine power at 1,600 HP, it could sail at a speed of 12 kn with a daily coal consumption of 36 tons and passenger capacity of 639. The vessel was used along the route between Shanghai and Qingdao after being built. It had been robbed by pirates on January 10, 1931 in Honghai Gulf near Shantou.

"新铭"轮于1937年抗日战争爆发后被征用，8月12日随同12艘老旧军舰、185艘被征用的民船沉塞在长江江阴航道，以阻绝日军向首都南京进犯。

After the Second Sino-Japanese War broke out, Xin Ming was requisitioned to sink itself on August 12, 1937 along with 12 old warships and 185 civil boats in Jiang Yin fairway of the Yangtze River to stop Japanese from invading Nanjing.

⚓ 同华、吉安、恒新　Tong Hua, Ji An and Heng Xin

"同华"轮、"吉安"轮为招商局1906年建造的海轮，排水量1176吨，长68.6米，宽10.2米，深5.8米，吃水4.9米，空船吃水2.3米，毛吨位1176吨，净吨位746吨，注册吨

位 1079 吨，功率 685 马力，航速每小时 9.5 海里，日耗煤 17 吨，载客 265 人。

Tong Hua and Ji An were China Merchants ocean vessels built in 1906 with a displacement of 1,176 tons for each. The length overall each was 68.6 meters, the beam was 10.2 meters and the depth was 5.8 meters with a draught of 4.9 meters (2.3 meters if unloaded). The vessel each measured 1,176 gross tons, 746 net tons and 1,079 registered tons. With its engine power at 685 HP, it could sail at a speed of 9.5kn with a daily coal consumption of 17 tons and passenger capacity of 265.

"同华"轮于 1937 年抗日战争爆发后被征用，8 月 12 日起随同 12 艘老旧军舰、185 艘被征用的民船沉塞在长江江阴航道，以阻绝日军向首都南京进犯。

Tong Hua dropped in the Jiangyin Fairway of the Yangtze River on August 12 after the Second Sino-Japanese War broke out along with 12 old warships and 185 civil boats requisitioned to stop Japanese from invading Nanjing.

"吉安"轮为招商局海轮，规格不详，1894 年 8 月 8 日晚应差载运湖南兵勇 1000 余名由江苏镇江至浙江温州海面时触礁，船身下沉。士兵有 700 人乘小艇登岸，有约 300 人因不习惯海上颠簸，落水死亡。

Ji An was a China Merchants ocean vessel. Specifications were not recorded. Ji An hit the reef near Wenzhou, Zhejiang on August 8, 1894 on an assignment to transport over a thousand Hunan troops from Zhenjiang, Jiangsu. The vessel sank and 700 of the troops were evacuated via life boats, 300 of them were not used to the bumpy boats and drowned after falling off the boats on the way.

"恒新"轮为招商局江轮，1909 年于上海求新船厂建造，长 90 英尺，主机马力 80 匹，航速每小时 9 海里。

Heng Xin was a China Merchants river steamer, built in 1909 by Shanghai Qiuxin Shipyard. Its length overall was 90 feet. With its engine power at 80 HP, it could sail at a speed of 9kn.

恒新　Heng Xin

江新 Jiang Xin

"江新"轮为招商局1903年在上海耶松船厂建造的江轮，造价387000两．排水量3571.2吨，船长99.1米，宽13.4米，深4.4米，吃水3.9米，空船吃水2.2米，毛吨位3372吨，净吨位2102吨，注册吨位1501吨，功率2200马力，航速每小时12.5海里，日耗煤34吨，载客1814人。

江新 Jiang Xin

Jiang Xin was a China Merchants river steamer built in Shanghai Yesong Shipyard in 1903 at a cost of 387,000 liang. Jiang Xin displaced 3,571.2 tons and its length overall was 99.1 meters, the beam was 13.4 meters and the depth was 4.4 meters with a draught of 3.9 meters (2.2 meters if unloaded). The vessel measured 3,372 gross tons, 2,102 net tons and 1,501 registered tons. With its engine power at 2,200 HP, it could sail at a speed of 12.5 kn with a daily coal consumption of 34 tons and passenger capacity of 1,814.

"江新"轮为抗战时撤入四川的六大江轮之一（即"江新"、"江顺"、"江汉"、"江安"、"江建"、"江华"），但因川江水浅无法航行而搁置，抗战胜利后于重庆就地整修，后复行驶于长江航线。

Jiang Xin was one of the six river steamers retreated into Sichuan during the Second Sino-Japanese War (the rest included Jiang Shun, Jiang Han, Jiang An, Jiang Jian and Jiang Hua), but it was laid aside because the river was not deep enough for its sail. After the Second Sino-Japanese War ended, Jiang Xin was repaired in Chongqing and put in sail along the route of the Yangtze River again.

"江新"轮在1949年5月22日曾被汤恩伯派兵持枪押往台湾，但出河口时被解放军炮击，押运军官搭小船逃命，该轮又开回上海而为解放军获得。该轮后来在上海浦东洋港码头被国民党空军飞机炸沉。1952年11月16日，中国海事部门将其打捞出水复用。

Jiang Xin was sent to Taiwan with armed force aboard by Tang Enbo on May 22, 1949 and was attached by the Communist Liberation Army at the estuary. The leaders fled by a boat. Jiang Xin returned to Shanghai and was obtained by Communist Liberation Army. It was later bombed by Kuomintang air force at the wharf of the Yanggang port, Pudong District, Shanghai, and then sank into the river . On November 16, 1952, the vessel was fished out and restored for use by the China maritime agency.

⚓ 兴盛 Xing Sheng

"兴盛"轮是1880年原招商局客货轮，花费约3万两白银将明轮改为暗轮并更新主机，改成货轮并更名为"兴盛"轮，排水量444吨。1883年5月23日在山东成山头被英国夹板船"噶地林马甸"号撞沉，死7人，伤船主及水手各1人，船货全部沉没。

Xing Sheng was built in 1880. Around 30,000 liang silver was spent to change the paddle wheel into screw propeller and replace the main steam engine. It was renovated into a cargo ship and renamed as Xing Sheng with a displacement of 444 tons. On May 23, 1883, Xing Sheng was hit down by a British decked boat named Ge Di Lin Ma Dian in Chengshantou of Shandong, causing 7 people dead as well as the vessel owner and a sailor injured. All the cargo aboard sunk along with the vessel.

⚓ 惠吉 Hui Ji

光绪四年三月，招商局接收由上海江南制造局建造的"中国第一号战舰""惠吉"轮（原名"恬吉"）。该轮长185尺，宽27尺，吃水8尺，船体木壳，明轮，老式蒸汽机，功率392马力，载重吨600，航速约每小时9.5海里。

In March, 1878, China Merchants took over Hui Ji (renamed from Tian Ji), the Number One Warship of China from Kiangnan Arsenal in Shanghai. Its length overall was 185 chi and the beam was 27 chi with a draught of 8 chi. The hull was made of wood and it was propelled by paddle wheel and old-style steam engine. With its engine power at 392 HP, it could sail at a speed of 9.5 kn and had a dead weight tonnage of 600 tons.

⚓ 江平 Jiang Ping

1893年"日新"轮与"江平"轮拆卸作为驳船。

Ri Xin and Jiang Ping were reassembled into barges in 1893.

江平　Jiang Ping

新安　Xin An

招商局内河拖轮，1909年上海求新船厂造，共10余艘，总长34英尺，拖重50吨，航速每小时9海里，主机功率30马力。

It was an inland river towboat, built in 1909 by Shanghai Qiuxin Shipyard. There were over ten of them. The length was 34 feet and the weight was 50 tons. With its engine power at 30 HP, it could sail at a speed of 9 kn.

新安　Xin An

江华　Kiang Hwa

英文名Kiang Hwa，铁壳客货船，属于大型江轮，1911年江南造船所为招商局建造的长江客轮，当时被誉为"长江各轮之冠"。价37万余两，船长330英尺，排水量4130吨，毛吨位3693吨，主机功率2400马力，航速每小时12—13海里，拥有货舱5间，各种客舱共76间，可载客998人，船身轻而灵活，吃水浅（满载吃水3.8米，空载吃水2.2米），载重

量大，耗煤省，行驶稳捷。

Built in 1911 by Kiangnan Arsenal at a cost of 370,000 liang, Kiang Hwa was a passenger and cargo river steamer with iron hull on the order of China Merchants. It was reputed to be Crown of Ships on the Yangtze River at that time. Its length overall was 330 feet, displacement 4,130 tons and gross tonnage 3,693 tons. With its engine power at 2,400 HP, it could sail at a speed of 12 to 13 kn. Kiang Hwa had 5 cargo holds and 76 passenger cabins that could accommodate 998 passengers. The vessel was light and easy to maneuver. Its draught was 3.8 meters fully loaded and 2.2 meters if unloaded. Heavy loaded, Kiang Hwa was also coal-saving and steady in sailing.

江华　Kiang Hwa

抗战时该轮连同"江新"等 5 艘大型江轮撤入川江，1941 年 8 月在万县附近被日机轰炸焚毁。

During the Second Sino-Japanese War, Kiang Hwa along with other 5 large river steamers retreated back to Chuanjiang River and was bombed by Japanese army near Wan County in August, 1941.

⚓ 江通　Jiang Tong

1878 年 4 月，"江通"轮开往宜昌。

In April, 1878, Jiang Tong sailed to Yi Chang.

⚓ 江源　Jiang Yuan

"江源"轮，曾用船名"俾物乐"，1878 年 5 月，"江源"同"江孚"投入汉口至宜昌航线。

Jiang Yuan, originally named as Bi Wu Le, was put into use in the route between Hankou and Yichang along with Jiang Fu in May, 1878.

美利　Mei Li

"美利"轮总吨472吨，1878年，"美利"开辟香港、海口线；1880年开辟上海、营口、烟台线，1883年3月在越南海面突遇大风，淹死大副7人，损失米数百吨。

Mei Li, with a gross tonnage of 472 tons, first sailed along Hong Kong and Haikou routes in 1878 and later Shanghai, Yingkou and Yantan routes in 1880. In March, 1883, Mei Li ran into a strong storm near Vietnam, causing 7 deaths and a loss of hundreds tons of rice.

康济　Kang Ji

1881年，"康济"开辟海口、海防线。

Starting from 1881, Kang Ji explored the routes to Haikou and Haiphong .

江表　Jiang Biao

"江表"轮为招商局江轮，1883年航行沪汉线。1890年，"江表"轮出售。

Jiang Biao was a China Merchants river steamer and sailed along the route between Shanghai and Hankou in 1883. The vessel was sold in 1890.

镇东　Zhen Dong

"镇东"轮是从美国旗昌洋行购买的海轮，1883年曾于春夏协运漕粮，秋冬则行驶牛庄、上海及厦门、汕头、香港、广州一带。为招商局服务至1896年。

Zhen Dong was an ocean vessel purchased by China Merchants from the U.S. Russell & Co. It was at firstly used for tribute grain transportation in the spring and summer time in 1883 and the vessel sailed along the areas like Niuzhuang, Shanghai, Xiamen, Shantou, HongKong and Guangzhou during the autumn and winter time. Zhen Dong had been in service for China Merchants until 1896.

海琛　Hai Chen

"海琛"轮是从美国旗昌洋行购买的海轮，曾用船名"直隶"。1883年"海琛"轮开福州线，1904年6月14日，"海琛"在马尾口外五星触雷失事。

Hai Chen, originally named as Zhi Li, was an ocean vessel purchased from U.S. Russell & Co. and sailed along the route of Fuzhou in 1883. On June 14, 1904, Hai Chen was hit by lightening and wrecked near Maweikou.

益东 Yi Dong

"益东"轮总吨位 507 吨，1879 年失事。

Yi Dong, with a gross tonnage of 507 tons, was wrecked in 1879.

镇西 Zhen Xi

"镇西"轮是招商局从旗昌洋行购买的海轮，1880 年卖给英商。

Zhen Xi was an ocean vessel purchased by China Merchants from U.S. Russell & Co. and was sold to a British trading company in 1880.

新盛 Xin Sheng

1888 年，添造"新盛"轮。1892 年 6 月 26 日，该船在山东烟台成山头遇风触礁，淹死妇女一人，船身沉没，货物全部损失。

Xin Sheng was added to China Merchants' fleet in 1888. On June 26, 1892, Xin Sheng hit the rocks and sunk due to the strong wind near Chengshantou of Yantai, Shandong, causing one woman died and a loss of all the cargos.

协和 Xie He

1900 年，添"协和"轮，净吨位 1082 吨，1905 年，该轮失事。

Xie He, with a net tonnage of 1,082 tons, was added to China Merchants' fleet in 1900 and wrecked in 1905.

美宫 Mei Gong

1911 年 4 月 23 日，"美宫"轮在三星灯山外被"广利"撞沉。

On April 23, 1911, Mei Gong was hit down by Guang Li near the mount of Sanxingdeng and wrecked.

海珊 Hai Shan

"海珊"轮，曾用名"江西"，是从旗昌洋行购买的海轮。

Hai Shan, originally named as Jiang Xi, was a China Merchants ocean vessel purchased from U.S. Russell & Co.

⚓ 江靖 Jiang Jing

"江靖"轮，曾用名"气拉渡"，是从旗昌洋行购买的江轮。

Jiang Jing, originally named as Hirado, was a river steamer purchased from U.S. Russell & Co.

⚓ 江汇 Jiang Hui

"江汇"轮，曾用名"快也坚"，是从旗昌洋行购买的江轮。

Jiang Hui, originally named as Kuai Ye Jian, was a river steamer purchased from U.S. Russell & Co.

⚓ 南浔、满洲、大有、汉阳 Nan Xun, Man Zhou, Da You and Han Yang

为招商局附局轮船。

They were all owned by China Merchants affiliates.

⚓ 宝康（保康） Bao Kang

1878年，招商局与太古轮船公司合购"宝康"（又称"保康"），到1881年该船全部归招商局所有，留在天津大沽作为驳运漕米之用。

In 1878, China Merchants and Swire co-purchased Bao Kang (Chinese: 保康 or 宝康). In 1881, the vessel was wholly owned by China Merchants and kept in Dagu, Tianjin to transport tribute grain.

⚓ 海镜 Hai Jing

"海镜"轮，总吨位409吨，1874年初，招商局向闽厂承领"海镜"号轮船，派往天津运漕，后又派往瓜州运兵，10月将该轮交还闽厂。

Hai Jing, with a gross tonnage of 409 tons, was borrowed from the shipyard in Fujian in early 1874 by China Merchants, and was sent to Tianjin to transport tribute grain and then to Guazhou to transport troops. Hai Jing was returned to the shipyard in Fujian in October, 1874.

第 二 章
民国时期

CHAPTER TWO
IN THE ERA OF THE REPUBLIC OF CHINA

第一节　时局动荡　艰难前行（1912—1936）

SECTION ONE
Arduous Growth in Chaotic Situation (1912-1936)

1911 年辛亥革命爆发，清王朝覆亡。1912 年 3 月，招商局在上海张园召开第二次股东常会，会议决定招商局改称"商办招商局轮船公司"，实行完全商办。进入商办以来，受时局变动、军阀混战等因素的影响，招商局轮运业务发展缓慢。

The Xinhai Revolution[31] broke out in 1911 and led to the fall of Qing Dynasty. In March 1912, China Merchants held its second regular shareholders' meeting in Zhang Yuan, Shanghai, and decided to rename it as "Commercialized China Merchants Steamship Company" and implement complete commercialization. Since then, influenced by the changes in political situation and incessant fightings among warlords, the shipping business of China Merchants developed very slowly.

1912 年上半年，招商局添置了"江华"轮及部分小轮和驳船。到 1914 年，招商局共有船舶 29 艘，其中江轮 9 艘，海轮 20 艘。1918 年招商局向耶松船厂订造海轮一艘，题名"新大"。1920 年，"新大"轮在成山石岛触礁沉没，该年添"嘉禾"海轮一艘。1921 年，招商局添置"江安"、"江顺"、"江庆"（后改名"峨眉"）、"新江天"、"新华"等 5 艘新轮，这一年也是招商局在整个商办时期（1912—1926 年）添加新轮最多、船舶总吨增长最快的一年。

The first half of 1912 witnessed the acquisition of Jiang Hua ship and some ferries and barges. To 1914, China Merchants had a total of 29 ships, including 9 river steamers and 20 ocean vessels. In 1918, China Merchants ordered a tailored ocean vessel from Yesong Shipyard and named it as Xin Da. In 1920, Xin Da ran into the reef in Chengshanshi Island and sunk. In the same year, an ocean vessel named Jia He was

---

1　The Xinhai Revolution, or the Hsin-hai Revolution, also known as the Revolution of 1911 or the Chinese Revolution, was a revolution that overthrew China's last imperial dynasty, the Qing dynasty, and established the Republic of China. The revolution was named Xinhai (Hsin-hai) because it occurred in 1911, the year of the Xinhai stem-branch in the sexagenary cycle of the Chinese calendar.

bought. In 1921, China Merchants purchased 5 new vessels, namely Jiang An, Jiang Shun, Jiang Qing (later renamed as E Mei), Xin Jiang Tian and Xin Hua. The year 1921 was the year when China Merchants enjoyed the largest number increase and the fastest gross tonnage growth throughout its commercial period (from 1912 to 1926).

1924年，招商局添置"华大"、"华利"两轮，改名"江大"、"江靖"。1929年，招商局将与太古、怡和公司合购的"联益"轮全部买断，改名"建国"。1932年，又向挪威购买"海瑞"、"海祥"两艘新式海轮。

In 1924, China Merchants acquired two ships named Hua Da and Hua Li, later renamed them as Jiang Da and Jiang Jing respectively. In 1929, China Merchants bought out the ship named Lian Yi which was co-purchased together with Swire and Jardine Matheson at first, and renamed it as Jian Guo. In 1932, two new-style ocean vessels named Hai Rui and Hai Xiang were bought from Norway.

1933年5月，招商局使用中英庚子赔款董事会的借款向英国订造"海元"、"海亨"、"海利"、"海贞"四艘海轮。1935年又从英国买进"达飞"号海轮，改名"海云"。同年，还购买了"鸿源"轮。

With the remittance remitted by Britain in Boxer Indemnity[1], China Merchants ordered four ocean vessels from Britain in May 1933, namely Hai Yuan, Hai Heng, Hai Li, and Hai Zhen. In 1935, an ocean vessel named Da Fei was bought from Britain and was renamed as Hai Yun. In the same year, China Merchants also purchased an ocean vessel named Hong Yuan.

到抗日战争前夕，招商局已建成了一支有相当规模的商业船队，拥有大小船舶84艘，计86381总吨，其中江海大轮29艘，69635总吨。

On the eve of the Second Sino-Japanese War, China Merchants had built a commercial fleet with a considerable scale, including 84 ships, with a gross tonnage of 86,381 tons, among which 29 are river steamers and ocean vessels with a gross tonnage of 69,635 tons.

---

1 Boxer Indemnity: The indemnity paid by China to Austria-Hungary, France, Germany, Italy, Japan, Russia, the United Kingdom, and the United States after the Boxer Protocol was signed on September 7, 1901.The Eight-Nation Alliance provided military forces into China after China's defeat in putting down the Boxer Rebellion.

嘉禾 Jia He

1920年购进的"嘉禾"轮，是一艘二手轮。1892年在格拉斯哥建造。船长72.8米，船宽11.6米，船深4.3米，吃水4.7米（空船吃水2米）。注册吨位977吨，毛吨位1588吨，净吨位977吨。功率860马力，航速每小时9海里，日煤耗18吨，可载客289人。1937年8月12日，沉船于江阴。

Jia He, purchased in 1920, was a second-hand ocean vessel built in Glasgow in 1892. Its length overall was 72.8 meters, the beam was 11.6 meters and depth 4.3 meters with a draught of 4.7 meters (2 meters if unloaded). The vessel measured 977 registered tons, 1,588 gross tons and 977 net tons. With its engine power at 860 HP, it could sail at a speed of 9 kn with a daily coal consumption of 18 tons and passenger capacity of 289. On August 12, 1937, it sunk in Jiangyin.

江安、江顺 Jiang An & Jiang Shun

"江安"、"江顺"是1921年在上海建造的新船。两船均长103.6米，船宽14.3米，船深4.7米。"江安"满载吃水3.7米、空船吃水2.3米；"江顺"满载吃水3.8米、空船吃水3.3米。两船注册吨位均为3141吨，毛吨位4327吨，净吨位2150吨。功率1570马力，航速每小时12.5海里，日耗煤41—45吨，可载客2022人。

Jiang An and Jiang Shun were new ships built in Shanghai in 1921. The length of ships in this level was 103.6 meters, the beam was 14.3 meters and the depth was 4.7 meters. Jiang An had a draught of 3.7 meters (2.3 meters if unloaded) while Jiang Shun 3.8 meters (3.3 meters if unloaded). The vessel each measured 3,141 registered tons, 4,327 gross tons and 2,150 net tons. With its engine power at 1,570 HP, the ship could sail at a speed of 12.5 kn with a daily coal consumption of 41-45 tons and passenger capacity of 2,022.

江安 Jiang An

江顺 Jiang Shun

"江顺"英文名 Kiang Shun，1949 年留在大陆。
With Kiang Shun as another English name, Jiang Shun was left in Mainland China in 1949.

抗日战争时期，六大江轮撤入川江。"江顺"轮是上驶川江的第一艘江轮。接着"江安"、"江新"、"江华"等轮陆续上驶抵达重庆。
During the Second Sino-Japanese War, six river steamers were withdrawn into the Chuanjiang River, the upstream of the Yangtze River. Jiang Shun was the first one sailing to Chuanjiang River. Later, Jiang An, Jiang Xin, Jiang Hua and other steamers arrived at Chongqing gradually.

江庆 Jiang Qing

"江庆"轮是 1920 年在上海建造的新船。船长 61.7 米，船宽 9.5 米，船深 3.1 米。满载吃水 2.4—2.5 米、空船吃水 1.1—1.7 米。该轮注册吨位 393 吨，毛吨位 1111 吨，净吨位 971 吨。功率 1555 马力，航速每小时 13 海里，日耗煤 54 吨，可载客 214 人。

Jiang Qing was a new ship built in Shanghai in 1920. Its length overall was 61.7 meters, the beam was 9.5 meters and the depth was 3.1 meters with a draught of 2.4-2.5 meters (1.1-1.7 meters if unloaded). With its engine power at 1,555 HP, it could sail at a speed of 13 kn with a daily coal consumption of 54 tons and passenger capacity of 214.

江庆 Jiang Qing

1921 年，"江庆"轮开始行驶川江，由于沿途土匪及军阀部队经常骚扰，只好"借重外人以自卫"，改悬法旗行驶。1925 年秋该轮曾在石门搁浅，到次年春季川水上涨时才脱浅，后更名"峨眉"，继续在川江从事运输活动。

In 1921, Jiang Qing began to sail along Chuanjiang River. However, it had to hang the French flag to protect itself due to the frequent harassment by bandits and warlord forces. In the autumn of 1925, the ship was stranded in Shimen and did not refloat until the next spring when the river water rose up. It was later renamed as E Mei and continued to engage in transportation activities in Chuanjiang River.

新江天 Xin Jiang Tian

新江天 Xin Jiang Tian

1921 年上海建造，客货轮，船长 91.4 米，船宽 14.6 米，船深 4.6 米。满载吃水 3.6 米，空船吃水 2.2 米。注册吨位 2594 吨，毛吨位 3659 吨，净吨位 2387 吨。功率 1800 马力，航速每小时 12 海里，日耗煤 36 吨，可载客 2326 人。

Built in Shanghai in 1921, Xin Jiang Tian was a passenger and cargo ship. Its length overall was 91.4 meters, the beam was 14.6 meters and the depth was 4.6 meters with a draught of 3.6 meters (2.2 meters if unloaded). The ship measured 2,594 registered tons, 3,659 gross tons and 2,387 net tons. With its engine power at 1,800 HP, it could sail at a speed of 12 kn with a daily coal consumption of 36 tons and passenger capacity of 2,326.

1938 年 4 月，沉船于镇海。

In April 1938, it sank in Zhenhai.

⚓ 新华 Xin Hua

1921 年在英国格拉斯哥造船厂建造的海轮。船长 82.3 米，船宽 12.2 米，船深 6.2 米，满载吃水 5.1—5.2 米，空船吃水 2.1—3.1 米，注册吨位 2310 吨，毛吨位 2056 吨，净吨位 1358 吨，功率 1100 马力，航速每小时 10.8 海里，日耗煤 28 吨，可载客 570 人。

Xin Hua was an ocean vessel built by Glasgow Shipyard of Britain in 1921. Its length overall was 82.3 meters, the beam was 12.2 meters and the depth was 6.2 meters with a draught of 5.1 meters to 5.2 meters (2.1 meters to 3.1 meters if unloaded). The ship measured 2,310 registered tons, 2,056 gross tons and 1,358 net tons. With its engine power at 1,100 HP, it could sail at a speed of 10.8 kn with a daily coal consumption of 28 tons and passenger capacity of 570.

1929 年 1 月 16 日，"新华"轮在离香港 10 余海里远的纬纶灯塔触礁沉没。

On January 16, 1929, Xin Hua hit the reef near Wei Lun lighthouse and sunk just 10-odd nautical miles away from Hong Kong.

⚓ 江大、江靖 Jiang Da & Jiang Jing

1924 年，招商局添置"华大"、"华利"两二手轮，改名"江大"、"江靖"。两轮于 1900 年在英国格拉斯哥造船厂建造。船长 75.5 米，船宽 9.1 米，船深 3.6 米。满载吃水 3.1 米，空船吃水 2.3 米。注册吨位 1160 吨，毛吨位 1680 吨，净吨位 710 吨。功率 400 马力，航速每小时 10 海里，日耗煤 21 吨，可载客 632 人。

In 1924, China Merchants acquired two second-hand ocean vessels named Hua Da and Hua Li, and renamed them as Jiang Da and Jiang Jing. They were built by Glasgow Shipyard of Britain in 1900. The length overall of each was 75.5 meters, the beam was 9.1 meters and the depth was 3.6 meters with a draught of 3.1 meters (2.3 meters if unloaded). The ship each measured 1,160 registered tons, 1,680 gross tons and

710 net tons. With its engine power at 400 HP, it could sail at a speed of 10 kn with a daily coal consumption of 21 tons and passenger capacity of 632.

"江大"1940年9月7日，在秭归被炸沉。"江靖"1940年10月，在秭归被炸沉。
Jiang Da was bombed and sunk in Zigui on September 7, 1940 and Jiang Jing in October 1940.

⚓ 海瑞、海祥 Hai Rui & Hai Xiang

1932年招商局向挪威购买"海瑞"、"海祥"两艘新式海轮，注册吨位分别为1852吨与1850吨，船长均为79.6米，吃水5.2米，航速每小时9海里，均系1881年所造。

In 1932, China Merchants bought two new-style ocean vessels from Norway, namely Hai Rui and Hai Xiang. The ships measured 1,852 registered tons and 1,850 registered tons respectively. Both of them were built in 1881 with a length of 79.6 meters and a draught of 5.2 meters. They could sail at a speed of 9 kn.

"海瑞"是铁壳客货船，主机功率250马力，总长122尺4寸，宽18尺8寸，2048.57载重吨，空船吃水8尺4寸，满载吃水9尺3寸，航速每小时8海里，1908年出厂，1938年6月入川时在葛洲坝搁浅，1946年4月30日发还航商刘梅村。

Hai Rui, completed and launched in 1908, was a passenger and cargo vessel with iron hull. Its length overall was 122.4 chi and the beam was 18.8 chi with a draught of 9.3 chi (8.4 chi if unloaded). With its engine power at 250 HP, it could sail at a speed of 8 kn and had a dead weight tonnage of 2,048.57 tons. In June 1938, it was stranded in Gezhou Dam when shipping to Sichuan Province. On April 30, 1946, it was returned to Liu Meicun, a shipping businessman.

"海祥"，2408.57载重吨，1941年8月13日，在秭归被炸沉。
Hai Xiang, with a dead weight tonnage of 2408.57 tons, was bombed and sunk in Zigui on August 13, 1941.

⚓ 海元、海亨、海利、海贞 Hai Yuan, Hai Heng, Hai Li and Hai Zhen

1933年5月，招商局使用中英庚子赔款董事会的借款向英国订造"海元"、"海亨"、"海利"、"海贞"四艘海轮，造价356800英镑。

With the remittance remitted by Britain in Boxer Indemnity, China Merchants ordered four ocean vessels from Britain in May 1933, namely Hai Yuan, Hai Heng, Hai Li, and Hai Zhen, at a price of 356,800 pounds in total.

本级轮船长 100—101 米，船宽 13.9 米，船深 6.9 米，吃水 5.3 米。总吨位 3395—3415 吨，净吨位 2078—2108 吨。功率 2500 马力，航速每小时 13.6 海里。本级轮有特等舱位 14 个，头等舱位 52 个，二等舱位 28 个，必要时甲板还可装载 900 人。

海亨　Hai Heng

The length overall of ships in this level was 100-101 meters, the beam was 13.9 meters, and the depth was 6.9 meters with a draught of 5.3 meters. The vessel of this level measured 3,395-3,415 gross tons and 2,078-2,108 net tons. With its engine power at 2,500 HP, it could sail at a speed of 13.6 kn. The vessel of this level had 14 superior-class seats, 52 first-class seats and 28 second-class seats. Another 900 passengers could be loaded on deck if necessary.

1937 年抗日战争起，招商局总经理蔡增基将上海业务委托美商卫利韩洋行代理，并将四大海轮连同总公司及资料账册迁往香港，1938 年 12 月四大海轮连同"海云"轮等五艘在香港出售予英商怡和洋行。

Since the Second Sino-Japanese War broke out, Mr. Cai Zengji, then General Manager of China Merchants entrusted Shanghai business to Hunt & Co.,William, an U.S. firm as the agent, and relocated these four ocean vessels, the headquarter as well as relevant documents and books to Hong Kong. In December 1938, these four vessels were sold to Jardine Matheson along with Hai Yun in Hong Kong.

⚓ 海云　Hai Yun

招商局于 1935 年以 7750 英镑，从英国买进"达飞"号海轮，改名"海云"，该轮长 99.1 米，宽 14.3 米，载重吨 5600，航速每小时 9 海里，适合装载各类货物，被派驶沪海（海州）线。

In 1935, China Merchants bought an ocean vessel named Da Fei from Britain at a cost of 7,750 pounds, and then renamed it as Hai Yun. Its length overall was 99.1 meters and the beam was 14.3 meters, with a dead weight tonnage of 5,600 tons. It could sail at a speed of 9 kn, suitable for transportation of all types of goods and sailing through the Shanghai-Haizhou route.

第二节　沉船御敌 江轮入川（1937—1945）

SECTION TWO
Shipwreck Against Enemy With River Steamers into Sichuan (1937-1945)

抗日战争爆发后，招商局船队作为中国战时军事运输的主动脉，成为日军打击的主要目标。为了减轻局产的损失，招商局采取了一系列应变措施：上海沦陷之前，总经理蔡增基率最好的 5 艘海轮"海元"、"海亨"、"海利"、"海贞"、"海云"撤退香港，暂避敌军锋芒；同时成立由副经理沈仲毅指挥的长江业务管理处，组织江海各轮向长江腹地后撤，并办理政府西迁的军公运输事宜。

After the Second Sino-Japanese War broke out, as the aorta of military transportation during wartime, China Merchants' fleet became the major attacking target to Japanese troops. In order to minimize the loss, China Merchants took a series of measures as follows. Before Shanghai was occupied, Mr. Cai Zengji, the General Manager of China Merchants retreated five best ocean vessels, namely Hai Yuan, Hai Heng, Hai Li, Hai Zhen and Hai Yun to Hong Kong to avoid enemy's attack. Meanwhile, China Merchants established Business Management Department of the Yangtze River at the command of Shen Zhongyi, Deputy General Manager of China Merchants, which was responsible for the retreat of river steamers and ocean vessels to the interior of the Yangtze River and transportation for migration of the government westward.

1937 年至 1939 年，为延缓日军的进攻，招商局在长江江阴、龙潭、马当等要塞共沉船 24 艘，其中江海大轮及大型趸船 18 艘，共计 34520 吨，占招商局江海船舶总吨数的 40%。

From 1937 to 1939, in order to hold back the attacks from Japanese army, 24 ships were ordered by China Merchants to sink themselves in the fortresses of the Yangtze River, such as Jiangyin, Longtan, and Madang, etc. Among the 24 ships, 18 were big river streamer, ocean vessels and large pontoons with a gross tonnage of 34,520 tons, accounting for 40% of the gross tonnage of China Merchants' fleet.

1943 年 4 月，招商局在重庆恢复总局，由徐学禹任总经理。此时，招商局仅有入川的大型江轮 6 艘、中型江轮 5 艘、小轮 7 艘。

In April 1943, China Merchants resumed its headquarter in Chongqing and Xu Xueyu was appointed as the General Manager. At this point, China Merchants only had six large river steamers, five medium-sized river steamers and seven small ones.

日本发动的侵华战争，给招商局带来了空前浩劫，从1937年到1945年，招商局共损失大小轮船、趸船、驳船73艘，计88952吨，其中江海轮船27艘，遭日军炸毁和掠走的船舶达55艘。

The aggression to China by Japan from 1937 to 1945 brought unprecedented catastrophe to China Merchants who lost a total of 73 steamers, pontoons and barges of various sizes with a gross tonnage of 88,952 tons during this period. Among the ships, 27 were river steamers and ocean vessels and 55 were bombed and robbed away by the Japanese invaders.

江汉 Kiang Han

"江汉"轮，英文名Kiang Han，铁壳客货船，属于大型江轮，用作客货运。原为日本日清汽船的"岳阳丸"。主机功率2400马力，船长94米，宽13.3米，3322.15总吨，1961.48净吨，仓容1850吨，吃水3.8米，航速每小时13海里。1907年出厂。在1937年战争爆发长江沉塞阻绝航道时被截获，交予招商局营运，改名为"江汉"。1949年该轮留在大陆。

江汉 Kiang Han

Kiang Han, a large passenger and cargo river steamer with iron hull, was formerly named as Yue Yang Maru and belonged to Japan Nissin Steam, Its length overall was 94 meters and the beam was 13.3 meters with a draught of 3.8 meters. The vessel measured 3,322.15 gross tons, 1,961.48 net tons and 1,850 tons of cargo capacity. With its engine power at 2,400 HP, it could sail at a speed of 13 kn. It was delivered in 1907. When the Second Sino-Japanese War broke out in 1937, Yue Yang Maru was captured in the fairway of the Yangtze River by Chinese army, later was handed over to China Merchants and renamed as Kiang Han. In 1949, the ship was left in Mainland China.

战争期间六大江轮退入四川后，因川江水浅无法营运，全部搁在重庆唐家沱。政府为保留战后航运力量，对这些船员仍发放粮食配给以为维系，但船只或久未营运失修，或被日机炸毁（如"江建"轮），所以当1944年战争快结束时政府曾拨发一亿四千万元整修，在1945年8月刚好修竣赶上复员的需要。

After retreat into Sichuan during the war, the six river steamers were put in Tangjiatuo, Chongqing because Chuanjiang River is not deep enough for sailing. In order to reserve the shipping power for postwar period, the government continued to distribute food to the crew members so as to keep these people. However, some of the ships were lack of maintenance after not being operated for a long time and some were bombed by Japanese aircrafts (such as Jiang Jian). So when the war came near to the end in 1944, the government allocated 140 million to repair these ships. Therefore, the ships could be put into operations when the war ended in August 1945.

随六大江轮入川的其他招商局轮船有："澄平"、"利济"、"江兴"、"景德"、"镇昌"、"恒吉"、"恒通"、"安宁"、"骏发"、"利源"、"河宽"、"飞龙"等12艘。

The Other 12 ships that were also reserved in Sichuan Province were: Cheng Ping, Li Ji, Jiang Xing, Jing De, Zhen Chang, Heng Ji, Heng Tong, An Ning, Jun Fa, Li Yuan, He Kuan and Fei Long.

⚓ 江建 Kiang Kien

英文名Kiang Kien，铁壳客货船，属于大型江轮，主机功率1500马力，总长285尺，宽42尺，2770.26总吨，1888.14净吨，仓容86418立方尺，空船吃水8尺，满载吃水12尺，航速每小时10.8海里，1905年出厂。1940年9月15日，该轮在巴东台子湾被炸沉没。

Kiang Kien was a large passenger and cargo river steamer with iron hull. Its length overall was 285 chi and the beam was 42 chi with a draught of 12 chi (8 chi if unloaded). The vessel measured 2,770.26 gross tons and 1,888.14 net tons, with a storage capacity 86,418 cubic feet. With its main engine power at 1,500 HP, it could sail at a speed of 10.8 kn. It was completed and delivered in 1905 and sunk in Taizi Gulf, Badong after being bombed on September 15, 1940.

江建　Kiang Kien

⚓ 遇顺　Yu Shun

载重吨 1696，1937 年 8 月 12 日，沉船于江阴。

Yu Shun had a dead weight tonnage of 1,696 tons. On August 12, 1937, it sunk in Jiangyin.

⚓ 津通　Jin Tong

载重吨 188，1939 年 12 月 20 日，在沙市招商局码头中弹沉没。

Jin Tong had a dead weight tonnage of 188 tons. On December 20, 1939, it was shot and sunk at the dock of China Merchants in Shashi, Hunan.

⚓ 岷江　Min Jiang

客货轮，载重吨 1100。

Min Jiang was a passenger and cargo ship with a dead weight tonnage of 1,100 tons.

⚓ 巴江　Ba Jiang

客货轮，载重吨 1100。

Ba Jiang was a passenger and cargo ship with a dead weight tonnage of 1,100 tons.

大业　Da Ye

客货轮，载重吨 1600。

Da Ye was a passenger and cargo ship with a dead weight tonnage of 1,600 tons.

大运　Da Yun

客货轮，载重吨 1600。

Da Yun was a passenger and cargo ship with a dead weight tonnage of 1,600 tons.

大载　Da Zai

客货轮，载重吨 1600。

Da Zai was a passenger and cargo ship with a dead weight tonnage of 1,600 tons.

飞舸　Fei Ge

小轮，载重吨 100。

Fei Ge was a ferry with a dead weight tonnage of 100 tons.

江襄　Jiang Xiang

原属日军船舶，名"大夏丸"，后被国民政府军俘获，1938 年 8 月 5 日，在湖北黄州附近中弹沉没。

Originally named as Daxia Maru, it was a Japanese ship that was captured by the National Revolutionary Army. On August 5, 1938, it was shot and sunk in the vicinity of Huangzhou, Hubei Province.

澄平　Cheng Ping

客货船，船长 47.6 米，宽 9.5 米，主机功率 650 马力，512 总吨，154 净吨，空船吃水 2.4 米，满载吃水 3.7 米，航速每小时 9 海里，1920 年出厂。

Cheng Ping was a passenger and cargo ship. Its length overall was 47.6 meters and the beam was 9.5 meters with a draught of 3.7 meters (2.4 meters if unloaded). The ship measured 512 gross tons and 154 net tons. With its main engine power at 650 HP, it could sail at a speed of 9 kn. It was delivered in 1920.

江济 Kiang Chi

英文名 Kiang Chi，属于大型江轮，客货船，原名"利济"。主机功率 440 马力，355 总吨，100 净吨，船长 44 米，空船吃水 1.5 米，满载吃水 1.9 米，航速每小时 8.5 海里，1922 年出厂。

Kiang Chi, originally named as Li Ji, was a large passenger and cargo river steamer. Its length overall was 44 meters with a draught of 1.9 meters (1.5 meters if unloaded). The vessel measured 355 gross tons and 100 net tons. With its main engine power at 400 HP, it could sail at a speed of 8.5 kn. It was delivered in 1922.

江济 Kiang Chi

安宁 An Ning

客货船，船长 27.4 米，宽 5.5 米，主机功率 240 马力，116 总吨，35 净吨，空船吃水 2.3 米，满载吃水 2.6 米，航速每小时 9 海里，1926 年出厂。

An Ning was a passenger and cargo ship. Its length overall was 27.4 meters and the beam was 5.5 meters with a draught of 2.6 meters (2.3 meters if unloaded). The ship measured 116 gross tons and 35 net tons. With its main engine power at 240 HP, it could sail at a speed of 9 kn. It was delivered in 1926.

第三节 战后复员 航产剧增（1946—1949）

SECTION THREE
Post War Recovery & Dramatic Growth (1946-1949)

抗战胜利后，招商局在国民党政府的全力支持下，接收了大量敌伪船舶，并从国外购买了大批剩余船舶。

After China defeated Japan in the Second Sino-Japanese War, supported by the Kuomintang government, China Merchants took over a large number of ships from the enemy and the puppet regime, and bought a lot of remaining ships from abroad after the World War II.

招商局接收船舶的主要对象是日资侵华航运企业，另有少量汪伪企业。截至1946年7月，累计接收敌伪船舶2158艘，239141吨。这些船只均归招商局统一处理，一部分留局自用，一部分作其他处理。1947年，招商局对留局船只重新进行了处理，留用船只共314艘，凡留用船只，江轮一律冠以"江"字，海轮冠以"海"字，其余小轮、拖轮、铁驳、特种机船、木驳、油驳等则另行命名。

China Merchants mainly took over ships from Japanese shipping companies who invaded China, as well as companies set up by the puppet regime led by Wang Jingwei[1]. By July 1946, a total of 2,158 vessels with a gross tonnage of 239,141 tons were taken over by China Merchants. All of these ships were allocated by China Merchants with some staying within China Merchants for its own use and others for other purpose. In 1947, China Merchants clarified the staying 314 ships by renaming the river steamers started by "Jiang"[2] and ocean vessels stated by "Hai"[3]. The remaining ferries, tugs, iron barges, special machine boats, wooden barges, and oil barges, etc. were named separately.

1　Wang Jingwei: or Wang Ching-wei (1883-1944), was initially a member of the Kuomintang but accepted an invitation from the Japanese Empire to form a Japanese-supported collaborationist government in Nanjing after the Sino-Japanese War broke out in 1937.
2　Jiang, "江" in Chinese, means river.
3　Hai, "海" in Chinese, means sea.

同时，招商局从美国、加拿大购买大量二战后的剩余船舶，这些外国船舶构成了招商局船舶的主体，其吨位约占招商局船舶总吨位的70%—76%。其中有代表性的船舶有自由轮10艘，分别是"海天"、"海地"、"海玄"、"海黄"、"海宇"、"海宙"、"海辰"、"海宿"、"海列"、"海张"；澳菲旧轮16艘，分别是"海苏"、"海浙"、"海皖"、"海赣"、"海鄂"、"海湘"、"海川"、"海康"、"海滇"、"海黔"、"海桂"、"海粤"、"海辽"、"海冀"、"海鲁"、"海陇"；N-3型货轮18艘，分别是"其美"、"黄兴"、"蔡锷"、"邓铿"、"执信"、"仲恺"、"延闿"、"培德"、"汉民"、"林森"、"铁桥"、"教仁"、"成功"、"鸿章"、"郑和"、"廷枢"、"继光"、"宣怀"；B-TYPE货轮7艘，分别是"海穗"、"海甬"、"海杭"、"海汉"、"海沪"、"海津"、"海平"；快速客轮3艘，分别是"锡麟"、"秋瑾"、"元培"；GREP-TYPE货轮3艘，分别是"自忠"、"登禹"、"麟阁"；L.S.T坦克登陆艇5艘，依次命名为"中字101—105"；L.S.M中型登陆艇12艘，依次命名为"华201"—"华212"；另外还有大量铁驳、木驳、拖小轮等。到1948年6月，招商局拥有大小船舶469艘（具体详见下表），计409200总吨，达到了招商局成立以来船舶拥有量的最高点。

Meanwhile, China Merchants purchased a large number of remaining ships from the United States and Canada after the World War II. These foreign ships were the major body of China Merchants' fleet, accounting for about 70%-76% of the gross tonnage. Among those ships, the ones with typical features included: ten liberty ships, namely, Hai Tien, Hai Ti, Hai Hsuan, Hai Huang, Hai Yu, Hai Chiao, Hai Chen, Hai Siu, Hai Lien and Hai Chang; sixteen Second-hand Lake Steamers, namely Hai Su, Hai Chch, Hai Wan, Hai Kang, Hai Er, Hai Xiang, Hai Chuan, Hai Kang, Hai Dean, Hai Chien, Hai Kwei, Hai Yueh, Hai Liao, Hai Chi, Hai Lu and Hai Lung; eighteen N-3 type freighters, namely, Chi Mei, Huang Hsing, Tsai Er, Teng Keng, Chih Hsin, Chung Kai, Yen Kai, Pei Teh, Han Min, Lin Shen, Tieh Chiao, Chiao Jen, Cheng Kong, Hung Chang, Zheng He, Ting Shu, Ji Guang and Xuan Huai; seven B-TYPE freighters, namely, Hai Shui, Hai Yun, Hai Hang, Hai Han, Hai Hu, Hai Tsin and Hai Ping; three Fast Speed Passenger Liners, namely, Shih Lin, Chiu Chin and Yuan Pei; three GREP-TYPE freighters, namely, Zi Zhong, Deng Yu and Lin Ge; five L.S.T, namely, Zhong 101, Zhong 102, Zhong 103, Zhong 104 and Zhong 105 and twelve L.S.M, namely Hua 201- 212. Besides, there were also a lot of iron barges, wooden barges and small tugs, etc. To June 1948, China Merchants had 469 ships of various size (see the table below), with a gross tonnage of 409,200 tons, the biggest number of ships since the establishment of China Merchants.

1947 年 2 月，招商局合资组建的专业油轮公司在上海成立，即为中国油轮公司。招商局将自美购得的 23 艘 (6 大 17 小) 油轮交予中国油轮公司运营。大油轮为驻美物资委员会在美国购入，价值 1152000 美元；小油轮为美军剩余物资，价值 5363238.58 美元。中国油轮公司专门以运油之油轮业务以和招商局客货运输业务做区分，以承运中国石油公司高雄炼油厂的油品为主。

In February 1947, China Merchants set up a joint venture in Shanghai named China Tanker Company to do oil transportation business. China Merchants purchased 23 oil tankers (6 large and 17 small) from U.S.A. and handed them over to this company for operation. The 6 large tankers were purchased in United States by Materials Committee stationed in US at a price of 1,152,000 US dollars while the 17 small tankers were remainders of US army after the World War II, pricing at 5,363,238.58 US dollars. While passenger and cargo transportation business were operated by the other units of China Merchants, Chinese Tanker Company was only dedicated to oil transportation business with oil tankers and mainly transport oil products for oil refinery factory of China National Petroleum Corporation in Kaohsiung, Taiwan.

1949 年，随着解放战争的节节胜利，国民党的统治面临总崩溃。1949 年 4 月，招商局总公司开始随国民党军队、机关一起迁住台湾。撤至台湾的船只共计 95 艘，其中海轮 80 艘，占该公司原有海轮总数的 81%。所有的自由轮、大湖轮及格莱型船只全部迁往台湾。

In 1949, with continuous victory by forces led by Communist Party of China in the Chinese Civil War, the Kuomintang's rule faced with collapse. In April 1949, China Merchants began to move to Taiwan together with Kuomintang army and the government. A total of 95 ships were brought to Taiwan, of which 80 were ocean vessels, accounting for 81% of all the ocean vessels. All liberty ships, Great Lake ships and the GREP-TYPE vessels were all brought to Taiwan.

1948年6月招商局船舶统计表
Lists of Ships of China Merchants in June, 1948

项目（船型） Project (Type of Ship)		船舶数量（艘） (Number)
抗战胜利前原有船舶 Ships before the Second Sino-Japanese War	江轮　River steamer	9
	拖小轮　Small tug	8
	木驳　Wooden barge	7
	铁驳　Iron barge	3
	小计　Subtotal	27
添购船舶 Newly purchased ships	海轮　Ocean vessel	2
	Truck Ferry	2
	小计　Subtotal	4
国外交来船舶 Ships bought from abroad	自由轮　Liberty ship	10
	澳菲旧轮　Second-hand Lake Steamer	15
	N-3	18
	G型轮　G-Type	3
	B型轮　B-Type	7
	Corrrttes	3
	Cisayi	4
	LST等各型船只　LST of various sizes	86
	小计　Subtotal	146
接收敌伪船舶 Ships received from enemies and the puppet regime	江轮　River steamer	7
	海轮　Ocean vessel	2
	拖小轮　Small tug	105
	铁驳　Iron barge	132
	特种机船　Special machine ship	12
	木驳　Wooden barge	33
	机帆船　Motor sailer	1
	小计　Subtotal	292
总计　Total		469

注：本表根据1948年9月30日国营招商局移交招商局轮船股份有限公司接收财产目录制定。
资料来源：招商局档案馆藏，B020-WS-19/1。
Note: This table was based on Property Catalog Received by China Merchants Ship Limited from State-owned China Merchants on September 30, 1948.
Source: China Merchants Archives, B020-WS-19/1.

招商局接收美登陆艇时的仪式

Takeover ceremony of US landing craft

接收人员在接收船上机器时的情景

China Merchants staff taking over machines on ship

国营招商局高级船员合影

Senior crew members of China Merchants

自由轮 Liberty Ships

⚓ 海天　Hai Tien

英文名 Hai Tien，曾用名 James J.Mckay，1943 年 8 月建造于美国威明顿。该船长 134.6 米，宽 17.4 米，2500 马力，航速每小时 11 海里，载重吨 10970。1946 年 2 月 13 日，由招商局接收。1947 年 2 月 12 日，开航中印线。1949 年迁往台湾，1950 年出售抵偿美债。

海天　Hai Tien

Originally named as James J.Mckay, the ship was built in August 1943 in Wilmington, U.S.A. Its length overall was 134.6 meters and the beam was 17.4 meters. With its engine power at 2,500 HP, it could sail at a speed of 11 kn and had a dead weight tonnage of 10,970 tons. On February 13, 1946, China Merchants took over the ship. One year later, the ship made its first sail to India on February 12, 1947. It was moved to Taiwan in 1949 and sold in 1950 to compensate for the debts to U.S.A.

⚓ 海地　Hai Ti

英文名 Hai Ti，原名 Jacob Perkins，1944 年 2 月建造于美国休斯敦。该船长 134.6 米，宽 17.4 米，2500 马力，航速每小时 11 海里，载重吨 10970。1946 年 2 月 15 日，由招商局接收。1947 年 2 月 25 日，"海地"轮开航关岛。1949 年迁往台湾，1963 年出售给兴业航运公司。

Originally named as Jacob Perkins, the ship was built in February 1944 in Huston, U.S.A. Its length overall was 134.6 meters and the beam was 17.4 meters. With its engine power at 2,500 HP, it could sail at a speed of 11 kn and had a dead weight tonnage of 10,970 tons. On February 15, 1946, China Merchants took over the ship. One year later, it made the first sail to Guam on February 25, 1947. It was moved to Taiwan in 1949 and sold to Xing Ye Shipping Company in 1963.

海地　Hai Ti

⚓ 海玄 Hai Hsuan

英文名 Hai Hsuan，原名 Ben Ruffin，1944 年 4 月建造于美国里士满。该船长 134.6 米，宽 17.4 米，2500 马力，航速每小时 11 海里，载重吨 10970。1946 年 2 月 15 日由招商局接收。1950 年"海玄"轮在新加坡起义回国。

海玄 Hai Hsuan

Originally named as Ben Ruffin, the ship was built in April 1944 in Richmond Calf, U.S.A. Its length overall was 134.6 meters and the beam was 17.4 meters. With its engine power at 2,500 HP, it could sail at a speed of 11 kn and had a dead weight tonnage of 10,970 tons. On February 15, 1946, China Merchants took over the ship. Later in 1950, the ship returned to Mainland China after a successful uprising in Singapore.

1947 年 10 月 24 日，国营招商局"海玄"轮航行印度，在印度惠安实业公司欢迎"海玄"轮的仪式上，双方人员合影留念

On October 24th of 1947, Hai Hsuan sailed to India. This photo was taken on the welcome ceremony held by the Indian company.

海黄 Hai Huang

英文名 Hai Huang，原名 Joha B. Ash，1942年6月，建造于美国加利福尼亚。该船长134.6米，宽17.4米，2500马力，航速每小时11海里，载重吨10970。1946年2月21日由招商局接收。1949年迁往台湾。

Originally named as Joha B. Ash, the ship was built in June 1942 in California, U.S.A. Its length overall was 134.6 meters and the beam was 17.4 meters. With its engine power at 2,500 HP, it could sail at a speed of 11 kn and had a dead weight tonnage of 10,970 tons. China Merchants took over the ship on February 21, 1946 and moved it to Taiwan in 1949.

海黄　Hai Huang

海宇 Hai Yu

英文名 Hai Yu，原名 Stephen Long，1941年10月，建造于美国加利福尼亚。该船长134.6米，宽17.4米，2500马力，航速每小时11海里，载重吨10970。1946年2月24日由招商局接收。1949年迁往台湾。

Originally named as Stephen Long, the ship was built in October 1941 in California, U.S.A. Its length overall was 134.6 meters and the beam was 17.4 meters. With its engine power at 2,500 HP, it could sail at a speed of 11 kn and had a dead weight tonnage of 10,970 tons. China Merchants took over the ship on February 24, 1946, and moved it to Taiwan in 1949.

1946年2月20日，国营招商局总经理徐学禹在接收新购"海宇"轮时与美方人员合影

On February 20th of 1946, General Manager of China Merchants Xu Xueyu meeting with US staff when taking over the newly-purchased Hai Yu.

1946年2月20日，国营招商局总经理徐学禹在接收新购"海宇"轮时与美方人员合影。

On February 20th of 1946, General

Manager of China Merchants Xu Xueyu meeting with US staff when taking over the newly-purchased Hai Yu.

⚓ 海宙 Hai Chiao

英文名 Hai Chiao，原名 Michael Sinnot，1943年6月建造于美国俄勒冈州。该船长134.6米，宽17.4米，2500马力，航速每小时11海里，载重吨10970。1946年2月27日由招商局接收。1949年迁往台湾。

"海宙"轮（在澳洲装运矿砂）

Hai Chiao (loading ore sand in Australia)

Originally named as Michael Sinnot, the ship was built in June 1943 in Oregon, U.S.A. Its length overall was 134.6 meters and the beam was 17.4 meters. With its engine power at 2,500 HP, it could sail at a speed of 11 kn and had a dead weight tonnage of 10,970 tons. China Merchants took over the ship on February 27, 1946, and moved it to Taiwan in 1949.

⚓ 海辰 Hai Chen

英文名 Hai Chen，原名 Lyman Beecher，1942年11月建造于美国旧金山，该船长134.6米，宽17.4米，2500马力，航速每小时11海里，载重吨10970。1946年3月26日由招商局接收。

1947年4月21日，国营招商局"海辰"轮首航新加坡，当地公司在欢迎船长暨高级船员时合影留念

On April 21st of 1947, Hai Chen made its maiden voyage to Singapore, this photo was taken on the welcome ceremony held by local company.

1949年迁往台湾，1950年1月"海辰"轮在离台赴日途中，船长张丕烈率船员起义，因特务告密，回归途中被国民党军队拦截，起义失败。1951年7月11日张丕烈在高雄英勇就义。而"海辰"轮1950年出售抵偿美债。

Originally named as Lyman Beecher, the ship was built in November 1942 in San Francisco, U.S.A. Its length overall was 134.6 meters and the beam was 17.4 meters. With its engine power at 2,500 HP, it could sail at a speed of 11 kn and had a dead weight tonnage of 10,970 tons. China Merchants took over the ship on March 26, 1946, and moved it to Taiwan in 1949. In January 1950, Mr. Zhang Pilie, the Captain of Hai Chen ship, staged an uprising with the ship crew during a voyage to Japan and decided to return to Mainland China. However, the plan was discovered by the Kuomintang agents and the ship was intercepted by the army on its way to Mainland China. Due to the aborted uprising, Mr. Zhang Pilie was executed by the Kuomintang army in Kaohsiung on July 11, 1951. The ship itself was sold in 1950 to compensate for the debts to U.S.A.

1950年，"海辰"轮起义失败，船长张丕烈光荣牺牲

In 1950, Hai Chen failed in the uprising, the captain Zhang Pilie died.

海宿　Hai Siu

英文名Hai Siu，原名Ancel F. Hains，1944年8月建造于美国新奥尔良。该船长134.6米，宽17.4米，2500马力，航速每小时11海里，载重吨10970。1946年3月30日由招商局接收，1949年迁往台湾，1963年出售给济运轮船公司。

Originally named as Ancel F. Hains, the ship was built in August 1944 in New Orleans, U.S.A. Its length overall was 134.6 meters and the beam was 17.4 meters. With its engine power at 2,500 HP, it could sail at a speed of 11 kn and had a dead weight tonnage of 10,970 tons. China Merchants took over the ship on March 30, 1946, and moved it to Taiwan in 1949. Later in 1963, the ship was sold to Jiyun Ship Company.

海宿　Hai Siu

海列　Hai Lien

英文名 Hai Lien，原名 Author Dobbs，1943 年 7 月建造于美国北卡罗来纳州。该船长 134.6 米，宽 17.4 米，2500 马力，航速每小时 11 海里，载重吨 10970。1946 年 4 月 5 日，由招商局接收。1950 年因案在日本被盟军没收，1951 年交涉回台湾招商局。1955 年售予台湾航业公司，改名"基隆"。

Originally named as Author Dobbs, the ship was built in July 1943 in North Carolina, U.S.A. Its length overall was 134.6 meters and the beam was 17.4 meters. With its engine power at 2,500 HP, it could sail at a speed of 11 kn and had a dead weight tonnage of 10,970 tons. China Merchants took over the ship on April 5, 1946. Later due to a conflict in Japan, the ship was confiscated by the Allied army in 1950, but China Merchants Taiwan branch managed to get it back one year later after rounds of negotiations. In 1955, the ship was sold to Taiwan Navigation Co., Ltd. and renamed as Keelung.

海张　Hai Chang

英文名 Hai Chang，原名 Chif Josph，1943 年 8 月建造于美国俄勒冈州。该船长 134.6 米，宽 17.4 米，2500 马力，航速每小时 11 海里，载重吨 10970。1946 年 4 月 18 日，由招商局接收。1949 年迁往台湾；1962 年运矿砂由高雄至基隆，在澎湖失踪，船上 43 人无一生还。

海张　Hai Chang

Originally named as Chif Josph, the ship was built in August 1943 in Oregon, U.S.A. Its length overall was 134.6 meters and the beam was 17.4 meters. With its engine power at 2,500 HP, it could sail at a speed of 11 kn and had a dead weight tonnage of 10,970 tons. China Merchants took over the ship on April 18, 1946, and moved it to Taiwan in 1949. In 1962, the ship disappeared near Penghu Island on its way of shipping ore sand from Kaohsiung to Keelung. 43 people aboard died.

澳菲旧轮（也称大湖轮） Second-hand Lake Steamers

⚓ 海苏 Hai Su

英文名 Hai su，原名 Wichita Falls，该船长 79.6 米，宽 17.4 米，1650 马力，2499.5 总吨，航速每小时 8 海里。1946 年 1 月 17 日，招商局接收的第一艘大湖级轮船。1949 年迁往台湾，1960 年出售拆解。

Originally named as Wichita Falls, its length overall was 79.6 meters and the beam was 17.4 meters. With its engine power at 1,650 HP, it could sail at a speed of 8 kn and had a gross tonnage of 2,499.5 tons. On January 17, 1946, the ship became the first Lake Steamer taken over by China Merchants. It was moved to Taiwan in 1949 and was disassembled for sale in 1960.

海苏　Hai Su

⚓ 海浙 Hai Chch

英文名 Hai Chch，原名 City of Philadelphia，该船长 79.6 米，宽 17.4 米，1500 马力，2600 总吨，航速每小时 9 海里。1947 年 1 月 24 日接收，"海浙"后改名"海吉"。1949 年迁往台湾，1951 年出售拆解。

Originally named as City of Philadelphia, its length overall was 79.6 meters and the beam was 17.4 meters. With its engine power at 1,500 HP, it could sail at a speed of 9 kn and had a gross tonnage of 2,600 tons. China Merchants took over the ship on January 24, 1947 and renamed it Hai Ji. It was moved to Taiwan in 1949 and was disassembled for sale in 1951.

⚓ 海皖 Hai Wan

英文名 Hai Wan，该船长 79.6 米，宽 17.4 米，1650 马力，2689.64 总吨，航速每小时 9 海里，1919 年建造于美国马尼托沃克。1947 年 1 月 24 日，由招商局接收。1949 年迁往台湾，1954 年出售拆解。

Built in Manitowoc, U.S.A., its length overall was 79.6 meters and the beam was 17.4 meters. With its engine power at 1,650 HP, it could sail at a speed of 9 kn and had a gross tonnage of 2,689.64 tons. China

Merchants took over the ship on January 24, 1947, and moved it to Taiwan in 1949. Later in 1954, the ship was disassembled for sale.

海赣 Hai Kang

英文名 Hai Kang，原名 Ozark，该船长 79.6 米，宽 17.4 米，1500 马力，2687.64 总吨，航速每小时 8.5 海里。1919 年建造于美国马尼托沃克。1947 年 1 月 29 日，由招商局接收。1949 年迁往台湾。1950 年被售予台湾银行抵债。后来，又成了台湾航业公司的"屏东"轮。

Originally named Ozark, the ship was built in Manitowoc, U.S.A in 1919. Its length overall was 79.6 meters and the beam was 17.4 meters. With its main engine power at 1,500 HP, it could sail at 8.5 kn and had a gross tonnage of 2,687.64 tons. China Merchants took over the ship on January 29, 1947, and moved it to Taiwan in 1949. In 1950, the ship was sold to Bank of Taiwan to compensate for the debts. Later, it was sold again to Taiwan Navigation Co., Ltd. and renamed as Pingtung.

海鄂 Hai Er

英文名 Hai Er，原名 Chippea，该船长 79.6 米，宽 17.4 米，1200 马力，2309 总吨，航速每小时 8 海里。1947 年 2 月 8 日，由招商局接收。1949 年迁往台湾。1950 年 5 月 1 日，在海南岛被防卫司令部征收改名为"阳明"号运输舰，交"海军部"使用，一个月后解编发还招商局。1954 年出售拆解。

海鄂 Hai Er

Originally named as Chippea, its length overall was 79.6 meters and the beam was 17.4 meters. With its engine power at 1,200 HP, it could sail at a speed of 8 kn and had a gross tonnage of 2,309 tons. China Merchants took over the ship on February 8, 1947, and moved it to Taiwan in 1949. On May 1, 1950, the ship was requisitioned by the Kuomintang Defense Command in Hainan Island, renamed as Yang Ming and used by the Kuomintang Navy Department in Taiwan. After one month, it was dismissed and returned to China Merchants. In 1954, the ship was disassembled for sale.

海湘　Hai Xiang

英文名 Hai Xiang，原名 Norlago，该船长 79.6 米，宽 17.4 米，1500 马力，2664 总吨，航速每小时 8 海里。1920 年建造于美国明尼苏达州。1947 年 2 月 12 日，由招商局接收。1949 年迁往台湾。1950 年被售予台湾银行抵债。后来，又成了台湾航业公司的"彰化"轮。

Originally named as Norlago, the ship was built in Minnesota, U.S.A in 1920. Its length overall was 79.6 meters and the beam was 17.4 meters. With its engine power at 1,500 HP, it could sail at a speed of 8 kn and had a gross tonnage of 2,664 tons. China Merchants took over the ship on February 12, 1947 and moved it to Taiwan in 1949. In 1950, the ship was sold to Bank of Taiwan to compensate for the debts. Later, it was sold again to Taiwan Navigation Co., Ltd. and renamed as Chang Hua.

海川　Hai Chuan

英文名 Hai Chuan，原名 West Texas，该船长 79.6 米，宽 17.4 米，1500 马力，2686 总吨，航速每小时 9.1 海里。1947 年 2 月 14 日，由招商局接收。1949 年迁往台湾。1950 年被售予台湾银行抵债。后来，又成了台湾航业公司的"新竹"轮。

Originally named as West Texas, its length overall was 79.6 meters and the beam was 17.4 meters. With its engine power at 1,500 HP, it could sail at a speed of 9.1 kn and had a gross tonnage of 2,686 tons. China Merchants took over the ship on February 14, 1947 and moved it to Taiwan in 1949. In 1950, the ship was sold to Bank of Taiwan to compensate for the debts. Later, it was sold again to Taiwan Navigation Co., Ltd. and renamed as Hsin Chu.

海康　Hai Kang

英文名 Hai Kang，原名 International，该船长 79.6 米，宽 17.4 米，1500 马力，2704 总吨，航速每小时 8 海里。1919 年建造于美国。1947 年 2 月 16 日，由招商局接收。1951 年 1 月在香港起义归国。

Originally named as International, the ship was built in the U.S.A. in 1919. Its length overall was 79.6 meters and the beam was 17.4 meters. With its main engine power at 1,500 HP, it could sail at a speed of 8 kn and had a gross tonnage of 2,704 tons. China Merchants took over the ship on February 16, 1947, but it returned to Mainland China in January 1951 after a successful uprising in Hong Kong.

海康　Hai Kang

"海康"轮起义船员合影
The uprising crew members of Hai Kang

⚓ 海滇　Hai Dean

英文名 Hai Dean，原名 Colorado，该船长 79.6 米，宽 17.4 米，1500 马力，2727.4 总吨，航速每小时 8 海里。1949 年迁往台湾，1954 年出售拆解。

Originally named as Colorado, its length overall was 79.6 meters and the beam was 17.4 meters. With its engine power at 1,500 HP, it could sail at a speed of 8 kn and had a gross tonnage of 2,727.4 tons. It was moved to Taiwan in 1949 and disassembled for sale in 1954.

⚓ 海黔　Hai Chien

英文名 Hai Chien，原名 Point Dan Pedro，该船长 79.6 米，宽 17.4 米，1500 马力，3718.9 总吨，航速每小时 10 海里。1920 年建造于美国亚拉巴马州木比耳。1949 年迁往台湾，1959 年出售拆解。

Originally named as Point Dan Pedro, the ship was built in 1920 in Mobile Ala, U.S.A. Its length overall was 79.6 meters and the beam was 17.4 meters. With its engine power at 1,500 HP, it could sail at a speed of 10 kn and had a gross tonnage of 3,718.9 tons. It was moved to Taiwan in 1949 and disassembled for sale in 1959.

⚓ 海桂　Hai Kwei

英文名 Hai Kwei，原名 Carrib Queen，该船长 79.6 米，宽 17.4 米，1600 马力，2705.3 总吨，

海黔　Hai Chien

航速每小时 9 海里。1919 年建造于美国 Minford。1949 年迁往台湾，1951 年出售拆解。

Originally named as Carrib Queen, the ship was built in Minford, U.S.A in 1919. Its length overall was 79.6 meters and the beam was 17.4 meters. With its engine power at 1,600 HP, it could sail at a speed of 9 kn and had a gross tonnage of 2,705.3 tons. It was moved to Taiwan in 1949 and disassembled for sale in 1951.

⚓ 海粤　Hai Yueh

英文名 Hai Yueh，原名 Norindies，该船长 79.6 米，宽 17.4 米，1600 马力，2677 总吨，航速每小时 9 海里。1949 年迁往台湾，1954 年出售拆解。

Originally named as Norindies, its length overall was 79.6 meters and the beam was 17.4 meters. With its engine power at 1,600 HP, it could sail at a speed of 9 kn and had a gross tonnage of 2,677 tons. It was moved to Taiwan in 1949 and disassembled for sale in 1954.

⚓ 海冀　Hai Chi

英文名 Hai Chi，原名 Port worth，该船长 79.6 米，宽 17.4 米，1650 马力，2671.8 总吨，航速每小时 8 海里。1919 年建造于美国费城。1948 年 2 月 28 日，由招商局移交"海军部"接管，并改名"昆仑"轮。

Originally named as Port worth, the ship was built in 1919 in Philadelphia, U.S.A. Its length overall was 79.6 meters and the beam was 17.4 meters. With its engine power at 1,650 HP, it could sail at a speed of 8 kn and had a gross tonnage of 2,671.8 tons. On February 28, 1948, it was handed over from China Merchants to the Kuomintang Navy Department and renamed as Kun Lun.

⚓ 海鲁　Hai Lu

英文名 Hai Lu，原名 Alomo，该船长 79.6 米，宽 17.4 米，1350 马力，2767 总吨，航速每小时 10 海里。1919 年建造于美国，1949 年迁往台湾。

Originally named as Alomo, the ship was built in 1919 in the U.S.A. Its length overall was 79.6 meters and the beam was 17.4 meters. With its engine power at 1,350 HP, it could sail at 10 kn and had a gross tonnage of 2,767 tons. It was moved to Taiwan in 1949.

⚓ 海陇　Hai Lung

英文名 Hai Lung，原名 Greylag，该船长 79.6 米，宽 17.4 米，1726 马力，3349 总吨，航速每小时 8 海里。1910 建造于美国 W. Hartlepool。1949 年迁往台湾，1959 年出售拆解。

Originally named as Greylag, the ship was built in 1910 in W. Hartlepool, U.S.A. Its length overall was 79.6 meters and the beam was 17.4 meters. With its engine power at 1,726 HP, it could sail at a speed of 8 kn and had a gross tonnage of 3,349 tons. It was moved to Taiwan and disassembled for sale in 1959.

海陇　Hai Lung

海辽 Hai Liao

英文名 Hai Liao，原名 San Antonio、"海闽"轮，该船长 79.6 米，宽 17.4 米，1500 马力，2677 总吨，航速每小时 8 海里。1920 年建造于美国马尼托沃克。1947 年 9 月 19 日，"海闽"轮改名为"海辽"轮。1949 年 9 月 19 日，"海辽"轮从香港赴汕头应差途中起义，回到大连解放区，成为招商局起义归国的第一艘海轮。1953 年，为了纪念这一次成功起义，我国发行的五分钱纸币的背景图案就是以"海辽"轮作为模型。

Originally named as San Antonio and later Hai Min, the ship was built in 1920 in Manitowoc, U.S.A. Its length overall was 79.6 meters and the beam was 17.4 meters. With its engine power at 1,500 HP, it could

海辽 Hai Liao

1953年发行的五分纸币上印制的"海辽"轮

Hai Liao was printed on the five-cent currency note issued in 1953

1949年9月28日，起义归来的"海辽"轮挂上了中华人民共和国国旗

Hai Liao, the first China Merchants ship returning from Hongkong through uprising with the national flag on September 28th, 1949.

"海辽"轮船长方枕流宣布起义成功

The captain of Hai Liao, Fang Zhenliu declaring the success of uprising

"海辽"轮船员 Crew members of Hai Liao

"海辽"轮全体人员合影 The uprising crew members of Hai Liao

sail at a speed of 8 kn and had a gross tonnage of 2,677 tons. On September 19, 1947, the ship was renamed as Hai Liao. Exactly two years later, an uprising was staged on the ship during its voyage from Hong Kong to Shantou and Hai Liao ship returned to the Communist Dalian liberated area. It was the first ocean vessel that successfully returned to Mainland China. To commemorate the successful uprising of the ship, Hai Liao ship was designed as the background picture of the 5 cent currency note issued by Mainland China in 1953.

N-3 型货轮　N-3 type Freighters

⚓ 其美　Chi Mei

英文名 Chi Mei，曾用名"海忠"，该船长 78.9 米，宽 12.7 米，功率 1300 马力，载重吨 2750，航速每小时 11 海里。1949 年迁往台湾，1951 年出售给泰国。

Originally named as Hai Zhong, its length overall was 78.9 meters and the beam was 12.7 meters. With its engine power at 1,300 HP, it could sail at a speed of 11 kn and had a gross tonnage of 2,750 tons. The ship was moved to Taiwan in 1949 and sold to Thailand in 1951.

该轮以历史名人命名。陈其美（1878—1916），字英士，浙江湖州人。近代民主革命志士，青帮代表人物，于辛亥革命初期与黄兴同为孙中山的股肱。陈其美与蒋介石关系密切，为蒋介石拜把之兄，将蒋介石引荐于孙中山。1916 年 5 月 18 日，受袁世凯指使的张宗昌派出程国瑞，假借签约援助讨袁经费，于日本人上田纯三郎寓所中将陈其美当场枪杀。陈其美遇刺后，孙中山高度赞扬陈其美是"革命首功之臣"。

The ship was named after a historic figure. Chen Chimei(1878-1916),also named Chen Yingshi, from Huzhou, Zhejiang. He was a democratic revolutionary in modern China, a representative of Green Gang, as well as an arm to Sun Yat-sen with Huang Hsing at the early stage of the 1911 Revolution. Chen Chimei was close with Chiang Kai-shek, a brother to Chiang Kai-shek by oath, introducing Chiang Kai-shek to Sun Yat-sen. On May 18th of 1916, Zhang Zongchang under Yuan Shih-kai's direction sent Cheng Guorui to kill Chen Chimei by gun on the spot in a Japanese apartment in the name of signing an agreement to borrow money to fight against Yuan Shih-kai. After Chen Chimei was assassinated, Sun Yat-sen highly praised him as "the top contributor to the revolution".

⚓ 黄兴 Huang Hsing

英文名 Huang Hsing，曾用名"海孝"，该船长 78.9 米，宽 12.7 米，功率 1300 马力，载重吨 2750，航速每小时 11 海里。1949 年迁往台湾。

Originally named as Hai Xiao, its length overall was 78.9 meters and the beam was 12.7 meters. With its engine power at 1,300 HP, it could sail at a speed of 11 kn and had a gross tonnage of 2,750 tons. The ship was moved to Taiwan in 1949.

该轮以历史名人命名。黄兴（1874—1916），湖南长沙人，近代民主革命家，中华民国的创建者之一，孙中山先生的第一知交。南京临时政府成立时，任陆军总长。袁世凯称帝时，任讨袁总司令。1916 年 10 月 31 日，黄兴病故于上海。1917 年 4 月 15 日，受民国元老尊以国葬葬于湖南长沙岳麓山。有《黄克强先生全集》、《黄兴集》、《黄兴未刊电稿》及《黄克强先生书翰墨迹》刊行。

The ship was named after a historic figure.Huang Hsing(1874-1916),from Changsha,Hunan.He was a democratic revolutionary in modern China, one of the founders of the Republic of China, the closest friend of Sun Yat-sen. He served as the chief of army when Nanjing Provisional Government was setup. When Yuan Shih-kai claimed to be the emperor, Huang Hsing was worked as the top commander of the army to fight against Yuan Shih-kai. On October 31st of 1916, Huang Hsing died of illness in Shanghai. On April 15th of 1917, he was buried as the founder of the Republic of China in the form of a state funeral in Yuelu Mountain in Changsha,Huanan. Works left by Huang Hsing were published like *Full Collection of Mr Huang Hsing*, *Huang Hsing Collection*, *Huang Hsing's Unpublished Telegraph Files*, *Huang Hsing's Calligraphy*.

黄兴 Huang Hsing

蔡锷 Tsai Er

英文名 Tsai Er，曾用名"海仁"，该船长 78.9 米，宽 12.7 米，功率 1300 马力，载重吨 2750，航速每小时 11 海里。1950 年 1 月，该船在香港起义归国。

Originally named as Hai Ren, its length overall was 78.9 meters and the beam was 12.7 meters. With its engine power at 1,300 HP, it could sail at a speed of 11 kn and had a gross tonnage of 2,750 tons. In January 1950, the ship returned to Mainland China after a successful uprising in Hong Kong.

该轮以历史名人命名。蔡锷（1882—1916），原名艮寅，字松坡，湖南宝庆（即今邵阳市）人。蔡锷曾经响应辛亥革命，发动反对袁世凯洪宪帝制的护国战争，是中华民国初年的杰出军事领袖。遗著被编为《蔡松坡集》。

The ship was named after a historic figure.Tsai Er(1882-1916), also named Tsai Songpo, originally named Tsai Genyin,from Baoqing,Hunan. Tsai Er once responded to the 1911 Revolution, initiated the war to fight against Yuan Shih-kai. He was an outstanding military leader in the early years of the Republic of China. His works left were compiled to *Tsai Songpo Collection*.

"蔡锷"轮全体船员起义纪念　The uprising crew members of Tsai Er

邓铿　Teng Keng

英文名 Teng Keng，曾用名"海信"，该船长 78.9 米，宽 12.7 米，功率 1300 马力，载重吨 2750，航速每小时 11 海里。1950 年 1 月香港起义归国。

Originally named as Hai Xin, its length overall was 78.9 meters and the beam was 12.7 meters. With its engine power at 1,300 HP, it could sail at a speed of 11 kn and had a gross tonnage of 2,750 tons. In January 1950, the ship returned to Mainland China after a successful uprising in Hong Kong.

该轮以历史名人命名。邓仲元（1886—1922），原名邓士元，别名邓铿。原籍嘉应（今梅县），7 岁随父居惠阳淡水。早年就读于惠阳，后肄业于崇雅学堂。19 岁入读广州将弁学堂，早年参加辛亥革命，曾任广东军政府陆军司司长、粤军总部参谋长兼陆军第一师师长，参加过讨伐袁世凯、驱除龙济光等战役，功绩卓著。

邓铿　Teng Keng

"邓铿"轮全体起义船员纪念   The uprising crew members of Teng Keng

The ship was named after a historic figure.Teng Zhongyuan(1886-1922),originally named Teng Shiyuan, also named Teng Keng. Originally from Jiaying, he went to Danshui,Huiyang with his father at 7. Having education in Huiyang,and graduated from ChongYa School,Teng Keng entered Jiangbian School at 19. Joining in the 1911 Revolution, he was served as the director of department of the army of Guangdong and the chief of staff of the headquarter of Guangdong army and the division commander of the 1st army, taking part in the wars to fight against Yuan Shih-kai and Long Jiguang, making outstanding contributions.

执信 Chih Hsin

英文名 Chih Hsin，曾用名"海悌"，该船长 78.9 米，宽 12.7 米，功率 1300 马力，载重吨 2750，航速每小时 11 海里。1949 年迁往台湾。1951 年发生海损，全部报废。

Originally named as Hai Ti, its length overall was 78.9 meters and the beam was 12.7 meters. With its engine power at 1,300 HP, it could sail at a speed of 11 kn and had a gross tonnage of 2,750 tons. The ship was moved to Taiwan in 1949 and totally scrapped in 1951 due to severe damages.

该轮以历史名人命名。朱执信（1885—1920），名大符，字执信。祖籍浙江萧山，出生于广东番禺（今广州市越秀区豪贤路）。中国近代革命家、理论家。1904 年官费留学日本，结识孙中山、廖仲恺等革命党人。1905 年 8 月，被选为中国同盟会评议部议员兼书记。先后担任过《民报》、《建设》等刊物的编辑，从事资产阶级革命理论宣传工作。1920 年 9 月 21 日被桂系军阀杀害。朱执信生平著述甚多，遗著编有《朱执信集》。

The ship was named after a historic figure.Zhu Chih-hsin(1885-1920), also named Zhu Dafu,was from Panyu,Guangdong. He was a revolutionary and theorist in modern China. Zhu Chih-hsin studied in Japan with government support and got to know Sun Yat-sen and Liao Chung-kai in 1904. In August of 1905,he was selected to be the representative and the secretary of Advisory department in Tung Meng Hui. He successively worked as the editor of the magazine *People's Daily* and monthly *Jianshe* to propagandize bourgeois revolutionary theories. On September 21st of 1920, he was killed by the Gui clique. Zhu Chil-hsin wrote a lot in his life. His articles left were compiled to *Zhu Chih-hsin Collection*.

⚓ 仲恺 Chung Kai

英文名 Chung Kai，曾用名"海和"，该船长 78.9 米，宽 12.7 米，功率 1300 马力，载重吨 2750，航速每小时 11 海里。1949 年迁往台湾，1964 年该船在日本失事沉没。

Originally named as Hai He, its length overall was 78.9 meters and the beam was 12.7 meters. With its engine power at 1,300 HP, it could sail at a speed of 11 kn and had a gross tonnage of 2,750 tons. The ship was moved to Taiwan in 1949. 15 years later, the ship sunk in Japanese Sea in an accident.

仲恺 Chung Kai

该轮以历史名人命名。廖仲恺（1877—1925），资产阶级民主革命政治家、国民党左派领袖。广东归善（今惠阳）人。曾参加"二次革命"和护法运动，是孙中山改组国民党、实行国共合作的积极参与者和忠实支持者。先后任国民政府委员、国民党中央工人部长、省港大罢工委员会顾问等职，积极支持工农运动。

The ship was named after a historic figure.Liao Chung-kai(1877-1925), a politician of the bourgeois democratic revolution, as well as the KMT leftist leader.He was from Guishan,Guangdong,attending the second revolution and Constitution Protection Movement. Liao Chung-kai was a loyal supporter and active participator for Sun Yat-sen's reconstruction on KMT and push for KMT-CPC cooperation. He was successively served as the member of National Government, the minister of KMT central workers, the consultant to the committee of Canton-Hong Kong Strike, actively supporting the movement for workers and peasants.

延闿 Yen Kai

英文名 Yen Kai，曾用名"海平"，该船长 78.9 米，宽 12.7 米，功率 1300 马力，载重吨 2750，航速每小时 11 海里。1949 年迁往台湾，1951 年出售给泰国。

Originally named as Hai Ping, its length overall was 78.9 meters and the beam was 12.7 meters. With its engine power at 1,300 HP, it could sail at a speed of 11 kn and had a gross tonnage of 2,750 tons. The ship was moved to Taiwan in 1949 and sold to Thailand in 1951.

该轮以历史名人命名。谭延闿（1880—1930），字组庵、祖安，号无畏、切斋，湖南茶陵人，民国初年政治人物，曾任湖南都督、国民政府主席、第一任行政院院长。亦擅长书法，有"近代颜书大家"之称。著述有《祖庵诗集》等。

The ship was named after a historic figure. Tan Yen Kai(1880-1930), also named Tan Zu'an, Tan Wuwei, Tan Qiezhai, from Chaling, Hunan. He was a political figure in the early years of Republic of China, once worked as the governor in Hunan, the president of National Government, the 1st president of the Executive Yuan. He was good at calligraphy and was rewarded as the modern master of Yan Style, with works like *Zu'an Poetry Collection*.

培德 Pei Teh

英文名 Pei Teh，曾用名"海礼"，该船长 78.9 米，宽 12.7 米，功率 1300 马力，载重吨 2750，航速每小时 11 海里。1949 年迁往台湾。

Originally named as Hai Li, its length overall was 78.9 meters and the beam was 12.7 meters. With its engine power at 1,300 HP, it could sail at a speed of 11 kn and had a gross tonnage of 2,750 tons. The ship was moved to Taiwan in 1949.

该轮以历史名人命名。朱培德(1888—1937)，字益之，国民革命军南京中央军校校务委员，国民政府军训总监部总监，国民革命军陆军一级上将。朱培德在云南讲武堂时期就和朱德并称模范二朱，历经护国战争、护法战争，始终追随

孙中山先生，后作为第三军军长参加北伐战争，战功卓著，官至江西省主席、参谋总长、代理总司令、军委办公厅主任。

The ship was named after a historic figure. Zhu Pei Teh(1888-1937),also named Zhu Yizhi. He was committee member of the national revolutionary army Nanjing central academy, the director of military training department of the National Government,the senior general of the national revolutionary army.Zhu Pei Teh was honored as "Double Zhu Model" with Zhu De in the period of Jiangwutang in Yunnan. He had been following Sun Yat-sen through the National Protection War and the Constitution Protection Movement, later then he was served as the 3rd army commander in the Northern Expedition with outstanding performance. He worked as the commander officer to Jiangxi Province, chief of the general staff, deputy commander and director of the general office of CMC.

培德　Pei Teh

⚓ 汉民　Han Min

英文名 Han Min，曾用名"海义"，该船长 78.9 米，宽 12.7 米，功率 1300 马力，载重吨 2750，航速每小时 11 海里。1949 年载黄金、国宝自上海迁往台湾，1951 年出售给泰国。

Originally named as Hai Yi, its length overall was 78.9 meters and the beam was 12.7 meters. With its engine power at 1,300 HP, it could sail at a speed of 11 kn and had a gross tonnage of 2,750 tons. The ship was moved from Shanghai to Taiwan in 1949, responsible for shipping gold and national treasures. It was later sold to Thailand in 1951.

该轮以历史名人命名。胡汉民（1879—1936）广东番禺（今广州）人，原名衍鸿，字展堂。曾在日本留学。1905 年秋加入同盟会，任书记部书记、《民报》编辑。1909 年任同盟会南方支部长。在孙中山领导的几次起义中负责筹饷运械工作。9 月孙中山北上后，代理大元帅兼广东省省长。1927 年与蒋介石同谋进行"清党"，任南京国民党中央政治会议主席，立法院院长。1931 年与蒋介石争权被囚禁。九一八事变后释放，在广东策动陈济棠反蒋。1935 年任国民党中常会主席。后病逝于广州。

The ship was named after a historic figure.Hu Hanmin(1879-1936), from Panyu, Guangdong, also named Yanhong or Zhantang. He studied in Japan and joined in Tung Meng Hui in autumn of 1905, serving as the secretary of Secretary Department, the editor of *People's Daily*.He became the director of Southern branch of Tung Meng Hui in 1909 and was responsible for fund collection and machinery transportation in some uprisings led by Sun Yat-sen.After Sun Yat-sen marched northward, he was appointed the acting marshal and the governor of Guangdong Province. In 1927, planning with Chiang Kai-shek to purge within the party, Hu Hanmin became the chairman of Nanjing KMT central political conference and the president of legislative yuan. He was put in jail because of the power struggle with Chiang Kai-shek in 1931. After setting free after the September 18th Incident in 1931, he stirred up Chen Jitang to fight against Chiang Kai-shek. He served as the chairman of KMT central standing committee and died of illness later in Guangzhou.

林森 Lin Shen

英文名 Lin Shen，曾用名"海廉"，该船长 78.9 米，宽 12.7 米，功率 1300 马力，载重吨 2750，航速每小时 11 海里。1950 年 1 月，该船在香港起义归国。

Originally named as Hai Lian, its length overall was 78.9 meters and the beam was 12.7 meters. With its engine power at 1,300 HP, it could sail at a speed of 11 kn and had a gross tonnage of 2,750 tons. In January 1950, the ship returned to Mainland China after a successful uprising in Hong Kong.

该轮以历史名人命名。林森（1868—1943），字子超，号长仁。福建林森县（今闽侯县）人。1914 年在东京加入中华革命党。林森幼居福州，入英华学堂，因反清被开除，后参加反割让台湾斗争，并加入兴中会；中国同盟会成立时率会加盟。辛亥革命中，领导九江起义，并促海军反正，派兵援鄂、皖，稳定革命大局，被举为民国开国参议院议长。1932 年起接替蒋介石任国民政府主席。1943 年 8 月 1 日因车祸在重庆逝世。

The ship was named after a historic figure.Lin Shen(1868-1943), also named Zichao and Changren. From Linsen County,Fujian, he joined in Chinese Revolution Party in Tokyo in 1914. Linshen lived in Fuzhou when he was young and studied in Yinghua School,but was dismissed because of the fight against Qing dynasty. Later he joined in the movement to anti-cede Taiwan and became a member of Society for the Revival of China. When Tung Meng Hui was setup, he joined in with the society. During the Revolution of 1911, Lin Shen initiated Jiujiang Uprising and pushed the navy to send troops to Hubei and Anhui to stabilize the revolution, and was elected to be the founding president of the senate of Republic of China. Since 1932, he succeeded Chiang Kai-shek as the president of the National Government. On August 1st of 1943, he died of an car accident in Chongqing.

林森　Lin Shen

"林森"轮起义船员合影　The uprising crew members of Lin Shen

铁桥　Tieh Chiao

英文名 Tieh Chiao，曾用名"Teng1405"，该船长 78.9 米，宽 12.7 米，功率 1300 马力，载重吨 2750，航速每小时 11 海里。1947 年 10 月 11 日，由招商局接收。1949 年迁往台湾。

Originally named as Teng1405, its length overall was 78.9 meters and the beam was 12.7 meters. With its engine power at 1,300 HP, it could sail at a speed of 11 kn and had a gross tonnage of 2,750 tons. China Merchants took over the ship on October 11 of 1947 and it was moved to Taiwan in 1949.

该轮以历史名人命名。赵铁桥（1886—1930），同盟

1947 年国营招商局接收新购"铁桥"轮时中美双方人员合影
China Merchants takeover ceremony of newly-purchased Tieh Chiao in 1947

会会员，四川反清起义及反袁斗争首领之一。1928 年 1 月，以国民党政府交通部参事身份担任招商局总管理处总办，全面负责局务。在他担任招商局总管理处总办期间，进行了许多重大改革。首先改革了管理体制；第二是改革会计制度，揭露出了轰动一时的招商局三大案；第三是设立各种专业委员会。此外，他还冲破各种阻力，改革招商局公学，增开航海专科，大力培养本国航海技术人才。他的改革触动了许多人的既得利益，1930 年 7 月 24 日，他在总局门口遇刺身亡，为招商局的发展献出了宝贵的生命。

The ship was named after a historic figure.Zhao Tieh-chiao(1886-1930), a member of Tung Meng Hui, one of the leaders in the uprising to fight against Qing dynasty and Yuan Shih-kai. In January of 1928, as the counselor of the Ministry of Transport of KMT government,Zhao Tieh-chiao worked as the executive officer for the general administration of China Merchants.During the period in China Merchants, he made a lot of significant reforms,firstly focusing on administration reform, then the accounting system, revealing three bribery cases within China Merchants,and setting up various professional committees. Besides that, he broke through the obstacles to make reforms on China Merchants Public School, adding shipping specialty to raise the shipping talents for China. His reforms affected many people's vested interest, unfortunately he was assassinated before the gate of China Merchants headquarter on July 24th of 1930, sacrificing his life to the development of China Merchants.

教仁 Chiao Jen

英文名 Chiao Jen，曾用名"Teng1401"，该船长 78.9 米，宽 12.7 米，功率 1300 马力，载重吨 2750，航速每小时 11 海里。1947 年 10 月 18 日，由招商局接收。1950 年 1 月，该船在香港起义归国。

Originally named as Teng1401, its length overall was 78.9 meters and the beam was 12.7 meters. With its engine power at 1,300 HP, it could sail at a speed of 11 kn and had a gross tonnage of 2,750 tons. On October 18, 1947, the ship was taken over by China Merchants. In January 1950, it returned to Mainland China after a successful uprising in Hong Kong.

该轮以历史名人命名。宋教仁（1882—1913），字遁初，号渔父，湖南常德市桃源人。中国"宪政之父"，与黄兴、孙中山并称，主持第一次改组国民党。伟大的民主

教仁　Chiao Jen

"教仁"轮全体起义船员纪念　The uprising crew members of Chiao Jen

革命先行者、中华民国的主要缔造者，民国初期第一位倡导内阁制的政治家。中华民国临时政府唐绍仪内阁的农林部总长，国民党的主要筹建人。1913年被暗杀于上海，终年31岁。

The ship was named after a historic figure.Song Chiao Jen(1882-1913),also named Dunchu and Yufu,from Taoyuan,Changde of Hunan. He was honored as "the Father of Constitution" in China with Huang Hsing and Sun Yat-sen,managing the 1st reconstruction of KMT. He was a great democratic revolutionary forerunner, the main founder of the Republic of China, the first politician to advocate cabinet system in the early of the republic of China.He worked as the Minister of Agriculture in Tang Shaoyi's cabinet of the interim government of the Republic of China, and he was also the main builder for KMT. He was assassinated in Shanghai in 1913 at his age of 31.

⚓ 成功　Cheng Kung

英文名Cheng Kung，曾用名"Teng1406"，该船长78.9米，宽12.7米，功率1300马力，载重吨2750，航速每小时11海里。1947年11月1日，由招商局接收。1950年1月，该船在香港起义归国。

Originally named as Teng1406, its length overall was 78.9 meters and the beam was 12.7 meters. With its engine power at 1,300 HP, it could sail at a speed of 11 kn and had a gross tonnage of 2,750 tons. On November 1, 1947, the ship was taken over by China Merchants. In January 1950, it returned to Mainland China after a successful uprising in Hong Kong.

成功　Cheng Kung

该轮以历史名人命名。郑成功（1624—1662），福建泉州南安人，明末抗清名将、民族英雄。其父郑芝龙，其母名田川氏。因受隆武帝赐明朝国姓"朱"，赐名成功，故世称"国姓爷"，又因蒙永历帝封延平王，故又称"郑延平"。1645年清军攻入江南，不久郑芝龙降清、田川氏在乱军中自尽。郑成功率领父亲旧部在中国东南沿海抗清，成为南明后期主要军事力量之一。1661年率军横渡台湾海峡，经过数月英勇战斗，打败侵占台湾达38年之久的荷兰殖民者，还给了台湾人民自由，开启郑氏在台湾的统治。战后他鼓励垦荒种田，大力发展生产，兴办学校，促进了台湾的发展。

The ship was named after a historic figure.Zheng Cheng kung(1624-1662),from Nan'an,Quanzhou of Fujian. He was a famous general to fight against Qing Army in late Ming dynasty, as well as a national hero. His father was Zheng Zhilong, his mother was Tain Chuanshi. He was granted to have the emperor's surname "Zhu" by Emperor Longwu. Later he was called Zheng Yanping after Emperor Yongli posted him "Yanping King". When Qing army entered Jiangnan, Zheng Zhilong surrendered and Tian Chuanshi committed suicide

"成功"轮全体起义船员纪念　The uprising crew members of Cheng Kung

in the war. Zheng Cheng kung led the rest troops to fight against Qing army in the southern coastal regions in China, which was the one of the main forces in the late period of South Ming Dynasty. In 1661, he led the troops to cross the Taiwan Strait and fought back the Dutch Colonists who had seized Taiwan for 38 years. In his period of Taiwan, Zheng Chengkung encouraged to farm the land and develop production, setup schools,accelerating the development of Taiwan.

⚓ 鸿章 Hung Chang

英文名 Hung Chang，曾用名"Teng1407"，该船长 78.9 米，宽 12.7 米，功率 1300 马力，载重吨 2750，航速每小时 11 海里。1947 年 11 月 8 日，由招商局接收，专门行驶北洋线。1950 年 1 月香港起义归国。

Originally named as Teng1407, its length overall was 78.9 meters and the beam was 12.7 meters. With its engine power at 1,300 HP, it could sail at a speed of 11 kn and had a gross tonnage of 2,750 tons. On November 8, 1947, the ship was taken over by China Merchants and dedicated to the transportation along the Beiyang route. In January 1950, it returned to Mainland China after a successful uprising in Hong Kong.

该轮以历史名人命名。李鸿章（1823—1901），本名章铜，字渐甫，号少荃，晚年自号仪叟，安徽合肥人。早年师从曾国藩。1847 年中进士，后组建淮军，并建立淮系政治集团。1870 年担任直隶总督兼北洋通商大臣，后参与掌管清政府外交、军事、经济大权，成为清末权势最为显赫的封疆大吏。任内兴建大批近代企业，创办北洋海军，派遣留学生等等，开启了中国近代化的首轮浪潮。由于国力限制以及自身认识的局限，被迫代表清政府签订

鸿章 Hung Chang

了一系列的不平等条约。1901年，病逝于北京。李鸿章是招商局的主要创办者，并对招商局早期发展给予了积极的支持。

The ship was named after a historic figure.Li Hungchang(1823-1901), also named Zhangtong, Jianfu and Shaoquan, Yisou,from Hefei, Anhui. He was taught by Zeng Guofan in his early years. He obtained Chin-Shih in 1847 and then formed Huai Army and setup Huai political group. He worked as the viceroy of Zhili and the northern trade minister, and then was of the one who control the diplomatics,army and economy of Qing government.He was the most prominent figure among different powers in late Qing period. During his administration, Li Hungchang setup lots of modern enterprises, formed the Northern Navy and dispatched Chinese students to study abroad, initiating the first wave of Chinese modernization. Due to the limitation of national power and self-recognition, he was forced to sign a series of unfair treaties on behalf of Qing government. He died of illness in Beijing in 1901. Li Hungchang was the main founder of China Merchants and had been supporting a lot to the development of China Merchants at early stage.

"鸿章"轮起义船员纪念合影　　The uprising crew members of Hung Chang

郑和　Zheng He

⚓ 郑和　Zheng He

曾用名"Teng1403"，该船长 78.9 米，宽 12.7 米，功率 1300 马力，载重吨 2750，航速每小时 11 海里。1949 年 4 月该船留在南京，后被国民党政府派飞机炸沉。

Originally named as Teng 1403, its length overall was 78.9 meters and the beam was 12.7 meters. With its engine power at 1,300 HP, it could sail at a speed of 11 kn and had a gross tonnage of 2,750 tons. The ship stayed in Nanjing in April 1949 but was bombed to sink by the aircraft sent by the Kuomintang government.

该轮以历史名人命名。郑和（1371—1433），原名马三保。出身云南咸阳世家，明朝伟大的航海家。1381 年冬，明军进攻云南。10 岁的马三保被掳入明营，受宫刑成为太监，后进入朱棣的燕王府。靖难之变中，在河

北郑州（今河北任丘北）为朱棣立下战功。1404年明成祖朱棣认为马姓不能登三宝殿，因此在南京御书"郑"字赐马三保郑姓，改名为和，任为内官监太监，官至四品，地位仅次于司礼监。1405—1433年，郑和七下西洋，完成了人类历史上伟大的壮举。

The ship was named after a historic figure.Zheng He(1371-1433), originally named Ma Sanbao. He was born in an aristocratic family in Xianyang, Yunnan. He was a great navigator in Ming Dynasty. In the winter of 1381, Ming army attacked Yunnan. The 10-year old Ma Sanbao was captured into Ming's camp and became an eunuch and later served in Prince Yan's(Zhu Di) residence. During Jing-nan Rebellion, he made achievements in the war for Zhu Di in Zhengzhou, Hebei. In 1404, he was granted to change name to "Zheng He" by the Emperor Zhu Di, and was appointed the imperial eunuch, 4-level officer,just lower than courtesy eunuch. From 1405 to 1433, Zheng He made 7 times of expeditions to western oceans,accomplishing a great feat in human history.

1948年8月30日，国营招商局接收新购"郑和"轮时中美双方人员合影
China Merchants takeover ceremony of newly purchased Zheng He on August 30th, 1948

⚓ 廷枢　Ting Shu

曾用名"Teng1404"，该船长78.9米，宽12.7米，功率1300马力，载重吨2750，航速每小时11海里。1948年4月24日，由招商局接收。1949年担任军运时被击毁。

Originally named as Teng1404, its length overall was 78.9 meters and the beam was 12.7 meters. With its engine power at 1,300 HP, it could sail at a speed of 11 kn and had a gross tonnage of 2,750 tons. The ship was taken over by China Merchants on April 24, 1948, but was attacked and wrecked in a military transportation in 1949.

该轮以历史名人命名。唐廷枢（1832—1892），字景星，广东香山县（今中山市）人，清代洋务运动的代表人物之一。1873年6月4日，唐廷枢被李鸿章札委担招商局总办，成为招商局的第二位掌门人，负责劝股、添船、造栈、揽载、开拓航路、设立码头等事务。1875年，唐廷枢设立保险招商局。1881年，唐廷枢与徐润等合办天津塘沽耕植畜牧公司。1885年，唐廷枢卸任离局，奉命北上专主开平煤矿。唐廷枢一生致力于发展中国的航运业、矿冶业、铁路运输业，热心筹办各类近代新式企业，为中国近代经济发展做出了杰出的贡献。

The ship was named after a historic figure.Tang Tingshu(1832-1892), also named Jingxing, from Xiangshan County, Guangdong,one of the representatives of Self-strengthening Movement. On June 4th of 1873, Tang Tingshu was assigned to be the general director of China Merchants by Li Hungchang, the 2nd president of China Merchants.He was responsible for fund collection, ship increase, warehouse building, business running, shipping lines exploration and setting up wharves. Tang Tingshu setup insurance company in 1875 and jointly setup Tianjin Tanggu Planting and Farming company with Xu Run in 1881. He left China Merchants in 1885 and was assigned to be the director of Kaiping Coal Mine. He dedicated his life to the development of shipping, mining, transportation industries in modern China, making outstanding contributions to the economic development of modern China.

宣怀 Xuan Huai

曾用名"Teng1402",该船长 78.9 米,宽 12.7 米,功率 1300 马力,载重吨 2750,航速每小时 11 海里。1947 年 12 月 24 日,由招商局接收,驶往天津。1948 年 11 月在营口发生爆炸。

Originally named as Teng1402, its length overall was 78.9 meters and the beam was 12.7 meters. With its engine power at 1,300 HP, it could sail at a speed of 11 kn and had a gross tonnage of 2,750 tons. The ship was taken over by China Merchants on December 24, 1947 and assigned to sail to Tianjin. In November 1948, the ship was destroyed in an explosion in Yingkou.

宣怀　Xuan Huai

该轮以历史名人命名。盛宣怀(1844—1916),生于江苏武进,字杏荪。清末官员,官办商人,洋务派代表人物,被誉为"中国实业之父"和"中国商父"。1872 年夏,盛宣怀受命创办招商局,草拟《轮船章程》。1873 年 9 月 9 日被委任为该局会办。1875 年奉调督办湖北煤铁矿务。1879 年 11 月,署天津河间兵备道。1884 年署天津海关道。1885 年初,被李鸿章委任为招商局督办,成为招商局的第三位掌门人。1892 年创办北洋大学堂。1894 年在上海整理被大火焚烧的机器织布局,设立华盛纺织总局,任督办。1895 年奏设天津中西学堂。1896 年奏设上海南洋公学。1898 年创办中国通商银行。1908 年 3 月就任邮传部右侍郎,1911 年元月被补授邮传部尚书,名义上不再担任招商局会长职务。1913 年 6 月 22 日,招商局在上海张园召开股东常年大会,当选为招商局副会长。其著有《愚斋存稿》、《盛宣怀未刊信籍》。

The ship was named after a historic figure.Sheng Xuanhuai(1844-1916), from Wujin,Jiangsu, also named Xingsun. He was an official in late Qing government, an official businessman, a representative figure in Self-strengthening Movement,who was awarded as "the Father of Industry" and "the Father of Commerce" in China. In the summer of 1872, Sheng Xuanhuai was appointed to setup China Merchants and drew up the "shipping regulation and rules". On September 9th of 1873, he was appointed the vice-director of China

Merchants. He was assigned to supervise Hubei Coal-iron business, and he became the customs officer in Tianjin in 1884. Early in 1885, he was appointed as the supervisor of China Merchants by Li Hungchang, the 3rd president of China Merchants. Sheng Xuanhuai founded BeiYang College in 1892, setup Huasheng Textile Company on the base of the burnt Shanghai Machine Weaving Company in 1894,found Tientsin Sino-West School in 1895 and Nanyang Public School in 1896. He founded the Commercial Bank of China in 1898. In March of 1908, Sheng Xuanhuai was appointed as the Youshilang(assistant) of the Ministry of Post and Transportation and promoted to Shangshu(chief) of the Ministry of Post and Transportation, no longer worked as the president of China Merchants.On June 22nd of 1913,China Merchants held annual shareholder conference in Zhangyuan,Shanghai, Sheng Xuanhuai was selected as the vice president of China Merchants. He had left works like *Yu Zhai Drafts* and Sheng *Xuanhuai Unpublished Letters*.

继光　Ji Guang

曾用名"Teng1414"，该船长78.9米，宽12.7米，功率1300马力，载重吨2750，航速每小时11海里。1948年1月8日，由招商局接收。1949年迁往台湾，1965年售予万丰轮船公司。

Originally named as Teng1414, its length overall was 78.9 meters and the beam was 12.7 meters. With its engine power at 1,300 HP, it could sail at a speed of 11 kn and had a gross tonnage of 2,750 tons. The ship was taken over by China Merchants on January 8, 1948 and moved to Taiwan in 1949. It was sold to Wanfeng Shipping Company in 1965.

该轮以历史名人命名。戚继光（1528—1588），字元敬，号南塘，山东烟台蓬莱人，祖籍安徽定远。明朝军事家，抗倭名将。出身将门，初任登州卫指挥佥事，1555年调浙江

继光　Ji Guang

抵抗倭寇，他招募编练新军，人称"戚家军"，为抗倭主力。1561年在台州大胜倭寇，次年捣毁倭寇在横屿的老巢，解除东南倭患。1567年调往北方镇守。1583年调往广东，后罢归登州，不久病卒。自戚家军成立开始，他率军于浙、闽、粤沿海诸地抗击来犯倭寇，历10余年，大小80余战，终于扫平倭寇之患，被誉为民族英雄。著有《纪效新书》、《练兵实纪》、《止止堂集》等书传世。

The ship was named after a historic figure.Qi Jiguang(1528-1588), also named Yuanjing,Nantang, from Penglai,Yantai of Shandong,originally from Dingyuan,Anhui. He was a militarist in Ming dynasty, as well as a famous general to fight against Japanese pirates. He was born in a general family, firstly served as a director in Dengzhou, then assigned to fight against Japanese pirates in Zhejiang in 1555, he recruited and trained a lot of new soldiers who were called "Qi Army". In 1561 in Taizhou, he made a victory over the enemy, in the following year he smashed the enemy in Hengyu, cleaning the Japanese pirates in Southeast area.He was appointed to guard in the northern area and then transferred to Guangdong, at last he quit in Dengzhou and died of illness later. Since the establishment of "Qi Army", Qi Jiguang had been leading the army to fight against Japanese pirates in different coastal areas of Zhejiang,Fujian and Guangdong for more than 10 years, undergoing more than 80 wars, and finally smashed away the Japanese pirates. He was rewarded as the national hero in China. He had works left like *Ji Xiao Xin Shu*, *Lian Bing Shi Ji*, and *Zhizhi Tang Ji*.

B 型轮　Type B Freighters

⚓ 海穗　Hai Shui

英文名 Hai Shui 曾用名"Ottawa Paget"，1946年建造于加拿大 Vancover。该船排水量1351.48吨，载重吨1684，长224尺，吃水16尺。航速每小时10海里，日耗油11吨。1946年9月17日，招商局接收。1949年迁往台湾。

海穗　Hai Shui

Originally named as Ottawa Paget, the ship was built in 1946 in Vancover, Canada. With a displacement of 1,351.48 tons and a dead weight tonnage of 1,684 tons, it was 224 chi long with a draught of 16 chi. It could sail at a speed of 10 kn with a daily fuel consumption of 11 tons. The ship was taken over by China Merchants on September 17, 1946 and moved to Taiwan in 1949.

⚓ 海甬 Hai Yun

英文名 Hai Yun，曾用名"Ottawa Palette"，1946 年建造于加拿大。该船排水量 1351.48 吨，载重吨 1684，长 224 尺，吃水 16 尺。航速每小时 10 海里，日耗油 11 吨。1946 年 9 月 26 日，由招商局接收，定期行驶上海至青岛线。1949 年留在大陆，改名为"民主七号"、"和平七十号"。

Originally named as Ottawa Palette, the ship was built in Canada in 1946. With a displacement of 1,351.48 tons and a dead weight tonnage of 1,684 tons, it was 224 chi long with a draught of 16 chi. It could sail at a speed of 10 kn with a daily fuel consumption of 11 tons. The ship was taken over by China Merchants on September 26, 1946 and served as a regular shipping liner between Shanghai and Qingdao. It stayed in Mainland China in 1949 and was renamed as Democracy No.7 and later Peace No.70.

⚓ 海杭 Hai Hang

英文名 Hai Hang，曾用名"Ottawa Parade"，1946 年建造于加拿大 Vancouver。该船排水量 1351.48 吨，载重吨 1684，长 224 尺，吃水 16 尺。航速每小时 10 海里，日耗油 11 吨。1946 年 10 月 8 日由招商局接收，1949 年迁往台湾。

Originally named as Ottawa Parade, the ship was built in Vancouver, Canada in 1946. With a displacement of 1,351.48 tons and a dead weight tonnage of 1,684 tons, it was 224 chi long with a draught of 16 chi. It could sail at a speed of 10 kn with a daily fuel consumption of 11 tons. The ship was taken over by China Merchants on October 8, 1946 and moved to Taiwan in 1949.

⚓ 海汉 Hai Han

英文名 Hai Han，曾用名"Ottawa Paeque"，1945 年建造于加拿大 Victoria。该船排水量 1351.48 吨，载重吨 1684，长 224 尺，吃水 16 尺。航速每小时 10 海里，日耗油 11 吨。1946 年 10 月 11 日由招商局接收，1950 年 1 月于香港起义归国。

Originally named as Ottawa Paeque, the ship was built in Victoria, Canada in 1945. With a displacement

海汉 Hai Han

of 1,351.48 tons and a dead weight tonnage of 1,684 tons, it was 224 chi long with a draught of 16 chi. It could sail at a speed of 10 kn with a daily fuel consumption of 11 tons. The ship was taken over by China Merchants on October 11, 1946. Later in January 1950, it returned to Communist Mainland China after a successful uprising in Hong Kong.

"海汉"轮起义船员纪念合影　The uprising crew members of Hai Han

⚓ 海沪 Hai Hu

英文名 Hai Hu，曾用名"Ottawa Palmer"，1946 年建造于加拿大 Victoria。该船排水量 1351.48 吨，载重吨 1684，长 224 尺，吃水 16 尺。航速每小时 10 海里，日耗油 11 吨。1946 年 10 月 16 日由招商局接收，1949 年迁往台湾。

Originally named as Ottawa Palmer, the ship was built in Victoria, Canada in 1946. With a displacement of 1,351.48 tons and a dead weight tonnage of 1,684 tons, it was 224 chi long with a draught of 16 chi. It could sail at a speed of 10 kn with a daily fuel consumption of 11 tons. The ship was taken over by China Merchants on October 16, 1946 and moved to Taiwan in 1949.

⚓ 海津 Hai Tsin

英文名 Hai Tsin，曾用名"Ottawa Painter"，1946 年建造于加拿大 Victoria。该船排水量 1351.48 吨，载重吨 1684，长 224 尺，吃水 16 尺。航速每小时 10 海里，日耗油 11 吨。1946 年 10 月 22 日由招商局接收，1949 年迁往台湾。

Originally named as Ottawa Painter, the ship was built in Victoria, Canada in 1946. With a displacement of 1,351.48 tons and a dead weight tonnage of 1,684 tons, it was 224 chi long with a draught of 16 chi. It could sail at a speed of 10 kn with a daily fuel consumption of 11 tons. The ship was taken over by China Merchants on October 22, 1946 and moved to Taiwan in 1949.

⚓ 海平 Hai Ping

英文名 Hai Ping，曾用名"Ottawa Pandora"，1946 年建造于加拿大 Victoria。该船排水量 1351.48 吨，载重吨 1684，长 224 尺，吃水 16 尺。航速每小时 10 海里，日耗油 11 吨。1946 年 10 月 29 日由招商局接收，1949 年迁往台湾。

Originally named as Ottawa Pandora, the ship was built in Victoria, Canada in 1946. With a displacement of 1,351.48 tons and a dead weight tonnage of 1,684 tons, it was 224 chi long with a draught of 16 chi. It could sail at a speed of 10 kn with a daily fuel consumption of 11 tons. The ship was taken over by China Merchants on October 29, 1946 and moved to Taiwan in 1949.

Corvettes 快速客轮 Corvettes / Fast Speed Passenger Liners

⚓ 锡麟 Shih Lin

英文名 Shih Lin，曾用名"Orangeville"，该船长 76.9 米，宽 11.1 米，2750 马力，载重吨 2000。由加拿大 Henry Robb 公司所建造。1949 年迁往台湾，1950 年交由台湾地区"海军部"，"锡麟"改名"德安"。

Originally named as Orangeville, the ship was built by a Canadian ship company called Henry Robb. Its length overall was 76.9 meters and the beam was 11.1 meters. With its engine power at 2,750 HP, its dead weight tonnage reached 2,000 tons. The ship was moved to Taiwan in 1949 and handed over to the Kuomintang Navy Department in 1950. The name of the ship was also changed from Shih Lin to De An.

锡麟 Shin Lin

该轮以历史名人命名。徐锡麟（1873—1907），字伯荪，浙江绍兴人。1901年任绍兴府学堂教师，后升副监督。1903年应乡试，名列副榜。同年以参观大阪博览会名义赴日本，于东京结识陶成章、龚宝铨，积极参加营救因反清入狱的章炳麟的活动。回国后先在绍兴创设书局，传播新译书报，宣传反清革命。1904年在上海加入光复会。1905年在绍兴创立体育会，后又创立大通学堂，规定入校学生均为光复会会员，参加兵操训练。同年冬赴日本学军，因患眼疾未能如愿。1906年归国，赴安徽任武备学堂副总办、安徽巡警学堂会办。1907年7月6日，徐锡麟在安庆刺杀安徽巡抚恩铭，率领学生军起义，攻占军械所，激战4小时，失败被捕，次日慷慨就义。

The ship was named after a historic figure.Xu Shinlin(1873-1907), also named Bosun, from Shaoxing, Zhejiang. He worked as a teacher in Shaoxing School and then was promoted to be the vice-supervisor. He took the provincial examination and got listed. In the same year, he went to Tokyo in the name of attending Osaka Exposition and met with Tao Chengzhang and Gong Baoquan, actively joining in the activity to rescue Zhang Binglin who was kept in prison because of anti-Qing activity. After returning to China, he setup a publishing house to propagate translated books and newspaper to advocate the revolution to fight agaist Qing government. He joined in Restoration Society in Shanghai in 1904. Xu Shinlin founded Sports Society in Shaoxing in 1905 and later founded Datong School,enrolled students should be the member of Restoration Society and have the military training. In winter of the same year, he went to Japan to learn how to train military, but he didn't make it due to the eye trouble. Returning in 1906, he worked as the chief of military preparatory school in Anhui and the vice chief of Anhui Patrol School.On July 6th of 1907, Xu Shinlin assassinated Anhui Governor En Ming and initiated an uprising made up of students, fighting for 4 hours and occupying armory, but finally failed, and Xu Shinlin was killed after being arrested.

⚓ 秋瑾 Chiu Chin

英文名Chiu Chin，曾用名"Tillsonburg"，该船长76.9米，宽11.1米，2750马力，载重吨2000。由加拿大Laware金属公司建造。1949年迁往台湾，1950年交由台湾地区"海军部"，"秋瑾"改名"高安"。

Originally named as Tillsonburg, the ship was built by a Canadian metal company called Laware. Its length overall was 76.9 meters and the beam was 11.1 meters. With its engine power at 2,750 HP, its dead weight tonnage reached 2,000 tons. The ship was moved to Taiwan in 1949 and handed over to the Kuomintang Navy Department in 1950. The name of the ship was also changed from Chiu Chin to Gao An.

该轮以历史名人命名。秋瑾（1875—1907），原名秋闺瑾，字璇卿。祖籍浙江山阴（今绍兴），生于福建厦门。中国女权和女学思想的倡导者，近代民主革命志士，提倡女权。曾自费东渡日本留学。积极投身革命，先后参加过三合会、光复会、同盟会等革命组织，联络会党计划响应萍浏醴起义未果。1907年，她与徐锡麟等组织光复军，拟于7月6日在浙江、安徽同时起义，事泄被捕。7月15日从容就义于绍兴轩亭口。

The ship was named after a historic figure.Chiu Chin(1875-1907), originally named Chiu Guijin, also named Xuanqing.Her family was originally from Shanyin,Zhejiang, and she was born in Xiamen,Fujian. She was the advocator of China's women rights and thoughts, modern democratic revolutionary. Chiu Chin devoted herself to the revolution, joined the organizations like Triad Society, Restoration Society and Tung Meng Hui, contacted with other members trying to respond to Pingliuli Uprising but in vain. She organized Recovery Army with Xu Xilin in 1907, planning to initiate uprisings in Zhejiang and Anhui on the same day of July 6th, she was arrested due to the plan leaking. Chiu Chin was executed to death at Xuantingkou in Shaoxing on July 15th.

⚓ 元培 Yuan Pei

英文名Yuan Pei，曾用名"Nunney Castle"，该船长76.9米，宽11.1米，2750马力，载重吨2000。由加拿大Wm Pickersgill & Son厂建造。1949年留在大陆，交海军部使用，改名为"广州"。

Originally named as Nunney Castle, the ship was built by a Canadian ship company called Wm Pickersgill & Son. Its length overall was 76.9 meters and the beam was 11.1 meters. With its engine power at 2,750 HP, its dead weight tonnage reached 2,000 tons. The ship stayed in Mainland China in 1949 and was later handed over to the Navy Department. The name of the ship was also changed from Yuan Pei to Guangzhou.

元培　Yuan Pei

该轮以历史名人命名。蔡元培（1868—1940），字鹤卿，浙江绍兴山阴县（今浙江绍兴）人，近代革命家、教育家、政治家，也是我国近代民族学研究的先驱。中华民国首任教育总长，1916年至1927年任北京大学校长，革新北大，开"学术"与"自由"之风；1920年至1930年，蔡元培同时兼任中法大学校长。1928年至1940年专任中央研究院院长，贯彻对学术研究的主张。他早年参加反清朝帝制的斗争，民国初年主持制定了中国近代高等教育的第一个法令——《大学令》。

The ship was named after a historic figure.Cai Yuanpei(1868-1940), also named Heqing, from Shanyin county, Shaoxing of Zhejiang.He was a modern revolutionary, educator and politician, as well as the pioneer of modern China ethnology research. Cai Yuanpei was the 1st Minister of Education, the president of Peking University from 1916 to 1927, making reforms in the university and initiating the trend of "academic research" and "freedom". From 1920 to 1930, Cai Yuanpei was also worked as the president of Sino-French University. He was the dean of Academia Sinica from 1928 to 1940, implementing the assertion to academic research. He joined in the fight against Qing Monarchy in his early years, and made "University Law"—the first Law for China Modern Higher Education in the early period of the Republic of China.

CISAYI 型海轮
CISAYI Type Ocean Liners

⚓ 海亚、海美、海欧、海澳
Hai Ya, Hai Mei, Hai Ou, Hai Ao

"海亚"轮在基隆港　Hai Ya ship in Keelung Port

LST 坦克登陆艇　Landing Ship, Tank

⚓ 中 101　Zhong 101

曾用名"LST8040"，1944 年建造于美国 Indiana，该船长 97.8 米，宽 15.2 米，1800 马力，3326.64 总吨，航速每小时 10 海里。1946 年 5 月由招商局接收。

Originally named as LST8040, the ship was built in 1944 in Indiana, U.S.A. Its length overall was 97.8 meters and the beam was 15.2 meters. With its engine power at 1,800 HP and a gross tonnage of 3326.64 tons, the ship could sail at a speed of 10 kn. China Merchants took over the ship in May, 1946.

⚓ 中 102　Zhong 102

曾用名"LST929"，1944 年建造于美国 Hingham Mass，该船长 97.8 米，宽 15.2 米，1800 马力，3326.64 总吨，航速每小时 10 海里。1946 年 5 月由招商局接收。1949 年 4 月 13

中 102　Zhong 102

日征用军运时与舰上所载国民党伞兵第三总队一同开往连云港起义，后成为海军使用的主力舰，改名为"太行山"。

Originally named as LST929, the ship was built in 1944 in Hingham Mass, U.S.A. Its length overall was 97.8 meters and the beam was 15.2 meters. With its engine power at 1,800 HP and a gross tonnage of 3,326.64 tons, the ship could sail at a speed of 10 kn. China Merchants took over the ship in May 1946. On April 13, 1949, the ship sailed to Lianyungang city for the uprising with the Third Corps of Paratroops of Kuomintang on board on its military transportation. It then served as the Navy battleship, and was renamed as Taihang Mountain.

中 103　Zhong 103

中 103　Zhong 103

曾用名"LST945"，1944 年建造于美国，该船长 97.8 米，宽 15.2 米，1800 马力，3326.64 总吨，航速每小时 10 海里。1946 年 5 月由招商局接收，1949 年迁往台湾。

Originally named as LST945, the ship was built in 1944 in the U.S.A. Its length overall was 97.8 meters and the beam was 15.2 meters. With its engine power at 1,800 HP and a gross tonnage of 3,326.64 tons, the ship could sail at a speed of 10 kn. China Merchants took over the ship in May, 1946 and moved it to Taiwan in 1949.

中 104　Zhong 104

曾用名"LST656"，1944 年建造于美国，该船长 97.8 米，宽 15.2 米，1800 马力，3326.64 总吨，航速每小时 10 海里。1946 年 5 月由招商局接收。

Originally named as LST656, the ship was built in 1944 U.S.A. Its length overall was 97.8 meters and the beam was 15.2 meters. With its engine power at 1,800 HP and a gross tonnage

中 104　Zhong 104

of 3,326.64 tons, the ship could sail at a speed of 10 kn. China Merchants took over the ship in May, 1946.

中 105　Zhong 105

曾用名"LST658",1943年建造于美国Pennsylvania,该船长97.8米,宽15.2米,1800马力,3326.64总吨,航速每小时10海里。1946年5月由招商局接收。

Originally named as LST658, the ship was built in 1943 in the U.S.A. Its length overall was 97.8 meters, and the beam was 15.2 meters. With its engine power at 1,800 HP and a gross tonnage of 3,326.64 tons, the ship could sail at a speed of 10 kn. China Merchants took over the ship in May, 1946.

中 105　Zhong 105

中 106　Zhong 106

1943年建造于美国Pennsylvania,该船长97.8米,宽15.2米,1800马力,3326.64总吨,航速每小时10海里。1946年5月由招商局接收。由船长金鸿福率船于1950年2月在香港起义归国。

中 106　Zhong 106

"中106"艇全体起义船员纪念　The uprising crew members of Zhong 106

The ship was built in Pennsylvania, U.S.A. in 1943. Its length overall was 97.8 meters, and the beam was 15.2 meters. With its engine power at 1,800 HP and a gross tonnage of 3,326.64 tons, the ship could sail at a speed of 10 kn. China Merchants took over the ship in May, 1946. The Captain Jin Hongfu led the ship to uprise in Hong Kong in February 1950 and returned to Mainland China.

⚓ 中 107　Zhong 107

1944年建造于美国，该船长97.8米，宽15.2米，1800马力，3326.64总吨，航速每小时10海里。1946年5月由招商局接收。1949年起义归国。

The ship was built in 1944 U.S.A. Its length overall was 97.8 meters and the beam was 15.2 meters. With its engine power at 1,800 HP and a gross tonnage of 3,326.64 tons, the ship could sail at a speed of 10 kn. China Merchants took over the ship in May, 1946. It returned to Mainland China after an uprising in 1949.

⚓ 中 108　Zhong 108

1949年迁往台湾，1954年招商局将其作为登陆舰交予台"海军部"（1955年台"海军部"交还"中108"）。

The ship was moved to Taiwan in 1949. It was handed over by China Merchants to the Kuomintang Navy Department in Taiwan as a landing ship (the Kuomintang Navy Department in Taiwan returned Zhong 108 in 1955).

⚓ 中 109　Zhong 109

1949年迁往台湾，后于1955年移交台湾"海军部"。

The ship was moved to Taiwan in 1949 and handed over to the Kuomintang Navy Department in Taiwan in 1955.

⚓ 中 110　Zhong 110

1948年2月于撤退时被国民党军队凿沉于三江营堵塞港口。

The ship was scuttled at Sanjiangying by the Kuomintang army to block the port during their retreat in February 1948.

⚓ 中 112　Zhong 112

1949年被征召军运时被炮火击毁。

The ship was destroyed by gunfire when it was requisitioned as a military carrier in 1949.

⚓ 中 113　Zhong 113

1949年迁往台湾，后于1959年解体出售。

The ship was moved to Taiwan in 1949 and disassembled for sale in 1959.

⚓ 中 117　Zhong 117

1949年迁往台湾，后1955年移交台湾"海军部"。

The ship was moved to Taiwan in 1949 and handed over to the Kuomintang Navy Department in Taiwan in 1955.

⚓ 中 118　Zhong 118

1949年迁往台湾，1951年招商局将其售予民航空运队为"江流"号修理船。

The ship was moved to Taiwan in 1949. China Merchants sold it to the Civil Aviation Air Force to be used as the repair ship for Jiang Liu in 1951.

⚓ 中 111、中 114、中 115、中 116
Zhong 111, Zhong 114, Zhong 115, Zhong 116

1949年留在大陆。

These ships were left behind at Mainland China in 1949.

中 114　Zhong 114

LSM 中型登陆艇　LSM Landing Ship Medium

⚓ 华 201、华 202、华 203、华 204、华 205、华 206、
华 207、华 208、华 209、华 210、华 211、华 212

Hua 201, Hua 202, Hua 203, Hua 204, Hua 205, Hua 206,
Hua 207, Hua 208, Hua 209, Hua 210, Hua 211, Hua 212

这些船只是二战期间美军为施行登陆战而紧急大量建造的中型登陆舰，能驶入较浅海滩，建造于美国 Houston 船厂。船长 61.7 米，宽 10 米，3600 马力，865.67 总吨，航速每小时 14 海里。1946 年 5、6 月招商局以每艘 23.5 万美元引进了 12 艘，依次命名为"华 201—华 212"，改装后用作货轮。

These ships were a large number of LSMs made by the U.S. army. They were used in the emergency landing battle during the World War II for their capability of entering shallow beach. They were built in the Houston Shipyard in the U.S.A. The length overall of each of them was 61.7 meters and the beam was 10 meters. With its engine power at 3,600 HP and a gross tonnage of 865.67 tons, each ship could sail at a speed of 14 kn. China Merchants bought 12 ships at the price of $ 235,000 for each in May and June in 1946, named them numerically from Hua 201 to Hua 212, and used them as cargo ships after modification.

华 203　Hua 203

华 212（1949 年起义后，成为海军滦河舰）
Hua 212 (Became Luan River Ship of Navy after the 1949 uprising)

华 204　Hua 204

Gre-type 货轮　Gre-type Freighter

⚓ 自忠　Zi Zhong

原名"Baldwin Park"，1944 年建造于加拿大洛宗，属于登陆坦克艇，后改装为货运船。该船长 99.7 米，宽 11.4 米，1374 马力，3265.13 总吨，航速每小时 10 海里。1946 年 11 月由招商局接收，1949 年迁往台湾。

Originally named as Baldwin Park, the ship was built in Lauzon P.Q. of Canada in 1944. It was originally a tank landing ship, and was converted for freight transportation. Its length overall was 99.7 meters and the beam was 11.4 meters. With its engine power at 1,374 HP and a gross tonnage of 3,265.13 tons, the ship could sail at a speed of 10 kn. China Merchants took over the ship in November, 1946 and moved it to Taiwan in 1949.

该轮以历史名人命名。张自忠（1891—1940），字荩臣，山东临清唐园村人。以中华民国上将衔陆军中将之职殉国，牺牲后追授为陆军二级上将军衔，著名抗日将领，民族英雄。同时也是第二次世界大战中同盟国牺牲的最高将领。从 1917 年开始，入冯玉祥部，先后担任营长、团长、旅长、师长、军长、军团长、集团军总司令等职。1940 年战死，享年 49 岁。

The ship was named after a historic figure. Zhang Zizhong(1891-1940), also named Zhang Jinchen, from Tangyuan Village of Linqing, Shandong. He sacrificed his life as a lieutenant general of the Republic of China, and was awarded posthumously the 2nd level army general. Zhang Zizhong was a famous general to flight against Japanese invaders, as well as a national hero. He was the highest level general died in the Allies of World War-Ⅱ. He joined in Feng Yuxiang's army since 1917, and successively served as battalion commander, colonel, brigade, division commander, army commander, army chief, chief of army group. He died in the war in 1940 at his age of 49.

⚓ 登禹 Deng Yu

原名"Mulgrave Park",1945 年建造于加拿大 Levia Que,属于登陆坦克艇,后改装为货运船。该船长 99.7 米,宽 11.4 米,1176 马力,3265.13 总吨,航速每小时 10 海里。1946 年 11 月由招商局接收,1950 年 1 月在香港起义归国。

Originally named as Mulgrave Park, the ship was built in Levia Que of Canada in 1945. It was originally a tank landing ship, and was converted for freight transportation. Its length overall was 99.7 meters and the beam was 11.4 meters. With its engine power at 1,176 HP and a gross tonnage of 3,265.13 tons, the ship could sail at a speed of 10 kn. China Merchants took over the ship in November, 1946. It was returned to Mainland China in January of 1950 after the uprising in Hong Kong.

该轮以历史名人命名。赵登禹(1898—1937),字舜诚,山东省菏泽县赵楼村人。陆军上将,民族英雄。少年时因家境贫寒,未入私塾读书,在家务农并师从武术名家朱凤军练习武术。1914 年加入冯玉祥的部队,后任冯的随身护兵。1926 年参加北伐。1933 年,任第 29 军第 37 师第 109 旅旅长,后任第 132 师师长。在抗日战争(七七事变,卢沟桥保卫战)中壮烈殉国,是抗日殉国的第一位师长。

The ship was named after a historic figure. Zhao Dengyu (1898-1937), also named Zhao Shuncheng, was from Zhaolou Village, Heze County of Shandong Province, an army general as well as a national hero. He failed to have education at young age because of his poor family, and was a farmer and learned Wushu from a famous martial master Zhu Fengjun. Joined in Feng Yuxiang's army in 1914, he served as an escort of Feng Yuxiang. Zhao Dengyu joined in the Northern Expedition in 1926. And in 1933, he served as the brigade commander of the 109th brigade in 37th division of the 29th army, and then served as the division commander of the 132nd division. He died in the fighting of "7.7 Incident", who was the 1st division commander sacrificed his life for the country.

登禹 Deng Yu

麟阁 Lin Ge

原名"Rockland Park",1945 年建造于加拿大 Plotou N. S,属于登陆坦克艇,后改装为货运船。该船长 99.7 米,宽 11.4 米,1176 马力,3265.13 总吨,航速每小时 10 海里。1946 年 11 月由招商局接收,1949 年迁往台湾。

Originally named as Rockland Park, the ship was built in Plotou N. S of Canada in 1945. It was originally a tank landing ship, and was converted for freight transportation. Its length overall was 99.7 meters and the beam was 11.4 meters. With its engine power at 1,176 HP and a gross tonnage of 3,265.13 tons, the ship could sail at a speed of 10 kn. China Merchants took over the ship in November, 1946 and moved it to Taiwan in 1949.

该轮以历史名人命名。佟麟阁(1892—1937),河北省保定市高阳县人,中国抗日将领。七七事变时,指挥第 29 军浴血抗战,喋血南苑,壮烈殉国,是全面抗战爆发后捐躯疆场的第一位高级将领。国民政府追赠陆军二级上将,民族英雄。佟麟阁早年参加护国讨袁战争。曾任冯玉祥部陆军第 11 师第 21 混成旅旅长。1926 年 9 月五原誓师后,随部参加北伐。1928 年起,任国民革命军第 2 集团军第 35 军军长、暂编第 11 师师长、第 29 军副军长。1933 年率部参加长城抗战,取得喜峰口大捷。同年 5 月,参加察哈尔抗日同盟军,任第一军军长兼代理察哈尔省主席,跟随冯玉祥驰骋察省,打击日军,收复失地,为察省光复做出了贡献。

The ship was named after a historical figure.Tong Linge(1892-1937), was from Gaoyang County, Baoding of He Bei, a famous general to fight agaist Japanese invaders. After "7.7 Incident", he led 29th army to have fierce fight against the Japanese army and died in the war. Tong Linge was the 1st senior general who

麟阁 Lin Ge

devoted his life to the fight against the Japanese army after the outbreak of the Anti-Japanese war. He was awarded posthumously the 2nd level army general. Tong Linge once joined the war to fight against Yuan Shih-kai in his early years. After that, he served as brigade commander in 21st mixed brigade of the 11th division of the army led by General Feng Yuxiang. After the Wuyuan Pledging, he joined in the Northern Expedition. From 1928, he served as the army commander of 35th army of the 2nd group of the National Revolutionary Army, the division commander of the 11th division, the vice commander of the 29th army. He led the army to take part in the Great Wall Fighting in 1933 and got a success in Xifeng kou. In may of the same year, Tong Linge joined in the Anti-Japanese Allied Army in Chahar Province, served as the army commander of the 1st army and the acting president of Chahar Province, following General Feng Yuxiang to fight against Japanese army and gained back lost territory, making contributions to the recovery of Chahar Province.

AI 型海轮　AI-type ocean vessel

⚓ 海菲　Hai Fei

1920 年美国建造的通用型客货轮，该船长 129.8 米，宽 16.4 米，主机功率 2000 马力，排水量 6202 吨，吃水 10 米，航速每小时 10 海里。招商局购买自私营远洋贸易公司，主要行驶中美航线。

This ship was a passenger and cargo liner built in the U.S.A in 1920. Its length overall was 129.8 meters and the beam was 16.4 meters. It had a displacement of 6,202 tons and a draught of 10 meters. With its main engine power at 2,000 HP, the ship could sail at a speed of 10 kn. China Merchants purchased it from a private Ocean Trading Company and used it mainly for the Sino-US route.

海菲　Hai Fei

海厦 Hai Xia

1923年建造于香港，原名"源生"轮，属于货运驳船，该船长97.5米，宽13.9米，主机功率2000马力，排水量3179.21吨，吃水7米，航速每小时11海里。1946年招商局购买自"怡和"洋行。1950年，该轮在香港起义归国，改名"利生"（再改为"和平九号"与"和平十二号"）。本轮直到1980年才退役。

Hai Xia was a cargo barge built in Hong Kong in 1923 and was previously named as Yuan Sheng. Its length overall was 97.5 meters and the beam was 13.9 meters. It had a displacement of 3,179.21 tons and a draught of 7 meters. With its main engine power at 2,000 HP, the ship could sail at a speed of 11 kn. The ship was bought by China Merchants from Jardine Matheson in 1946 and returned to Mainland China in 1950 after the uprising in Hong Kong. After that, it was renamed as Li Sheng (and again He Ping 9 and He Ping 12) and had been in service until 1980.

海厦 Hai Xia

"海厦"轮全体起义船员纪念
The uprising crew members of Hai Xia

大型江轮　Large River Steamer

该 16 艘大型江轮，是招商局在长江航线的主要航运力量，其中江安、江顺、江华、江汉、江建、江庆、江济等 7 艘江轮在抗日战争期间就发挥过重要作用，且前一节已经有详细论述，在此就不一一列叙。另外的 9 艘江轮如下。

The 16 large river steamers were major shipping power of China Merchants along the Yangtze River. Among the 16 river steamers, 7 river steamers, namely Jiang An, Jiang Shun, Jiang Hua, Jiang Han, Jiang Jian, Jiang Qing, and Jiang Ji, had already played an important role during the Second Sino-Japanese War, with details elaborated in the previous section and would not be listed here again. The other 9 river steamers were as follows.

⚓ 江新　Kiang Hsin

英文名 Kiang Hsin，属于大型江轮，用作客货运。该船长 101 米，2200 马力，3372.91 总吨，吃水 3.8 米，航速每小时 12.5 海里。1949 年留在上海，后被国民党空军炸沉。1952 年 11 月重新打捞出水。

The ship was a large river steamer used for passenger and cargo transportation. Its length overall was 101 meters, with a gross tonnage of 3,372.91 tons and a draught of 3.8 meters. With its engine power at 2,000 HP, the ship could sail at a speed of 12.5 kn. The ship was kept in Shanghai in 1949, and later sunk due to the bombing of the Kuomintang air force. It was salvaged in November 1952.

⚓ 江亚　Kiang Ya

英文名 Kiang Ya，原名"兴亚"轮。属于大型江轮，用作客货运。该船长 102.4 米，宽 13.2 米，吃水 4.7 米，2500 马力，3365.17 总吨，航速每小时 12 海里。1946 年，招商局汉口分局接收的日伪船舶。1948 年 12 月 3 日在吴淞口外爆炸沉没。

Originally named as Xing Ya, the ship was a large river steamer used

江亚　Kiang Ya

for passenger and cargo transportation. Its length overall was 102.4 meters, the beam was 13.2 meters, with a gross tonnage of 3,365.17 tons and a draught of 4.7 meters. With its engine power at 2,500 HP, the ship could sail at a speed of 12 kn. It was taken over by the Hankou Branch of China Merchants from the Japanese puppet regime in 1946, and sunk in Wusong estuary after an explosion on December 3, 1948.

江静 Kiang Ging

英文名 Kiang Ging，曾用名"同华"、"宁波"。属于大型江轮，用作客货运输。该船长 97 米，2500 马力。总吨位 3784.54，吃水 3.8 米，航速每小时 13 海里。1946 年，招商局接收的日伪船舶。1949 年"江静"轮后因搭载蒋介石及蒋经国父子由上海至奉化而闻名。后迁往台湾，1959 年拆解出售。

Originally named as Tong Hua and Ning Bo, the ship was a large river steamer used for passenger and cargo transportation. Its length overall was 97 meters, with a gross tonnage of 3,784.54 tons and a draught of 3.8 meters. With its engine power at 2,500 HP, the ship could sail at a speed of 13 kn. It was taken over by China Merchants from the Japanese puppet regime in 1946. Kiang Ging became well-known after it was

江静 Kiang Ging

used by the father and son Chiang Kai-shek and Chiang Ching-kuo for their trip from Shanghai to Fenghua in 1949. It was moved to Taiwan, and disassembled for sale in 1959.

⚓ 江泰 Kiang Tai

英文名 Kiang Tai，曾用名"同盟"、"兴泰"。属于大型江轮，用作客货运。该船长 99.7 米，宽 14.5 米，3936 马力，3214.89 总吨，吃水 4.1 米，航速每小时 12.5 海里。1946 年，招商局接收的日伪船舶。1949 年被炸沉于芜湖港江边。1951 年 1 月，该船被打捞起。

Originally named as Tong Meng and Xing Tai, this ship was a large river steamer used for passenger and cargo transportation. Its length overall was 99.7 meters, the beam was 14.5 meters, with a gross tonnage of 3,214.89 tons and a draught of 4.1 meters. With its engine power at 3,936 HP, the ship could sail at a speed of 12.5 kn. It was taken over by China Merchants from the Japanese puppet regime in 1946. It was sunk in Wuhu Port waterfront in 1949 and salvaged in January 1951.

⚓ 江宁 Kiang Ning

英文名 Kiang Ning，曾用名"兴国"。属于大型江轮，用作客货运。该船长 104.3 米，2500 马力，3486.76 总吨，吃水 4.1 米，航速每小时 13 海里。1946 年招商局接收的日伪船舶，1949 年迁往台湾，后在 1959 年拆解出售。

江泰 Kiang Tai

Originally named as Xing Guo, the ship was a large river steamer used for passenger and cargo transportation. Its length overall was 104.3 meters, with a gross tonnage of 3,486.76 tons and a draught of 4.1 meters. With its engine power at 2,500 HP, the ship could sail at a speed of 13 kn. It was taken over by China Merchants from the Japanese puppet regime in 1946. It was moved to Taiwan in 1949, and disassembled for sale in 1959.

⚓ 江平　Kiang Ping

英文名 Kiang Ping，曾用名"兴平"。属于大型江轮，用作客货运。该船长 103 米，4000 马力，3214.89 总吨，吃水 4.3 米，航速每小时 12 海里。1946 年招商局接收的日伪船舶。

Originally named as Xing Ping, the ship was a large river steamer used for passenger and cargo transportation. Its length overall was 103 meters, with a gross tonnage of 3,214.89 tons and a draught of 4.3 meters. With its engine power at 4,000 HP, the ship could sail at a speed of 12 kn. It was taken over by China Merchants from the Japanese puppet regime in 1946.

⚓ 江隆　Kiang Lung

英文名 Kiang Lung，曾用名"兴隆"、"靖安"。属于大型江轮，用作客货运。该船长 97.8 米，4000 马力，3214.89 总吨，吃水 4.1 米，航速每小时 13.5 海里。1945 年抗战胜利后

江平　Kiang Ping

江隆　Kiang Lung

在青岛接收，后拨交海军应用，改名"靖安"。1949年迁往台湾，后在1959年拆解出售。

Originally named as Xing Long and Jing An, the ship was a large river steamer used for passenger and cargo transportation. Its length overall was 97.8 meters, with a gross tonnage of 3,214.89 tons and a draught of 4.1 meters. With its engine power at 4,000 HP, the ship could sail at a speed of 13.5 kn. The ship was taken over in Qingdao after the victory of the second Sino-Japanese War in 1945. It was then given to the Kuomintang Navy Department and renamed as Jing An. It was moved to Taiwan in 1949 and disassembled for sale in 1959.

⚓ 江陵　Kiang Ling

英文名Kiang Ling，曾用名"武陵丸"。属于大型江轮，用作客货运。该船长66.8米，2500马力，1361.92总吨，吃水2.5米，航速每小时9海里。该轮接收时海军曾留用为运输舰，后于1946年10月移交招商局。1949年留置大陆，改称为"江陵解放"号。

Originally named as Wuling Maru, the ship was a large river steamer used for passenger and cargo transportation. Its length overall was 66.8 meters, with a gross tonnage of 1,361.92 tons and a draught of 2.5 meters. With its engine power at 2,500 HP, the ship could sail at a speed of 9 kn. The ship was taken over by the navy as a transportation ship, and was handed over to China Merchants in October 1946. It was left behind in Mainland China in 1949, and was renamed as Jiang Ling Jie Fang.

江和　Kiang Ho

英文名Kiang Ho。属于大型江轮，用作客货运。该船长67.6米，2650马力，1361.61总吨，吃水3.3米，航速每小时13.5海里。1950年被征军运遭炮火击毁。

Kiang Ho was a large river steamer used for passenger and cargo transportation. Its length overall was 67.6 meters, with a gross tonnage of 1,361.61 tons and a draught of 3.3 meters. With its engine power at 2,650 HP, the ship could sail at a speed of 13.5 kn. The ship was destroyed by gunfire when it was taken over as a military carrier in 1950.

驳船　YE Barge

利101、利102、利103、利104、利105、利106、利107、利108、利109、利110

Li 101, Li 102, Li 103, Li 104, Li 105, Li 106, Li 107, Li 108, Li 109, Li 110

本级为招商局战后引进的驳船(YE Barge)，共引进十艘，排水量2228.89吨，1941年建造，其他情况不详。本级驳船部分留在大陆，其中"利110"于1949年12月23日由"民319"拖带时两船搁浅于长江殷州头十二圩至次年1月19日才救出。迁到台湾的"利106"号曾改装为修理船并于1958年拆解出售。

利106　Li 106

This section describes the ten YE barges introduced by China Merchants after the Second Sino-Japanese War. These barges were built in 1941, and the displacement was 2,228.89 tons for each. Other informations of the barges were unknown. Some of the barges were left in Mainland China. When Min 319 was towing Li 110 on December 23, 1949, the two ships were stranded in the Twelfth Dyke, Yinzhoutou of the Yangtze River, and were not rescued until the next January 19. Li 106 was moved to Taiwan, converted into a repair ship, and disassembled for sale in 1958.

Ocean Tug 船　Ocean Tug

⚓ 民 301、民 302、民 303、民 304、民 305、民 306、民 307、民 308、民 309、民 310、民 311、民 312、民 313、民 314、民 315、民 316、民 317、民 318

Min 301, Min 302, Min 303, Min 304, Min 305, Min 306, Min 307, Min 308, Min 309, Min 310, Min 311, Min 312, Min 313, Min 314, Min 315, Min 316, Min 317, Min 318

"民 302"，该船型属于远洋船，船长 43.4 米，1900 马力，596.8 总吨，吃水 4 米，航速每小时 12.5 海里。1950 年 1 月 15 日，"民 302"船在船长谷源松的率领下起义归国（另"民 301"、"民 303"、"民 304"、"民 305"、"民 306"、"民 307"、"民 308"、"民 309"、"民 310"型号一致）。

Min 302 was an ocean vessel. Its length overall was 43.4 meters, with a gross tonnage of 596.8 tons and a draught of 4 meters. With its engine power at 1,900 HP, the ship could sail at a speed of 12.5 kn. Min 302 returned to Mainland China after the uprising led by the captain Gu Yuansong on January 15, 1950. (Min 301, Min 303, Min 304, Min 305, Min 306, Min 307, Min 308, Min 309 and Min 310 were of the same model.)

"民 311"，该船属于柴油机拖轮，用作货运。该船长 37.3 米，宽 9.12 米，1225 马力，433.56 总吨，吃水 4 米，航速每小时 12 海里。1949 年留在大陆（另"民 314"、"民 315"与"民 311"型号一致，均迁往台湾）。

Min 311 was a diesel tug used for freight transportation. Its length overall was 37.3 meters and the beam was 9.12 meters, with a gross tonnage of 433.56 tons and a draught of 4 meters. With its engine power at 1,225 HP, the ship could sail at a speed of 12 kn. It was left in the Mainland China in 1949. (Min 314 and Min 315 were of the same model, and both were moved to Taiwan.)

"民 312"，该船属于蒸汽机拖轮，用作货运。该船长 45.2 米，宽 10 米，1200 马力，总吨位 497.45 吨，吃水 4 米，航速每小时 12 海里。原为美国海军救难拖船，招商局战后自美国引进。1947 年"民 312"改装为破冰船（另"民 317"、"民 320"、"济安"、"国庆"型号与"民 312"一致）。

Min 312 was a steam tug used for freight transportation. Its length overall was 45.2 meters, the beam was 10 meters, with a gross tonnage of 497.45 tons, and a draught of 4 meters. With its engine power at 1,200 HP, the ship could sail at a speed of 12 kn. It used to be a U.S. Navy rescue tug, and was introduced by China Merchants from the U.S.A. after the Second Sino-Japanese War. Min 312 was converted into an icebreaker in 1947. (Min 317, Min 320, Ji'an, and Guoqing were of the same model.)

民 302　Min 302

1950年1月15日，"民302"船在船长谷源松的率领下起义归国。图为"开路先锋"谷源松

On Jan. 15th, 1950, Min 302 initiated the uprising led by the captain Gu Yuansong and returned back to mainland China. This is the photo of Gu Yuansong who was awarded "the Uprising Pioneer"

"民302"轮全体起义船员纪念
The uprising crew members of Min 302

民 308　Min 308

民 306　Min 306

民 313　Min 313

YF-2 型轮　YF-2 Ship

⚓ 和 105、和 106、和 107、和 108、和 109、和 110
　He 105, He 106, He 107, He 108, He 109, He 110

该批次型号相同，总吨 500 吨。

These ships were of the same model with a gross tonnage of 500 tons for each.

YC 型轮　YC Ship

⚓ 和 101、和 102、和 103、和 104
　He 101, He 102, He 103, He 104

该批次型号相同，总吨 500 吨。

These ships were of the same model with a gross tonnage of 500 tons for each.

YW、YOG 型轮　YW and YOG Ship

⚓ 平 801、平 802、平 803、平 804、平 805、平 806
　Ping 801, Ping 802, Ping 803, Ping 804, Ping 805, Ping 806

该批次型号相同，总吨 593.29 吨。

These ships were of the same model with a gross tonnage of 593.29 tons for each.

L.C.T 型轮　L.C.T Ship

⚓ 胜 109、胜 110、胜 111、胜 112
　Sheng 109, Sheng 110, Sheng 111, Sheng 112

该批次型号相同，总吨 235 吨。

These ships were of the same model with a gross tonnage of 235 tons for each.

YR 型轮　YR Ship

⚓ 设 101、设 102　She 101, She 102

该批次型号相同，总吨 540 吨。

These ships were of the same model with a gross tonnage of 540 tons for each.

PB 型轮　PB Ship

⚓ 复 101、复 102　Fu 101, Fu 102

该批次型号相同，总吨 10 吨。

These ships were of the same model with a gross tonnage of 10 tons for each.

其他海轮　Other ocean vessels

⚓ 伯先　Bo Xian

1949 年建造于上海的海轮，客货兼运，该船长 83.9 米，宽 11.5 米，1300 马力，2200 总吨，吃水 4.5 米，航速每小时 10.5 海里。1950 年 2 月 20 日，被国民党飞机击中沉毁。1950 年 7 月 22 日，将其打捞出水，改名"工农兵 9 号"，行驶青岛、烟台、大连。

This ship was built in Shanghai in 1949 for passenger and cargo transportation. Its length overall was 83.9 meters, the beam was 11.5 meters, with a gross tonnage of 2,200 tons, and a draught of 4.5 meters. With its engine power at 1,300 HP, the ship could sail at a speed of 10.5 kn. The ship went down after being hit by the Kuomintang aircraft on February 20, 1950. It was salvaged on July 22, 1950, and was renamed as Gong Nong Bing 9 for the route to Qingdao, Yantai and Dalian.

该轮以历史名人命名。赵声（1881—1911），字伯先，因此又名赵伯先。江苏镇江大港人。赵伯先清末在新军中担任军官，为孙中山先生领导的同盟会主要领导人之一，是孙中山和黄兴的亲密战友。1911 年 4 月 27 日，赵伯先具体策划、组织并领导了震惊中外的黄

花岗起义。起义失败后,赵伯先因壮志未酬,悲愤成疾,于 1911 年 5 月 18 日病逝于香港。

The ship was named after a historic figure. Zhao Sheng (1881-1911), also named Zhao Boxian, was from Dagang, Zhenjiang of Jiangsu. Zhao Boxian served as an officer in the modernized army in late Qing Dynasty, he was also one of the main leaders in Tung-meng Hui led by Sun Yat-sen, the close comrade of Sun Yat-sen and Huang Hsing. On April 27th,1911, Zhao Boxian planned and organized the Guangzhou Uprising that shocked the world. He got sick after the failure of the uprising and died in Hongkong on May 18th,1911.

⚓ 海有 Hai You

1913 年建造于上海的海轮,客货兼运,该船长 43.9 米,宽 6.74 米,390 马力,426.75 总吨,吃水 3 米,航速每小时 7.5 海里。战后接收自日本产业。

This ship was built in Shanghai in 1913 for passenger and cargo transportation. Its length overall was 43.9 meters, the beam was 6.74 meters, with a gross tonnage of 426.75 tons, and a draught of 3 meter. With its engine power at 390 HP, the ship could sail at a speed of 7.5 kn. It was taken over from the postwar Japanese industry.

⚓ 海新 Hai Xin

1910 年美国建造的海轮,客货兼用。该船长 77.8 米,宽 12.7 米,功率 2000 马力,2515.02 总吨,吃水 3.6 米,航速每小时 12.5 海里。1949 年留在大陆。

This ship was built in the U.S.A. in 1910 for passenger and cargo transportation. Its length overall was 77.8 meters, the beam was 12.7 meters, with a gross tonnage of 2,515.02 tons, and a draught of 3.6 meters. With its engine power at 2,000 HP, the ship could sail at a speed of 12.5 kn. It was left in Mainland China in 1949.

⚓ 增利 Zeng Li

快速轮,961 总吨。1949 年 8 月由日本佐世保驶回,由招商局接收。

The gross tonnage of this fast ship was 961 tons. It was driven back from Sasebo of Japan in August 1949 and taken over by China Merchants.

增利 Zeng Li

⚓ 登州 Deng Zhou

原名"万寿花",二战时期美国建造。1946年,招商局从水运大队接收而来。该船属于小型货轮,载重吨500,吃水2.4米,航速每小时12海里。1949年由海军接管,改名"遵义"。

Originally named as Wan Shou Hua, the ship was built in the U.S.A. during the World War II. China Merchants took it over from the Marine Brigade in 1946. The dead weight tonnage of this small cargo ship was 500 tons, with a draught of 2.4 meters and a cruising speed of 12 kn. The Navy took it over in 1949, and changed the name from Deng Zhou into Zun Yi.

⚓ 青州 Qing Zhou

原名"紫罗蓝",二战时期美国建造。1946年,招商局从水运大队接收而来。该船属于小型货轮,载重吨500,吃水2.4米,航速每小时12海里。1949年,由海军接管,"青州"改称为"邯郸"。

Originally named as Zi Luo Lan, the ship was built in the U.S.A. during the World War II. China Merchants took it over from the Marine Brigade in 1946. The dead weight tonnage of this small cargo ship was 500 tons, with a draught of 2.4 meters and a cruising speed of 12 kn. The Navy took it over in 1949, and changed the name from Qing Zhou into Han Dan.

⚓ 杭州 Hang Zhou

原名"丁香",二战时期美国建造。1946年,招商局从水运大队接收而来。该船属于小型货轮,载重吨500,吃水2.4米,航速每小时12海里。1949年由海军接管,"杭州"改称为"盐城"。

Originally named as Ding Xiang, the ship was built in the U.S.A. during the World War II. China Merchants took it over from the Marine Brigade in 1946. The dead weight tonnage of this small cargo ship was 500 tons, with a draught of 2.4 meters, and a cruising speed of 12 kn. The Navy took it over in 1949, and changed the name from Hang Zhou into Yan Cheng.

⚓ 苏州 Su Zhou

原名"金香花",二战时期美国建造。1946年,招商局从水运大队接收而来。该船属于小型货轮,载重吨500,吃水2.4米,航速每小时12海里。1949年,由海军接管,"苏州"改称为"淮阳"。

Originally named as Jin Xiang Hua, the ship was built in the U.S.A. during World War II. China Merchants took it over from the Marine Brigade in 1946. The dead weight tonnage of this small cargo ship was 500 tons, with a draught of 2.4 meters and a cruising speed of 12 kn. The Navy took it over in 1949, and changed the name from Su Zhou into Huai Yang.

⚓ 常州　Chang Zhou

1944 年美国建造的海轮，客货兼用。该船长 53.5 米，宽 9.7 米，功率 1000 马力，547.85 总吨，吃水 2.4 米，航速每小时 7 海里。1949 年留在大陆。

The ship was built in the U.S.A. in 1944 for passenger and cargo transportation. Its length overall was 53.5 meters, the beam was 9.7 meters, with a gross tonnage of 547.85 tons and a draught of 2.4 meters. With its engine power at 1,000 HP, the ship could sail at a speed of 7 kn. It was left in Mainland China in 1949.

⚓ 兰州　Lan Zhou

1944 年美国建造的海轮，货运。该船长 52.5 米，宽 9.7 米，功率 600 马力，400 总吨，吃水 1.5 米，航速每小时 11 海里。1949 年留在大陆。

The ship was built in the U.S.A. in 1944 for cargo transportation. Its length overall was 52.5 meters, the beam was 9.7 meters, with a gross tonnage of 400 tons and a draught of 1.5 meters. With its engine power at 600 HP, the ship could sail at a speed of 11 kn. It was left in Mainland China in 1949.

⚓ 中州　Zhong Zhou

1944 年美国建造的海轮，货运。该船长 52.5 米，宽 9.7 米，功率 600 马力，601.5 总吨，吃水 1.5 米，航速每小时 11 海里。1949 年留在大陆。

The ship was built in the U.S.A. in 1944 for cargo transportation. Its length overall was 52.5 meters, the beam was 9.7 meters, with a gross tonnage of 601.5 tons and a draught of 1.5 meters. With its engine power at 600 HP, the ship could sail at a speed of 11 kn. It was left in Mainland China in 1949.

⚓ 万富　Wan Fu

1944 年美国建造的海轮，客货兼运。该船长 99.7 米，宽 15.2 米，功率 1800 马力，3326.64 总吨，吃水 1.2—3.4 米，航速每小时 10 海里。1949 年迁往台湾。

The ship was built in the U.S.A. in 1944 for passenger and cargo transportation. Its length overall was 99.7 meters, the beam was 15.2 meters, with a gross tonnage of 3,326.64 tons and a draught of 1.2/3.4 meters.

With its engine power at 1,800 HP, the ship could sail at a speed of 10 kn. It was moved to Taiwan in 1949.

⚓ 万国 Wan Guo

1944年美国建造的海轮，客货兼运。该船长99.7米，宽15.2米，功率1800马力，3326.64总吨，吃水1.2—3.4米，航速每小时10海里。1949年迁往台湾，1955年7月"万国"轮由台湾"海军部"接收，改名"中训"舰。

The ship was built in the U.S.A. in 1944 for passenger and cargo transportation. Its length overall was 99.7 meters, the beam was 15.2 meters, with a gross tonnage of 3,326.64 tons and a draught of 1.2-3.4 meters. With its engine power at 1,800 HP, the ship could sail at a speed of 10 kn. It was moved to Taiwan in 1949 and was taken over by the Kuomintang Navy Department in Taiwan in July 1955, and renamed it as Zhong Xun.

⚓ 万利 Wan Li

1944年美国建造的海轮，客货兼运。该船长99.7米，宽15.2米，功率1800马力，总吨位3326.64吨，吃水1.2—3.4米，航速每小时10海里。1949年迁往台湾。1959年解体出售。

The ship was built in the U.S.A. in 1944 for passenger and cargo transportation. Its length overall was 99.7 meters, the beam was 15.2 meters, with a gross of tonnage 3,326.64 tons and a draught of 1.2-3.4 meters. With its engine power at 1,800 HP, the ship could sail at a speed of 10 kn. It was moved to Taiwan in 1949, and disassembled for sale in 1959.

⚓ 万民 Wan Min

1944年美国建造的海轮，客货兼运。该船长99.7米，宽15.2米，功率1800马力，总吨位3326.64吨，吃水1.2—3.4米，航速每小时10海里。1949年迁往台湾，1955年移交台湾"海军部"。

The ship was built in the U.S.A. in 1944 for passenger and cargo transportation. Its length overall was 99.7 meters, the beam was 15.2 meters, with a gross tonnage of 3,326.64 tons and a draught of 1.2-3.4 meters. With its engine power at 1,800 HP, the ship could sail at a speed of 10 kn. It was moved to Taiwan in 1949 and handed over to the Kuomintang Navy Department in Taiwan in 1955.

万民 Wan Min

油 轮　Oil Tanker

战后，大部分油轮都由招商局接收，后转交由招商局合资组建的中国油轮公司。其中甲级油轮 6 艘，乙级油轮 17 艘，共 23 艘。

After the Second Sino-Japanese War, China Merchants took over most of the oil tankers and handed them over to its joint venture, China Tank Company. There were a total of 23 oil tankers, including 6 Class A tankers and 17 Class B tankers.

甲级油轮　Class A Tanker

⚓ 永渝　Yong Yu

曾用名"昆仑丸"，该船长 324.1 尺，宽 45.3 尺，功率 1100 马力，载重吨 4721，"永渝"轮为 1946 年招商局在香港购得的一艘"山东"号旧轮船，并以此船向上海宝昌洋行换得一艘 1944 年建造的油船"昆仑丸"，改名为"永渝"号（油 151 号）。

Originally named as Kunlun Maru, its length overall was 324.1 chi, and the beam was 45.3 chi. With its engine power at 1,100 HP, it had a dead weight tonnage of 4,721 tons. China Merchants brought an old steamer Shan Dong in Hong Kong in 1946, traded it with Shanghai Bowe & Co.,Inc. for the tanker Kunlun Maru built in 1944, and renamed the tanker as Yong Yu.

⚓ 永灏　Yong Hao

曾用名"黑潮丸"，载重吨 14960，航速每小时 16.5 海里。"永灏"轮是 1946 年第二次世界大战时被美军击沉的日本籍油轮"黑潮丸"，由中国油轮公司打捞拖往香港修理并改名"永灏"（油 205 号）。船长左文渊，"永灏"轮是香港 13 艘起义船舶之一。

Originally named as Heichao Maru, the ship had a gross tonnage of 14,960 tons, and a speed of 16.5 kn. The Japanese tanker Heichao Maru was hit down by the U.S. military

永灏　Yong Hao

during the World War II in 1946. It was later salvaged by China Tanker Company, repaired in Hong Kong, and renamed as Yong Hao (You 205). Its captain was Zuo Wenyuan, and the ship was one of the 13 ships participated in the Hong Kong uprising.

⚓ 永洪　Yong Hong

原名 Swift Light，1921年建造于美国。该船长481.2 尺，宽 60 尺，功率 3150 马力，载重吨 11900，吃水 26.7 尺，航速每小时 8 海里。1946 年 5 月，由招商局接收。1947 年中国油轮公司成立，招商局以股价方式移交中国油轮公司，作为伊朗运油来华之用。

永洪　Yong Hong

Originally named as Swift Light, the ship was built in the U.S.A. in 1921. Its length overall was 481.2 chi, the beam was 60 chi, with a dead weight tonnage of 11,900 tons, and a draught of 26.7 chi. With its engine power at 3,150 HP, the ship could sail at a speed of 8 kn. China Merchants took over the ship in May 1946. When China Tanker Company was established in 1947, China Merchants handed the ship over through share transfer for oil transportation from Iran to China.

⚓ 永澄　Yong Cheng

原名 Ardmore，1913 年建造于美国。该船长 470 尺，宽 59.6 尺，功率 2500 马力，载重吨 9815，吃水 27 尺，航速每小时 8 海里。1946 年 6 月，由招商局接收。1947 年中国油轮公司成立，招商局以股价方式移交中国油轮公司，作为伊朗运油来华之用。

Originally named as Ardmore, the ship was built in the U.S.A. in 1913. Its length overall was 470 chi, the beam was 59.6 chi, with a dead weight tonnage of 9,815 tons and a draught of 27 chi. With its engine power at 2,500 HP, the ship could sail at a speed of 8 kn. China Merchants took over the ship in June 1946. When China Tanker Company was established in 1947, China Merchants handed the ship over through share transfer for oil transportation from Iran to China.

⚓ 永泽 Yong Ze

原名 Matini Cock，1913年建造于美国。该船长460尺，宽60尺，功率2800马力，载重吨10680，吃水24.1尺，航速每小时8海里。1946年5月由招商局接收。1947年中国油轮公司成立，招商局以股价方式移交中国油轮公司，作为伊朗运油来华之用。

永泽　Yong Ze

Originally named as Matini Cock, the ship was built in the U.S.A. in 1913. Its length overall was 460 chi, the beam was 60 chi, with a dead weight tonnage of 10,680 tons and a draught of 24.1 chi. With its engine power at 2,800 HP, the ship could sail at a speed of 8 kn. China Merchants took over the ship in May 1946. When China Tanker Company was established in 1947, China Merchants handed the ship over through share transfer for oil transportation from Iran to China.

⚓ 永清 Yong Qing

原名John D. Rockefeller，1914年建造于美国。该船长474.8尺，宽60尺，功率2500马力，载重吨9630，吃水28.6尺，航速每小时8海里。1946年6月由招商局接收。1947年中国油轮公司成立，招商局以股价方式移交中国油轮公司，作为伊朗运油来华之用。

Originally named as John D. Rockefeller, the ship was built in the U.S.A. in 1914. Its length overall was 474.8 chi, the beam was 60 chi, with a dead weight tonnage of 9,630 tons and a draught of 28.6 chi. With its engine power at 2,500 HP, the ship could sail at a speed of 8 kn. China Merchants took over the ship in June 1946. When China Tanker Company was established in 1947, China Merchants handed the ship over through share transfer for oil transportation from Iran to China.

乙级油轮　Class B Tanker

⚓ 永涞、永洮、永潇、永湟、永叙、永淞、永潼、永涪、永汉、永滦、永泸、永淝、永淮、永湘、永漳、永渭、永洛

Yong Lai, Yong Tao, Yong Xiao, Yong Huang, Yong Xu, Yong Song, Yong Tong, Yong Fu, Yong Han, Yong Luan, Yong Lu, Yong Fei, Yong Huai, Yong Xiang, Yong Zhang, Yong Wei, Yong Luo

二战时期美国建造的油轮。该批油轮型号一致，船长 220.1 尺，宽 37.1 尺，功率 860 马力，载重吨 1339，吃水 12.1 米，航速每小时 8 海里。1946 年 6—12 月，由招商局陆续接收。

Bulit in U.S.A. during the World War II, these oil tankers were of the same model. Length overall of each was 220.1 chi, the beam was 37.1 chi, with a dead weight tonnage of 1,339 tons and a draught of 12.1 meters. With its engine power at 860 HP, it could sail at a speed of 8 kn. China Merchants took over these tankers gradually from May to November in 1946.

永汉　Yong Han

其中"永渭"、"永潇"、"永湘"、"永湟"、"永叙"1949 年后留在大陆，"永湟"轮交华东军区海军使用，改名为 602。

Among the above-mentioned tankers, Yong Wei, Yong Xiao, Yong Xiang, Yong Huang and Yong Xu were kept in Mainland China after 1949. Yong Huang was handed over to the navy of East China Military Area Command and was renamed as 602.

"永淮"、"永洛"、"永洮"三艘油轮是在中国油轮公司船务处长顾久宽起义时，自沉于黄浦江陆家嘴航道中。由于该沉船严重阻塞航行，1949 年 6 月底解放军解放上海后，将这三艘油轮进行打捞。"永洛"轮交华东军区海军使用，改名 601。

Yong Huai, Yong Luo and Yong Tao were ordered to sink themselves in the Lujiazui fairway of Huangpu River by Gu Jiukuan, the head of Shipping Business Department of China Tanker Company during the uprising. After the liberation of Shanghai by the end of June in 1949, these three tankers were salvaged

1946年12月5日，招商局接收"永洮"轮时与美方人员合影

Photo taken with US staff when China Merchants taking over Yong Tao on December 5th, 1946

because the fairway was totally blocked. Yong Luo was handed over to the navy of East China Military Area Command and was renamed as 601.

其他油轮都迁往台湾。招商局于1951年接管时小型油轮只得"永涞"、"永淞"、"永潼"、"永泸"、"永淝"、"永滦"、"永漳"、"永涪"、"永灨"等9艘，"永灨"于1958年，"永淞"、"永泸"、"永淝"于1959年分别拆解出售。

Other tankers were moved to Taiwan. China Merchants only took over 9 small oil tankers in 1951, namely: Yong Lai, Yong Song, Yong Tong, Yong Lu, Yong Fei, Yong Luan, Yong Zhang, Yong Fu and Yong Gan, among which Yong Gan was disassembled for sale in 1958, and Yong Song, Yong Lu and Yong Fei were disassembled in 1959.

建甲　Jian Jia

⚓ 建甲　Jian Jia

战后招商局接收自用的油轮，总吨位601.5吨，功率600马力。1949年8月1日，移交给海军成为"四明"舰，1975年退役。

The tanker was taken over by China Merchants for private use after the Second Sino-Japanese War with a gross tonnage of 601.5 tons and engine power of 600 HP. It was handed over to the navy and renamed as Si Ming. It has been on service until 1975.

抗日战争结束之后，招商局还接收了大量的拖小轮、铁驳、木驳、特种机船等。具体船名、船质、马力、总吨等情形，如下表。

After the Second Sino-Japanese War ended, China Merchants also took over a lot of small tugs, iron barges, wooden barges and special machine boats, etc. The specific information of these ships, including name, material, horse power and gross tonnage are as follows.

拖小轮
Small Tugs

序号 No.	船名 Name	船质 Material	马力 HP	序号 No.	船名 Name	船质 Material	马力 HP
1	国强 Guo Qiang	铁 Iron	750	16	飞彪 Fei Biao	木 Wood	25
2	国伟 Guo Wei	铁 Iron	260	17	飞厦 Fei Xia	木 Wood	54
3	国兴 Guo Xing	铁 Iron	144	18	飞皖 Fei Wan	铁 Iron	144
4	国本 Guo Ben	铁 Iron	120	19	飞长 Fei Chang	铁 Iron	60
5	国利 Guo Li	铁 Iron	170	20	飞渊 Fei Yuan	铁 Iron	40
6	国华 Guo Hua	铁 Iron	180	21	飞侠 Fei Xia	铁 Iron	75
7	国仲 Guo Zhong	铁 Iron	120	22	飞宁 Fei Ning	木 Wood	60
8	国丰 Guo Feng	铁 Iron	120	23	飞川 Fei Chuan	木 Wood	55
9	国富 Guo Fu	铁 Iron	300	24	飞赣 Fei Gan	木 Wood	80
10	国达 Guo Da	铁 Iron	200	25	飞康 Fei Kang	木 Wood	80
11	国盛 Guo Sheng	铁 Iron	330	26	飞鄂 Fei E	木 Wood	80
12	飞沪 Fei Hu	铁 Iron	110	27	飞桂 Fei Gui	木 Wood	80
13	飞亨 Fei Heng	铁 Iron	25	28	飞闽 Fei Min	木 Wood	66
14	飞杭 Fei Hang	木 Wood	25	29	飞粤 Fei Yue	铁 Iron	100
15	飞艇 Fei Ting	木 Wood	25	30	飞加 Fei Jia	木 Wood	80

续表

序号 No.	船名 Name	船质 Material	马力 HP	序号 No.	船名 Name	船质 Material	马力 HP
31	飞钟 Fei Zhong	木 Wood	80	46	飞青 Fei Qing	木 Wood	60
32	飞旭 Fei Xu	木 Wood	60	47	飞鹣 Fei Jian	木 Wood	17
33	飞虹 Fei Hong	木 Wood	56	48	国沧 Guo Cang	铁 Iron	400
34	国镇 Guo Zhen	木 Wood	130	49	飞雯 Fei Wen	铁 Iron	100
35	飞钜 Fei Ju	木 Wood	80	50	飞豹 Fei Bao	铁 Iron	120
36	飞镁 Fei Mei	木 Wood	100	51	国祥 Guo Xiang	铁 Iron	500
37	飞钰 Fei Yu	木 Wood	80	52	飞富 Fei Fu	铁 Iron	100
38	飞铃 Fei Ling	木 Wood	90	53	国宛 Guo Wuan	铁 Iron	320
39	飞镜 Fei Jing	木 Wood	80	54	飞龙 Fei Long		50
40	飞锋 Fei Feng	木 Wood	70	55	飞鹰 Fei Ying		60
41	国良 Guo Liang	铁 Iron	835	56	飞星 Fei Xing		70
42	国康 Guo Kang	铁 Iron	520	57	飞骏 Fei Jun		70
43	国运 Guo Yun	铁 Iron	320	58	飞天 Fei Tian	铁 Iron	420
44	飞鸠 Fei Jiu	木 Wood	60	59	飞波 Fei Bo	铁 Iron	300
45	飞州 Fei Zhou	木 Wood	80	60	飞新 Fei Xin	铁 Iron	200

续表

序号 No.	船名 Name	船质 Material	马力 HP	序号 No.	船名 Name	船质 Material	马力 HP
61	飞涛 Fei Tao	铁 Iron	260	76	国裕 Guo Yu	木 Wood	120
62	飞元 Fei Yuan	铁 Iron	130	77	飞盛 Fei Sheng	木 Wood	70
63	飞胜 Fei Sheng	铁 Iron	150	78	飞安 Fei An	木 Wood	120
64	飞快 Fei Kuai	铁 Iron	120	79	飞雪 Fei Xue	铁 Iron	55
65	飞淞 Fei Song	木 Wood	120	80	国怀 Guo Huai	铁 Iron	160
66	飞大 Fei Da	木 Wood	183	81	飞流 Fei Liu	铁 Iron	100
67	飞顺 Fei Shun	木 Wood	179	82	飞开 Fei Kai	木 Wood	50
68	飞福 Fei Fu	木 Wood	100	83	飞源 Fei Yuan	木 Wood	70
69	飞信 Fei Xin	木 Wood	176	84	飞礼 Fei Li	木 Wood	60
70	飞明 Fei Ming	铁 Iron	141	85	飞虎 Fei Hu	铁 Iron	490
71	飞云 Fei Yun	木 Wood	100	86	飞鮀 Fei Tuo	木 Wood	18
72	飞狮 Fei Shi	铁 Iron	120	87	飞国 Fei Guo	铁 Iron	30
73	飞荣 Fei Rong	木 Wood	60	88	飞邦 Fei Bang	木 Wood	80
74	飞中 Fei Zhong	木 Wood	120	89	飞永 Fei Yong	木 Wood	40
75	国光 Guo Guang	铁 Iron	120	90	飞兴 Fei Xing	木 Wood	45

续表

序号 No.	船名 Name	船质 Material	马力 HP	序号 No.	船名 Name	船质 Material	马力 HP
91	飞台 Fei Tai	木 Wood	80	103	国燕 Guo Yan	铁 Iron	130
92	飞高 Fei Gao	木 Wood	84	104	国朔 Guo Shuo	铁 Iron	250
93	国青 Guo Qing	铁 Iron	430	105	国冀 Guo Ji	铁 Iron	150
94	国洋 Guo Yang	铁 Iron	350	106	国栾 Guo Luan	铁 Iron	150
95	国安 Guo An	铁 Iron	540	107	国阳 Guo Yang	铁 Iron	20
96	国泰 Guo Tai	铁 Iron	400	108	国天 Guo Tian	铁 Iron	350
97	国山 Guo Shan	铁 Iron	420	109	国秦 Guo Qin	铁 Iron	310
98	国津 Guo Jin	铁 Iron	400	110	飞鸿 Fei Hong		70
99	国沽 Guo Gu	铁 Iron	250	111	飞汉 Fei Han		75
100	国芦 Guo Lu	铁 Iron	300	112	飞马 Fei Ma		100
101	国唐 Guo Tang	铁 Iron	100	113	飞勤 Fei Qin		25
102	国通 Guo Tong	铁 Iron	200				

铁 驳
Iron Barges

序号 No.	船名 Name	船质 Material	总吨 GT	序号 No.	船名 Name	船质 Material	总吨 GT
1	招商 5 Zhao Shang 5	铁 Iron	349.94	16	招商 38 Zhao Shang 38	铁 Iron	50
2	招商 11 Zhao Shang 11	铁 Iron	347.45	17	招商 39 Zhao Shang 39	铁 Iron	80
3	招商 12 Zhao Shang 12	铁 Iron	600	18	招商 40 Zhao Shang 40	铁 Iron	50
4	招商 20 Zhao Shang 20	铁 Iron	168.7	19	招商 41 Zhao Shang 41	铁 Iron	50
5	招商 21 Zhao Shang 21	铁 Iron	360.99	20	招商 46 Zhao Shang 46	铁 Iron	472.02
6	招商 25 Zhao Shang 25	铁 Iron	104.85	21	招商 47 Zhao Shang 47	铁 Iron	368.46
7	招商 26 Zhao Shang 26	铁 Iron	80	22	招商 48 Zhao Shang 48	铁 Iron	600
8	招商 27 Zhao Shang 27	铁 Iron	50	23	招商 102 Zhao Shang 102	铁 Iron	254.65
9	招商 29 Zhao Shang 29	铁 Iron	61.56	24	招商 103 Zhao Shang 103	铁 Iron	246.39
10	招商 30 Zhao Shang 30	铁 Iron	262.72	25	招商 104 Zhao Shang 104	铁 Iron	300
11	招商 31 Zhao Shang 31	铁 Iron	199	26	招商 105 Zhao Shang 105	铁 Iron	240
12	招商 32 Zhao Shang 32	铁 Iron	220	27	招商 107 Zhao Shang 107	铁 Iron	212.89
13	招商 33 Zhao Shang 33	铁 Iron	300	28	招商 110 Zhao Shang 110	铁 Iron	83.16
14	招商 36 Zhao Shang 36	铁 Iron	92.85	29	招商 113 Zhao Shang 113	铁 Iron	213.21
15	招商 37 Zhao Shang 37	铁 Iron	80	30	招商 460 Zhao Shang 460	铁 Iron	343.05

续表

序号 No.	船名 Name	船质 Material	总吨 GT	序号 No.	船名 Name	船质 Material	总吨 GT
31	招商 333 Zhao Shang 333	铁 Iron	600	46	招商 461 Zhao Shang 461	铁 Iron	600
32	招商 346 Zhao Shang 346	铁 Iron	107	47	招商 468 Zhao Shang 468	铁 Iron	100
33	招商 367 Zhao Shang 367	铁 Iron	120	48	招商 64 Zhao Shang 64	铁 Iron	368.78
34	招商 44 Zhao Shang 44	铁 Iron	357.02	49	招商 367 Zhao Shang 367	铁 Iron	107.05
35	招商 304 Zhao Shang 304	铁 Iron	750	50	招商 368 Zhao Shang 368	铁 Iron	108.9
36	招商 49 Zhao Shang 49	铁 Iron	700	51	供水 4 号 Gong Shui 4	铁 Iron	60
37	招商 302 Zhao Shang 302	铁 Iron	426.74	52	供水 5 号 Gong Shui 5	铁 Iron	60
38	招商 363 Zhao Shang 363	铁 Iron	300	53	招商 448 Zhao Shang 448	铁 Iron	106.95
39	招商 366 Zhao Shang 366	铁 Iron	348.56	54	招商 450 Zhao Shang 450	铁 Iron	88.68
40	招商 384 Zhao Shang 384	铁 Iron	250	55	招商 436 Zhao Shang 436	铁 Iron	375.21
41	招商 385 Zhao Shang 385	铁 Iron	450	56	招商 437 Zhao Shang 437	铁 Iron	153.69
42	招商 393 Zhao Shang 393	铁 Iron	200	57	招商 22 Zhao Shang 22	铁 Iron	110.8
43	招商 396 Zhao Shang 396	铁 Iron	346.72	58	招商 34 Zhao Shang 34	铁 Iron	168.05
44	招商 462 Zhao Shang 462	铁 Iron	80	59	招商 35 Zhao Shang 35	铁 Iron	129.43
45	招商 67 Zhao Shang 67	铁 Iron	350	60	招商 108 Zhao Shang 108	铁 Iron	254.65

续表

序号 No.	船名 Name	船质 Material	总吨 GT	序号 No.	船名 Name	船质 Material	总吨 GT
61	招商 364 Zhao Shang 364	铁 Iron	420	76	招商 50 Zhao Shang 50	铁 Iron	358.61
62	招商 466 Zhao Shang 466	铁 Iron	189.49	77	招商 53 Zhao Shang 53	铁 Iron	330.58
63	招商 472 Zhao Shang 472	铁 Iron	400	78	招商 55 Zhao Shang 55	铁 Iron	174.13
64	招商 316 Zhao Shang 316	铁 Iron	200	79	招商 56 Zhao Shang 56	铁 Iron	242.84
65	招商 83 Zhao Shang 83	铁 Iron	135.66	80	招商 57 Zhao Shang 57	铁 Iron	386.34
66	招商 383 Zhao Shang 383	铁 Iron	171.88	81	招商 60 Zhao Shang 60	铁 Iron	288.63
67	招商 465 Zhao Shang 465		350	82	招商 91 Zhao Shang 91	铁 Iron	360.2
68	招商 6 Zhao Shang 6	铁 Iron	346.16	83	招商 92 Zhao Shang 92	铁 Iron	300
69	招商 24 Zhao Shang 24	铁 Iron	60.75	84	招商 93 Zhao Shang 93	铁 Iron	321.61
70	招商 43 Zhao Shang 43	铁 Iron	160.16	85	招商 95 Zhao Shang 95	铁 Iron	200
71	招商 101 Zhao Shang 101	铁 Iron	254.65	86	招商 96 Zhao Shang 96	铁 Iron	130
72	招商 106 Zhao Shang 106	铁 Iron	240	87	招商 82 Zhao Shang 82	铁 Iron	450
73	供水 3 号 Gong Shui 3	铁 Iron	50	88	招商 84 Zhao Shang 84	铁 Iron	150
74	招商 380 Zhao Shang 380	铁 Iron	327.9	89	招商 87 Zhao Shang 87	铁 Iron	400
75	招商 45 Zhao Shang 45	铁 Iron	700	90	招商 98 Zhao Shang 98	铁 Iron	170

续表

序号 No.	船名 Name	船质 Material	总吨 GT	序号 No.	船名 Name	船质 Material	总吨 GT
91	招商 99 Zhao Shang 99	铁 Iron	800	106	招商 407 Zhao Shang 407	铁 Iron	439.51
92	招商 100 Zhao Shang 100	铁 Iron	700	107	招商 408 Zhao Shang 408	铁 Iron	393.87
93	招商 303 Zhao Shang 303	铁 Iron	850	108	招商 409 Zhao Shang 409	铁 Iron	401.26
94	招商 306 Zhao Shang 306	铁 Iron	900	109	招商 410 Zhao Shang 410	铁 Iron	415.06
95	招商 311 Zhao Shang 311	铁 Iron	200	110	招商 413 Zhao Shang 413	铁 Iron	101.42
96	招商 315 Zhao Shang 315	铁 Iron	100	111	招商 414 Zhao Shang 414	铁 Iron	132.48
97	招商 332 Zhao Shang 332	铁 Iron	390	112	招商 415 Zhao Shang 415	铁 Iron	388.88
98	招商 451 Zhao Shang 451	铁 Iron	151.3	113	招商 416 Zhao Shang 416	铁 Iron	419.6
99	招商 1 Zhao Shang 1	铁 Iron	322.92	114	招商 422 Zhao Shang 422	铁 Iron	366.67
100	招商 3 Zhao Shang 3	铁 Iron	515.43	115	招商 423 Zhao Shang 423	铁 Iron	132.04
101	招商 9 Zhao Shang 9	铁 Iron	482.31	116	招商 427 Zhao Shang 427	铁 Iron	419.6
102	招商 10 Zhao Shang 10	铁 Iron	494.76	117	招商 428 Zhao Shang 428	铁 Iron	372.63
103	招商 14 Zhao Shang 14	铁 Iron	487.31	118	招商 429 Zhao Shang 429	铁 Iron	419.6
104	招商 16 Zhao Shang 16	铁 Iron	370.64	119	招商 443 Zhao Shang 443	铁 Iron	372.63
105	招商 17 Zhao Shang 17	铁 Iron	346.24	120	招商 444 Zhao Shang 444	铁 Iron	365.82

续表

序号 No.	船名 Name	船质 Material	总吨 GT	序号 No.	船名 Name	船质 Material	总吨 GT
121	招商 445 Zhao Shang 445	铁 Iron	312.37	129	招商 13 Zhao Shang 13	铁 Iron	344.59
122	招商 4 Zhao Shang 4	铁 Iron	528	130	招商 440 Zhao Shang 440	铁 Iron	267.36
123	招商 94 Zhao Shang 94	铁 Iron	520	131	招商 7 Zhao Shang 7	铁 Iron	491.32
124	招商 387 Zhao Shang 387	铁 Iron	700	132	招商 425 Zhao Shang 425	铁 Iron	419.6
125	招商 391 Zhao Shang 391	铁 Iron	400	133	招商 473 Zhao Shang 473	铁 Iron	700
126	招商 471 Zhao Shang 471	铁 Iron	112.09	134	招商 464 Zhao Shang 464	铁 Iron	350
127	招商 424 Zhao Shang 424	铁 Iron	419.6	135	招商 469 Zhao Shang 469	铁 Iron	567
128	招商 426 Zhao Shang 426	铁 Iron	419.6				

特种机船
Special Vessel

序号 No.	船名 Name	总吨 GT	序号 No.	船名 Name	总吨 GT
1	飞程 Fei Cheng	10	7	交 16 Jiao 16	10
2	飞工 Fei Gong	10	8	交 17 Jiao 17	10
3	供水 1 号 Gong Shui 1	300	9	交 18 Jiao 18	5
4	起重 1 号 Qi Zhong 1	297	10	飞府 Fei Fu	20
5	飞歙 Fei Xi	53	11	洪利 Hong Li	150
6	飞禾 Fei He	18	12	旭 Xu	10

木 驳
Wooden Barges

序号 No.	船名 Name	船质 Material	马力 HP	序号 No.	船名 Name	船质 Material	马力 HP
1	招商 202 Zhao Shang 202	木 Wood	39.1	21	235	木 Wood	75
2	招商 204 Zhao Shang 204	木 Wood	60	22	237	木 Wood	44
3	招商 206 Zhao Shang 206	木 Wood	60	23	招商 242 Zhao Shang 242	木 Wood	120
4	招商 208 Zhao Shang 208	木 Wood	30	24	招商 243 Zhao Shang 243	木 Wood	100
5	招商 213 Zhao Shang 213	木 Wood	45	25	招商 247 Zhao Shang 247	木 Wood	90
6	招商 214 Zhao Shang 214	木 Wood	50	26	招商 248 Zhao Shang 248	木 Wood	90
7	招商 215 Zhao Shang 215	木 Wood	50	27	招商 256 Zhao Shang 256	木 Wood	100
8	招商 218 Zhao Shang 218	木 Wood	48.15	28	招商 257 Zhao Shang 257	木 Wood	100
9	招商 219 Zhao Shang 219	木 Wood	46.73	29	招商 258 Zhao Shang 258	木 Wood	100
10	招商 217 Zhao Shang 217	木 Wood	44.76	30	NO.1	木 Wood	12.38
11	招商 231 Zhao Shang 231	木 Wood	36	31	NO.2	木 Wood	13.01
12	招商 232 Zhao Shang 232	木 Wood	36	32	招商 212 Zhao Shang 212	木 Wood	20.5
13	招商 233 Zhao Shang 233	木 Wood	40	33	招商 283 Zhao Shang 283	木 Wood	
14	招商 234 Zhao Shang 234	木 Wood	13.9	34	招商 284 Zhao Shang 284	木 Wood	
15	招商 220 Zhao Shang 220	木 Wood	30	35	招商 285 Zhao Shang 285	木 Wood	
16	招商 221 Zhao Shang 221	木 Wood	46	36	招商 222 Zhao Shang 222	木 Wood	60
17	招商 259 Zhao Shang 259	木 Wood	56	37	招商 263 Zhao Shang 263	木 Wood	40
18	招商 260 Zhao Shang 260	木 Wood	40	38	招商 264 Zhao Shang 264	木 Wood	40
19	招商 261 Zhao Shang 261	木 Wood	40	39	招商 265 Zhao Shang 265	木 Wood	30
20	招商 262 Zhao Shang 262	木 Wood	40				

第 三 章
新中国成立后

CHAPTER THREE
AFTER THE FOUNDATION OF THE PEOPLE'S REPUBLIC OF CHINA

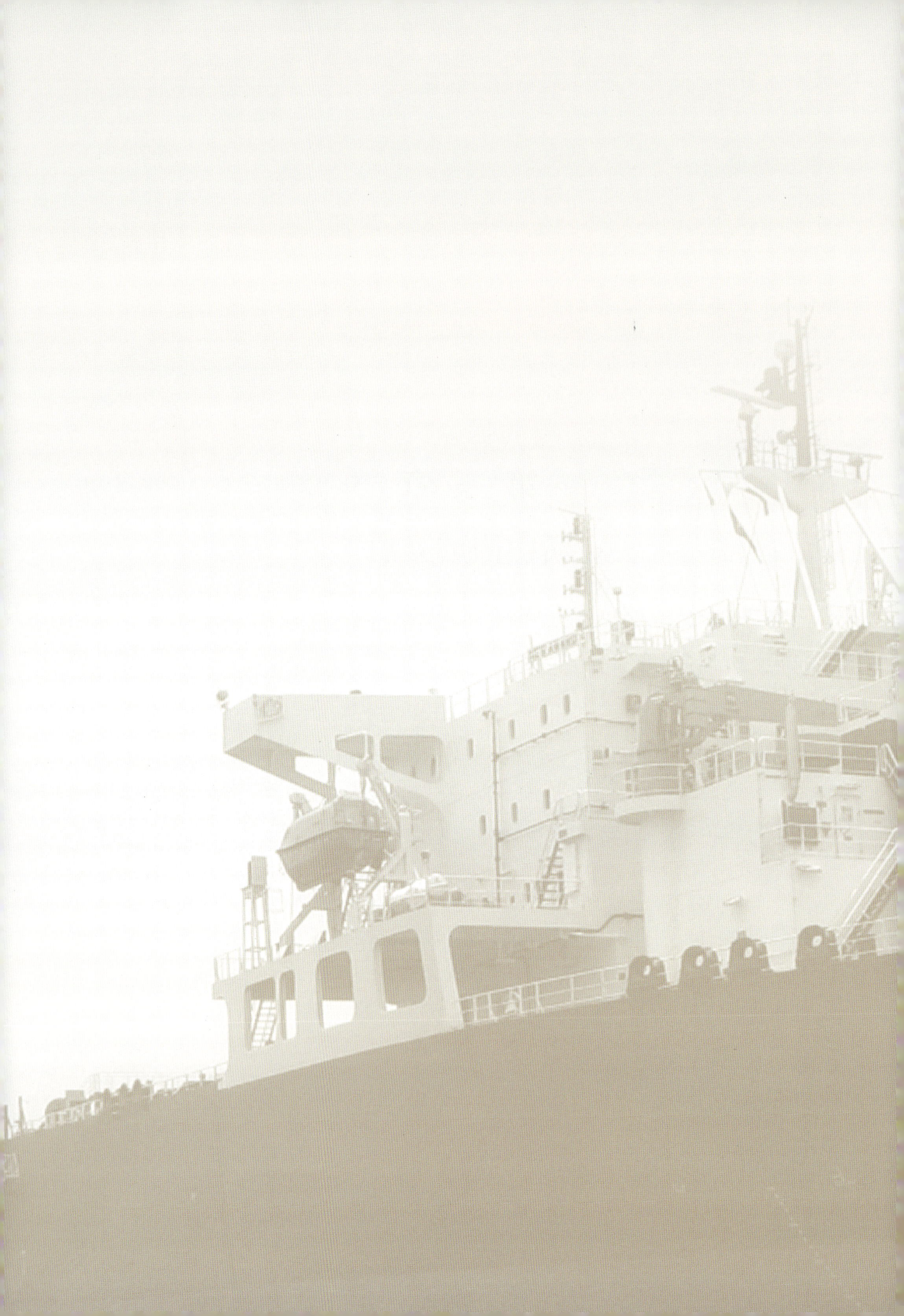

第一节　投向光明　航业新生（1950—1979）

SECTION ONE
Return to Mainland China and New Birth of Shipping Industry (1950-1979)

1949年10月，随着中华人民共和国的成立，除了迁往台湾的招商局轮船之外，留在大陆的招商局船舶都被各地军事管制委员会接管。1950年初，在中国共产党中央华南分局的统一部署和直接领导下，香港招商局和招商局集聚在香港的13艘海轮起义，毅然回归祖国。起义归来的船只，积极参与国家经济的恢复建设，成为新中国成立初期重要的水上运输力量。

In October 1949 with the establishment of the People's Republic of China, all the China Merchants' ships, except those moved to Taiwan, were taken over by the Military Control Commission respectively. In early 1950, under the unified deployment and direct leadership of Central South Branch of the Communist Party of China, China Merchants Hongkong, together with the 13 ocean vessels gathered in Hong Kong, started an uprising and returned to Mainland China resolutely. All the 13 vessels played an active role later in the recovery of China's economy and became the important shipping power for the newly established People's Republic of China.

1950年代末期，随国家的航政改革，招商局在各地的分公司逐渐演变为各地的航务局、港务局；而招商局香港分局却得以保留母体的名义继续开展业务，延续招商局的发展命脉。

In late 1950s, with the reform of navigation system of the People's Republic of China, branches and agencies of China Merchants in different areas were changed to the shipping authorities and port offices of the Ministry of Transport, while the Hong Kong branch of China Merchants was authorized to keep the original name "China Merchants" to continue its business.

从1949年至1979年，招商局零星地添置了些拖轮与铁驳船。这一时期，香港招商局的主要业务在于为中国远洋机构、远洋公司贷款购买船只以及经营船舶代理。

From 1949 to 1979, China Merchants only bought some tugs and iron barges at times. During this period, Hong Kong branch of China Merchants mainly served for China's ocean shipping agencies and companies to purchase ships via loans and acted as a ship agent.

1950年10月，香港招商局将"海康"（改名为"岷山"）、"海汉"（改名为"新门"），交运通公司直接经营。另外，招商局广州分公司调派拖轮3艘（"民302"、"飞华"、"钜昌"）与铁驳船6艘（"民泰"、"丰泰"、"国泰"、"裕泰"、"利105"、"YF325"）参与港穗航线运输。1959年，为配合中转业务的发展，招商局开办了第一艘港作铁驳船业务，投资57342港元，添置"招商1号"铁驳，11月20日竣工，12月份投入生产。1960年，招商局再添铁驳一艘，称为"2号铁驳"。1961年，添"飞星"号拖轮。1963年，投资212077港元，再建铁驳3艘；又投资120034港元建造"卫星"拖轮（150马力）。

回归后的船员参加运输任务
The crew members back to China Mainland taking part in the transportation task

In October 1950, Hong Kong branch of China Merchants handed Hai Kang (renamed as Min Shan) and Hai Han (renamed as Xin Men) over to Yuntong Company[1] for direct operations. Besides, another three tugs (Min 302, Fei Hua and Ju Chang) and six iron barges (Min Tai, Feng Tai, Guo Tai, Yu Tai, Li 105 and YF 325) were dispatched by Guangzhou branch of China Merchants to participate in the shipping route between Hong Kong and Guangzhou. In 1959, to cooperate with the transit business, China Merchants started the first iron barge business in Hong Kong and bought an iron barge named Zhao Shang 1 with an investment of 57,342 Hong Kong dollars, which was completed in November 20 and put into use in December 1959. Later, China Merchants bought another iron barge named Zhao Shang 2 in 1960, a tug named Fei Xing in 1961, and other three iron barges at a total cost of 212,077 HKD in 1963 and built a tug named Wei Xing (150 HP) with an investment of 120,034 HKD in the same year.

除了上述添置的几艘拖轮与铁驳船之外，招商局江海船舶的状况一直到1979年初招商局成立船务部才开始有所转变。

Besides the purchase of tugs and iron barges mentioned above, the shipping power in China Merchants remained no change till early 1979 when the Shipping Department was set up in China Merchants.

1　Yuntong Company: A shipping company set up by the East China Bureau in Hong Kong.

第二节　改革开放 轮运复苏（1980—2000）

SECTION TWO
The Reform and Opening-up & Recovery of Shipping (1980-2000)

1978年中共十一届三中全会召开，中国进入了改革开放的新时代。招商局在改革的风潮中，投资创办了中国对外开放的第一个工业园区——蛇口工业区，并且以"临江"轮——一艘小集装箱船起家重新组建自己的远洋船队。1980年，招商局在船务部的基础上成立了香港明华船务有限公司，经营船东、船舶代理，货物运输等业务。1980年，招商局拥有船舶9艘，244373吨。1981年，招商局又陆续购进船舶，各类船舶数量增至16艘，共409180吨，迎来了招商局航运业的复苏期。

With the convening of the third plenary session of 11th Central Committee of Communist Party of China in 1978, China embarked on the path of reform and opening-up as a new era. In the wave of this reform, China Merchants invested and created the first industrial park in China for opening-up – Shekou[1] Industrial Zone and rebuilt its ocean fleet starting with a small container ship named Lin Jiang. In 1980, on the basis of its Shipping Department, China Merchants set up Hong Kong Ming Wah Shipping Co., Ltd. to do business like ship owners, shipping agent and cargo transportation, etc. In the same year, China Merchants had nine ships, with a total tonnage of 244,373 tons. In 1981, China Merchants continued to procure ships, with the ship number increasing to sixteen with a total tonnage of 409,180 tons. China Merchants has ushered in the period of shipping recovery.

在80年代初期，招商局根据自身业务需要购买了一些散货船、杂货船。到80年代末期和90年代初期，招商局开始大量购进油轮，参与国家的石油运输。截至1999年，招商局拥有各种类型的轮船101艘。

Considering its business development, China Merchants purchased some bulk carriers and general cargo vessels in early 1980s. From late 1980s to early 1990s, China Merchants began to purchase a great number of

---

[1] Shekou: A port located in Guangdong Province.

oil tankers and took part in the petroleum transportation for China. By the year of 1999, China Merchants had possessed 101 ships of various types.

⚓ 临江　Lin Jiang

"临江"轮英文船名 Lin Jiang，多用途船，船长 110 米，船宽 19 米，吃水 6.5 米，载重吨 6700，主机功率 3880 千瓦，航速每小时 13.5 海里。

Lin Jiang is a multi-purpose carrier. Its length overall is 110 meters and the beam is 19 meters with a draught of 6.5 meters. With its main engine power at 3,880 kilowatts, it could sail at a speed of 13.5kn and has a dead weight tonnage of 6,700 tons.

"临江"轮由东德沃尔格斯特造船厂建造，1971 年 6 月出厂。1978 年 8 月，广州远洋运输公司组织船员到荷兰鹿特丹港接收了"临江"轮，营运于日本和中国华北各港。1979 年 4 月，根据交通部的指示，将"临江"轮从广州远洋运输公司调拨给香港招商局使用。当年 6 月 6 日在香港正式移交。船旗不变，船名不变，船员不变。招商局船务部发动船员和友联船厂一起，仅用一昼夜的时间就把"临江"轮由杂货船修缮成多用途船，可以承载集装箱

临江　Lin Jiang

100TEU。6月8日靠泊香港国际货箱码头装货，6月9日起航前往广州黄埔港，开辟了香港至广州的集装箱航线，这在中国经济贸易的历史上具有破冰式的开拓性意义。8月15日，"临江"轮开辟了香港至青岛的集装箱航线。11月1日，"临江"轮又开辟了香港至上海的集装箱航线。这些航线的开辟，都是集装箱航运史上的第一次。

Built by Walgast Shipyard of former East Germany in June 1971, the carrier was delivered to the crew of Guangzhou Ocean Shipping Co., Ltd. at the Port of Rotterdam of the Netherlands in August 1978 and was then used among the ports in North China and Japan. In April 1979, Lin Jiang was allocated to Hong Kong branch of China Merchants from Guangzhou Ocean Shipping Company according to the instructions from the Ministry of Transport of the People's Republic of China. On June 6, 1979, Lin Jiang was officially taken over by China Merchants with its flag, name and crew unchanged. Through the joint efforts of the crew and Yiu Lian Dockyards, it took only 24 hours to renovate Lin Jiang from a general cargo vessel into a multi-purpose carrier with a loading capacity of 100 TEU. It was loaded at Hong Kong International Container Terminal on June 8, 1979 and sailed to Huangpu Port of Guangzhou on June 9, 1979, which was an icebreaking sailing in the China's trading history. Lin Jiang opened up the first container route from Hong Kong to Qingdao on August 15 and the first route from Hong Kong to Shanghai on November 1, 1979.

"临江"轮是香港招商局重建远洋运输船队的第一艘船，由香港明华船务有限公司管理。1982年7月10日，按照交通部的指示，香港招商局将"临江"轮交给上海远洋运输公司。

Lin Jiang was the first ship after China Merchants rebuilt its ocean shipping fleet and was managed by Hong Kong Ming Wah Shipping Co., Ltd. at that time. On July 10, 1982, China Merchants handed Lin Jiang to Shanghai Ocean Shipping Co., Ltd. upon the instruction of the Ministry of Transport.

⚓ 顺江 Shun Jiang

"顺江"轮英文船名Shun Jiang，集装箱船，船长108.5米，船宽18.8米，吃水6.52米，载重吨6700，主机功率3880千瓦，航速每小时13.25海里。

Shun Jiang is a container vessel. Its length overall is 108.5 meters and the beam is 18.8 meters, with a draught of 6.52 meters. With its main engine power at 3,880 kilowatts, it could sail at a speed of 13.25 kn and has a dead weight tonnage of 6,700 tons.

"顺江"轮于1976年3月1日由日本大岛造船厂建造竣工出厂。1979年11月15日香港明华船务有限公司从中国远洋运输总公司接船，1980年1月投入营运，穿行于中国沿海

顺江　Shun Jiang

及远东和东南亚航线。1982年7月31日，按照交通部的指示，于大连港将"顺江"轮交给上海远洋运输公司。

　　Built by Oshima Shipbuilding Co.,Ltd of Japan on March 1, 1976, the vessel was taken over by Hong Kong Ming Wah Shipping from China Ocean Shipping Company on November 15, 1979 and put into operation in January 1980, serving the routes along the coast of China, Far East and Southeast Asia. On July 31, 1982, China Merchants handed Shun Jiang to Shanghai Ocean Shipping Co., Ltd. at Dalian Port upon the instruction of the Ministry of Transport.

⚓ 江图 Jiang Tu

"江图"轮英文船名 Jiang Tu，灵便型散货船，船长 150 米，船宽 20.3 米，吃水 8.7 米，载重吨 15300，主机功率 6800 千瓦，航速每小时 12.50 海里。

Jiang Tu is a handysize bulk carrier. Its length overall is 150 meters and the beam is 20.3 meters with a draught of 8.7 meters. With its main engine power at 6,800 kilowatts, it could sail at a speed of 12.50 kn and has a dead weight tonnage of 15,300 tons.

江图 Jiang Tu

"江图"轮由日本幸阳造船厂建造，1974 年 5 月出厂。1980 年 4 月 16 日由招商局购买接船，香港明华船务有限公司负责经营管理。1984 年 7 月 29 日出售并交船。

Built by Koyo Dockyard Co.,Ltd of Japan in May 1974, the carrier was sold and delivered to China Merchants on April 16, 1980 and managed by Hong Kong Ming Wah Shipping. The carrier was sold and delivered on July 29, 1984.

⚓ 华阳 Hua Yang

"华阳"轮英文船名 Hua Yang，灵便型散货船，船长 169 米，船宽 24.5 米，吃水 9.4 米，载重吨 29672，主机功率 8050 千瓦，航速每小时 13 海里。

Hua Yang is a handysize bulk carrier. Its length overall is 169 meters and the beam is 24.5 meters with a draught of 9.4 meters. With its main engine power at 8,050 kilowatts, it could sail at a speed of 13 kn and has a dead weight tonnage of 29,672 tons.

华阳 Hua Yang

"华阳"轮由日本佐世保造船厂建造，1980 年 4 月 11 日出厂进入招商局，香港明华船务有限公司负责管理经营。1982 年 7 月 2 日出售给广州远洋运输公司，于黄埔港交船。

Built by Sasebo Heavy Industries Co.,Ltd of Japan, the carrier was delivered to China Merchants on April 11,

1980 and managed by Hong Kong Ming Wah Shipping. The carrier was sold to Guangzhou Ocean Shipping Co., Ltd and delivered at Huangpu Port on July 2, 1982.

华富 Hua Fu

"华富"轮英文船名 Hua Fu，大灵便型油轮，船长 130.2 米，船宽 32 米，吃水 11.5 米，载重吨 45725，主机功率 8380 千瓦，航速每小时 14 海里。

Hua Fu is a handymax oil tanker. Its length overall is 130.2 meters and the beam is 32 meters with a draught of 11.5 meters. With its main engine power at 8,380 kilowatts, it could sail at a speed of 14 kn and has a dead weight tonnage of 45,725 tons.

"华富"轮是由瑞典造船厂 1963 年 7 月建造竣工出厂的，原名"金湖"轮，为天津远洋运输公司所有。招商局 1980 年 7 月 5 日购入并改为现名。香港明华船务有限公司负责管理。当时租给东方石油公司承运青岛至菲律宾的原油。1982 年 4 月 30 日出售并在香港交船。

Built by Sweden Shipbuilding Factory in July 1963, Hua Fu was owned by Tianjin Ocean Shipping Co., Ltd. with its original name as Jin Hu. On July 5, 1980, China Merchants bought it and changed it to the present name. It was managed by Hong Kong Ming Wah Shipping Co., Ltd. and rented to Feoso Oil Limited for crude oil shipment between Qingdao and Philippines. On April 30, 1982, the ship was sold and delivered in Hong Kong.

华富 Hua Fu

⚓ 华兴 Hua Xing

"华兴"轮英文船名 Hua Xing，灵便型散货船，船长 175.5 米，船宽 28.1 米，吃水 10.3 米，载重吨 35339，主机功率 7620 千瓦，航速每小时 13 海里。

Hua Xing is a handysize bulk carrier. Its length overall is 175.5 meters and the beam is 28.1 meters with a draught of 10.3 meters. With its main engine power at 7,620 kilowatts, it could sail at a speed of 13 kn and has a dead weight tonnage of 35,339 tons. .

"华兴"轮于 1966 年 9 月由日本常石造船厂建造竣工出厂。1980 年 8 月 11 日招商局购入改为现名，香港明华船务有限公司负责管理。1983 年 11 月 23 日出售并在香港交船。

Built by Tsuneishi Shipbuilding Co., Ltd of Japan in September, 1966, it was bought by China Merchants on August 11, 1980 and renamed to the present one. It was managed by Hong Kong Ming Wah Shipping Co., Ltd., and sold and delivered in Hong Kong on November 23, 1983.

⚓ 华朋 Hua Peng

"华朋"轮英文船名 Hua Peng，灵便型散货船，船长 175 米，船宽 28.3 米，吃水 10.3 米，载重吨 34260，主机功率 7706 千瓦，航速每小时 13 海里。

Hua Peng is a handysize bulk carrier. Its length overall is 175 meters and the beam is 28.3 meters with a draught of 10.3 meters. With its main engine power at 7,706 kilowatts, it could sail at a speed of 13kn with a dead weight tonnage of 34,260 tons.

"华朋"轮由挪威豪格松曼卡聂斯克造船厂建造，1966 年 7 月出厂。招商局于 1980 年 8 月 22 日购进接船，改为现名。集美航海专科学校曾在 1981 年 10 月 28 日派 31 名师生组成的船员队伍到该轮服务。1984 年 5 月 22 日出售给广州海运局，在大连港交船。

Built by Haugsunmen Kakeisk Shipyard of Norway and completed in July 1966, it was bought by China Merchants on August 22, 1980 and renamed to the present one. Jimei Navigation Technical College sent a crew of 31 teachers and students to serve the ship on October 28, 1981. The ship was sold to Guangzhou Maritime Transport Bureau and then delivered at Dalian Port on May 22, 1984.

华顺 Hua Shun

"华顺"轮英文船名 Hua Shun，灵便型散货船，船长 170 米，船宽 28.1 米，吃水 10.4 米，载重吨 34800，主机功率 7630 千瓦，航速每小时 13 海里。

Hua Shun is a handysize bulk carrier. Its length overall is 170 meters and the beam is 28.1 meters with a draught of 10.4 meters. With its main engine power at 7,630 kilowatts, it could sail at a speed of 13 kn and has a dead weight tonnage of 34,800 tons.

"华顺"轮于 1966 年 9 月由挪威豪格松曼卡聂斯克造船厂建造竣工出厂。招商局 1980 年 8 月 29 日购进改为现名。香港明华船务有限公司管理经营。1985 年 3 月 20 日出售给广州海运局，在黄埔港交船。

Built and completed by Haugsunmen Kakeisk Shipyard of Norway in September 1966, it was bought by China Merchants on August 29, 1980 and renamed to the present one. It was managed by Hong Kong Ming Wah Shipping Co., Ltd. and sold to Guangzhou Maritime Transport Bureau and then delivered at Huangpu Port on March 20, 1985.

华隆 Hua Long

"华隆"轮英文船名 Hua Long，灵便型散货船，船长 171.05 米，船宽 28 米，吃水 10.5 米，载重吨 35339，主机功率 7600 千瓦，航速每小时 13 海里。

Hua Long is a handysize bulk carrier. Its length overall is 171.05 meters and the beam is 28 meters with a draught of 10.5 meters. With its main engine power at 7,600 kilowatts, it could sail at a speed of 13 kn with a dead weight tonnage of 35,339 tons.

华隆 Hua Long

"华隆"轮是日本石川岛造船厂建造，1965 年 2 月出厂。招商局于 1980 年 9 月 30 日购进并在澳大利亚接船。1981 年 3 月 12 日，大连海运学院派出全套由师生组成的船员队伍上该轮服务。1983 年 11 月 29 日出售交船。

Built by Ishikawajima Shipbuilding Factory of Japan and completed in February, 1965, it was bought by China Merchants and was delivered in Australia on September 30, 1980. Dalian Maritime College sent a crew of teachers and students to the ship for service on March 12, 1981. The ship was sold and delivered on November 29, 1983.

华发 Hua Fa

"华发"轮英文船名 Hua Fa，灵便型散货船，船长 168 米，船宽 28 米，吃水 10.4 米，载重吨 34150，主机功率 7700 千瓦，航速每小时 13 海里。

Hua Fa is a handysize bulk carrier. Its length overall is 168 meters and the beam is 28 meters with a draught of 10.4 meters. With its main engine power at 7,700 kilowatts, it could sail at a speed of 13 kn and has a dead weight tonnage of 34,150 tons.

"华发"轮由德国不来梅造船厂建造，1967 年 6 月出厂。招商局 1980 年 12 月 1 日购进并在美国东海岸接船，改为现名。香港明华船务有限公司经营管理。1984 年 10 月 15 日出售交船。

Built by Bremer-Vulkan Shipbuilding Factory of Germany and completed in June, 1967, it was bought by China Merchants on December 1, 1980, delivered at the eastern coast of U.S.A. and renamed as its present name. It was managed by Hong Kong Ming Wah Shipping Co., Ltd., and was sold and delivered on October 15, 1984.

华乐 Hua Le

"华乐"轮英文船名 Hua Le，灵便型散货船，船长 173.5 米，船宽 28 米，吃水 10.5 米，载重吨 35339，主机功率 7705 千瓦，航速每小时 13 海里。

Hua Le is a handysize bulk carrier. Its length overall is 173.5 meters and the beam is 28 meters with a draught of 10.5 meters. With its main engine power at 7,705 kilowatts, it could sail at a speed of 13 kn and has a dead weight tonnage of 35,339 tons.

"华乐"轮是 1966 年 6 月由日本佐世保造船厂建造出厂的。招商局于 1981 年 1 月 29 日购进在上海港接船。香港明华船务有限公司经营管理。1981 年 6 月 21 日上海海运学院派出整套师生组成的船员队伍上该轮服务。1984 年 5 月 26 日出售给买家，在厦门港交船。

Built and completed by Sasebo Heavy Industries Co., Ltd of Japan in June, 1966. It was bought by China Merchants on January 29, 1981 and delivered at Shanghai Port. It was under the operation of Hong Kong Ming Wah Shipping Co., Ltd. On June 21, 1981, Shanghai Maritime College sent a group of teachers and students to the ship for service. The ship was sold and delivered at Xiamen Port On May 26, 1984.

⚓ 华江　Hua Jiang

"华江"轮英文船名 Hua Jiang，集装箱船，船长 105 米，船宽 18 米，吃水 6.5 米，载重吨 6450，主机功率 3800 千瓦，航速每小时 13.5 海里。

Hua Jiang is a container carrier. Its length overall is 105 meters and the beam is 18 meters with a draught of 6.5 meters. With its main engine power at 3,800 kilowatts, it could sail at a speed of 13.5 kn and has a dead weight tonnage of 6,450 tons.

"华江"轮是由日本佐世保造船厂 1975 年 3 月建造竣工出厂的。招商局 1981 年 2 月 3 日购入接船，香港明华船务有限公司经营管理。1982 年 7 月 27 日按照交通部的指示，出售给上海远洋运输公司并在张家港交船。

Built by Sasebo Heavy Industries Co., Ltd of Japan and completed in March, 1975, Hua Jiang was procured by China Merchants on February 3, 1981, and then operated and managed by Hong Kong Ming Wah Shipping Co., Ltd. On July 27, 1982, as instructed by the Ministry of Transport, the ship was sold to Shanghai Ocean Shipping Co., Ltd. and delivered at Zhangjiagang Port.

⚓ 华昌　Hua Chang

"华昌"轮英文船名 Hua Chang，杂货船，船长 120 米，船宽 20.2 米，吃水 7.55 米，载重吨 9124，主机功率 4650 千瓦，航速每小时 13 海里。

Hua Chang is a general cargo vessel. Its length overall is 120 meters and the beam is 20.2 meters with a draught of 7.55 meters. With its main engine power at 4,650 kilowatts, it could sail at a speed of 13 kn and has a dead weight tonnage of 9,124 tons.

"华昌"轮 1960 年 10 月从日本大阪造船厂建造完工出厂。招商局 1981 年 4 月 25 日购进，于香港接船。香港明华船务有限公司经营管理。1983 年 4 月 27 日出售给买家，于香港交船。

Built by Osaka Shipyard of Japan and completed in October, 1960, it was procured by China Merchants on April 25, 1981 and delivered in Hong Kong. It was under the operation of Hong Kong Ming Wah Shipping Co., Ltd.. The ship was sold and delivered in Hong Kong on April 27, 1983.

CHAPTER THREE AFTER THE FOUNDATION OF THE PEOPLE'S REPUBLIC OF CHINA \ 第三章 新中国成立后 \ **183**

华江 Hua Jiang

华昌 Hua Chang

华强　Hua Qiang

⚓ 华强　Hua Qiang

"华强"轮英文船名 Hua Qiang，杂货船，船长 120 米，船宽 20 米，吃水 7.6 米，载重吨 9180，主机功率 4620 千瓦，航速每小时 12.5 海里。

Hua Qiang is a general cargo vessel. Its length overall is 120 meters and the beam is 20 meters with a draught of 7.6 meters. With its main engine power at 4,620 kilowatts, it could sail at a speed of 12.5 kn and has a dead weight tonnage of 9,180 tons.

"华强"轮由瑞典造船厂于 1955 年 10 月建造完成出厂。该轮原属于上海远洋运输公司，船名"武都"。1981 年 12 月 11 日招商局购进接船，更名"华强"。香港明华船务有限公司经营管理。1982 年 4 月 30 日在科威特港出售交船给买家。

Built by Sweden Shipbuilding Factory and completed in October, 1955, Hua Qiang was originally owned by Shanghai Ocean Shipping Co., Ltd. with its former name as Wu Du. It was purchased by China Merchants on December 11, 1981 and renamed as Hua Qiang. Operated and managed by Hong Kong Ming Wah Shipping Co., Ltd., the ship was sold and delivered at Kuwait Port on April 30, 1982.

华都 Hua Du

"华都"轮英文船名 Hua Du，杂货船，船长 132 米，船宽 19.5 米，吃水 8.5 米，载重吨 12730，主机功率 5300 千瓦，航速每小时 13 海里。

Hua Du is a general cargo vessel. Its length overall is 132 meters and the beam is 19.5 meters with a draught of 8.5 meters. With its main engine power at 5,300 kilowatts, it could sail at a speed of 13 kn and has a dead weight tonnage of 12,730 tons.

"华都"轮 1957 年 8 月由瑞典造船厂建造成功出厂。招商局 1982 年 2 月 22 日购进，在上海接船。香港明华船务有限公司经营管理。1982 年 5 月 10 日出售给买家并交船。

Built by Sweden Shipbuilding Factory and completed in August, 1957, it was procured by China Merchants on February 22, 1982 and delivered in Shanghai. Operated and managed by Hong Kong Ming Wah Shipping Co., Ltd., Hua Du was sold and delivered on May 10, 1982.

华胜 Hua Sheng

"华胜"轮英文船名 Hua Sheng，散货船，船长 129.08 米，船宽 19.49 米，吃水 7.97 米，载重吨 8627，主机功率 2463 千瓦，航速每小时 13.8 海里。

Hua Sheng is a bulk carrier. Its length overall is 129.08 meters and the beam is 19.49 meters with a draught of 7.97 meters. With its main engine power at 2,463 kilowatts, it could sail at a speed of 13.8 kn and has a dead weight tonnage of 8,627 tons.

"华胜"轮由芬兰赫尔辛基造船厂建造，1971 年 11 月出厂。原名"延河"轮，属于上海远洋运输公司。该轮由于机械事故造成两台主机之一的机壳被打碎，只能单机工作。经请示交通部批准，上海远洋运输公司以 150 万美元的废钢价卖给香港招商局。香港明华船务有限公司派船员于 1982 年 9 月 12 日接船，船速每小

华胜 Hua Sheng

时仅有 2 海里。开到香港修理后，恢复到每小时 7 海里。该轮改名为"华胜"，航行香港至厦门线。船员在公司的指导配合下，边营运边自修，半年后航速恢复到每小时 12 海里。运行 13 年之后，于 1996 年 12 月 29 日将"华胜"轮出售给广东省拆船加工公司，收回人民币 415.50 万元。"华胜"轮的一只锚现陈列在蛇口明华国际会议中心 C 座楼前。

Built by Helsinki Shipbuilding Factory of Finland and completed in November, 1971, it was owned by Shanghai Ocean Shipping Co., Ltd. with its original name as Yan He. Due to mechanical accident, the enclosure for one of the two main engines was smashed, which led to single-engine work of the ship. As approved by the Ministry of Transport, Shanghai Ocean Shipping Co. Ltd. sold the ship at the price of $1.5 million as scrap steel to China Merchants. A crew sent by Hong Kong Ming Wah Shipping Co., Ltd. took over the ship on September 12, 1982, when the cruising speed was only 2 knots. After being repaired in Hong Kong, the ship could sail at 7 knots. With its name changed to Hua Sheng, the ship sailed along the route between Hong Kong and Xiamen. Under the instruction and coordination of the company, the crew continued to repair the ship along while in operation. Half a year later, the speed rose to 12 knots. After thirteen years of operation, Hua Sheng was sold to Guangdong Shipbreaking and Processing Company on December 29, 1996 at a price of RMB 4.155 million. One of its anchors is now presented in front of Tower C of Ming Wah International Conference Center in Shekou.

华盈　Hua Ying

"华盈"轮英文船名 Hua Ying，多用途船，船长 124.5 米，船宽 17.6 米，吃水 7.58 米，载重吨 7245，主机功率 4705 千瓦，航速每小时 13 海里。

Hua Ying is a multi-purpose carrier. Its length overall is 124.5 meters and the beam is 17.6 meters with a draught of 7.58 meters. With its main engine power at 4,705 kilowatts, it could sail at a speed of 13 kn and has a dead weight tonnage of 7,245 tons.

华盈　Hua Ying

"华盈"轮由德国不来梅造船厂建造，1969 年 6 月出厂。香港明华船务有限公司于 1983 年 12 月 28 日在荷兰法院以 50 万美元拍得该轮，自修后投入营运。1996 年 7 月 29 日出售给买家并交船。

Built by Bremer-Vulkan Shipbuilding Factory of Germany and completed in June, 1969, it was bid by Hong Kong Ming Wah Shipping Co., Ltd. at Dutch Court at a price of US$500,000 and then put into operation after being repaired. The ship was sold and delivered on July 29, 1996.

华琼 Hua Qiong

"华琼"轮英文船名 Hua Qiong，多用途船，船长 124.5 米，船宽 18 米，吃水 8.12 米，载重吨 8100，主机功率 4776 千瓦，航速每小时 13.5 海里。

Hua Qiong is a multi-purpose carrier. Its length overall is 124.5 meters and the beam is 18 meters with a draught of 8.12 meters. With its main engine power at 4,776 kilowatts, it could sail at a speed of 13.5 kn and has a dead weight tonnage of 8,100 tons.

华琼　Hua Qiong

"华琼"轮由德国不来梅船厂建造，1972 年 3 月出厂。1985 年 3 月 16 日招商局签约购入，原名 Green Ocean，更名为"华琼"。香港明华船务有限公司管理。1996 年 7 月 23 日出售交船。

Built by Bremer-Vulkan Shipbuilding Factory of Germany and completed in March, 1972, Hua Qiong was purchased by China Merchants with a contract on March 16, 1985. With its original name as Green Ocean, it was renamed to Hua Qiong and operated by Hong Kong Ming Wah Shipping Co., Ltd. The ship was sold and delivered on July 23, 1996.

华佳　Hua Jia

⚓ 华佳　Hua Jia

"华佳"轮英文船名 Hua Jia，多用途船，船长 100.91 米，船宽 15.2 米，吃水 6.77 米，载重吨 4478，主机功率 2985 千瓦，航速每小时 11 海里。

Hua Jia is a multi-purpose carrier. Its length overall is 100.91 meters and the beam is 15.2 meters with a draught of 6.77 meters. With its main engine power at 2,985 kilowatts, it could sail at a speed of 11 kn and has a dead weight tonnage of 4,478 tons.

"华佳"轮由德国舒斯沃特造船厂制造，1970 年 3 月出厂。原名 Weser Broker，后改名 Scandutch Asia。1985 年 7 月 5 日招商局购进，更名"华佳"，由香港明华船务有限公司经营管理。1996 年 12 月 9 日出售给香港买家并在港交船。

Built by Schichau-Werft Shipbuilding Factory of Germany and completed in March, 1970, it was originally named as Weser Broker and then changed to Scandutch Asia. China Merchants procured it on July 5, 1985 and renamed it as Hua Jia, which was operated by Hong Kong Ming Wah Shipping Co., Ltd. The ship was sold to a Hong Kong buyer and delivered in Hong Kong on December 9, 1996.

华川　Hua Chuan

华川　Hua Chuan

"华川"轮英文船名 Hua Chuan，多用途船，船长 120.94 米，船宽 19.23 米，吃水 7.9 米，载重吨 10091，主机功率 4478 千瓦，航速每小时 13 海里。

Hua Chuan is a multi-purpose carrier. Its length overall is 120.94 meters and the beam is 19.23 meters with a draught of 7.9 meters. With its main engine power at 4,478 kilowatts, it could sail at a speed of 13 kn and has a dead weight tonnage of 10,091 tons.

"华川"轮是日本太平造船厂建造并于 1975 年 9 月出厂的。招商局 1986 年 11 月 3 日购进，香港明华船务有限公司管理经营。1997 年 3 月 11 日出售并在黄埔港交船。

Built by Japanese Shin Kurushima Dockyard Co., Ltd and completed in September, 1975, it was procured by China Merchants on November 3, 1986 and managed by Hong Kong Ming Wah Shipping Co., Ltd. The ship was sold and delivered at Huangpu Port on March 11, 1997.

华河　Hua He

"华河"轮英文船名 Hua He，多用途船，船长 123.32 米，船宽 20.54 米，吃水 8.11 米，载重吨 11598，主机功率 4627 千瓦，航速每小时 14 海里。

Hua He is a multi-purpose carrier. Its length overall is 123.32 meters and the beam is 20.54 meters with a draught of 8.11 meters. With its main engine power at 4,627 kilowatts, it could sail at a speed of 14 kn and has a dead weight tonnage of 11,598 tons.

华河　Hua He

"华河"轮由日本太平造船厂建造,1974年4月出厂。招商局1987年4月14日购入,香港明华船务有限公司管理营运。1997年3月3日出售,在印度港口交船。

Built by Japanese Shin Kurushima Dockyard Co., Ltd and completed in April, 1974, it was procured by China Merchants on April 14, 1987 and managed by Hong Kong Ming Wah Shipping Co., Ltd. The ship was sold and delivered at Port in India on March 3, 1997.

⚓ 华泉 Hua Quan

"华泉"轮英文船名Hua Quan,多用途船,船长123.32米,船宽20.5米,吃水8.11米,载重吨11598,主机功率5400千瓦,航速每小时14海里。

Hua Quan is a multi-purpose vessel. Its length overall is 123.32 meters and the beam is 20.5 meters with a draught of 8.11 meters. With its main engine power at 5,400 kilowatts, it could sail at a speed of 14 kn and has a dead weight tonnage of 11,598 tons.

"华泉"轮由日本太平造船厂于1976年7月建造完工出厂。招商局1987年5月4日购进,香港明华船务有限公司管理经营。1997年12月23日出售并交船。

Built by Japanese Shin Kurushima Dockyard Co.,Ltd and completed in July, 1976, it was procured by China Merchants on May 4, 1987 and managed by Hong Kong Ming Wah Shipping Co., Ltd. The ship was sold and delivered on December 23, 1997.

华泉 Hua Quan

华利　Hua Li

⚓ 华利　Hua Li

"华利"轮英文船名 Hua Li，多用途船，船长 131.81 米，船宽 19.04 米，吃水 8.3 米，载重吨 11128，主机功率 5270 千瓦，航速每小时 13 海里。

Hua Li is a multi-purpose vessel. Its length overall is 131.81 meters and the beam is 19.04 meters with a draught of 8.3 meters. With its main engine power at 5,270 kilowatts, it could sail at a speed of 13 kn and has a dead weight tonnage of 11,128 tons.

"华利"轮由日本太平造船厂于 1976 年 5 月建造竣工出厂。原名 Jasmine 1，挂巴拿马船旗。招商局 1988 年 4 月 5 日签约购进，香港明华船务有限公司管理经营，改挂中国船旗。1995 年 10 月申改新加坡船籍，更名为 Marina Lauri。1997 年 12 月 12 日出售给印度买家并交船。由招商局船员协助，在印度 Alang 冲滩。

Built by Japanese Shin Kurushima Dockyard Co., Ltd and completed in May, 1976 with an original name as Jasmine 1 and Panamanian flag, it was procured by China Merchants with a contract on April 5, 1988 and managed by Hong Kong Ming Wah Shipping Co., Ltd. with Chinese flag. In October, 1995, the nationality of the ship was changed to Singapore and its name was changed to Marina Lauri. On December 12, 1997, the ship was sold and delivered to an Indian buyer. Aided by China Merchants crew, the ship was taken to the land at Alang in India.

⚓ 华宝 Hua Bao

"华宝"轮英文船名 Hua Bao，多用途船，船长 131.81 米，船宽 19.04 米，吃水 8.3 米，载重吨 10880，主机功率 5270 千瓦，航速每小时 13 海里。

Hua Bao is multi-purpose vessel. Its length overall is 131.81 meters and the beam is 19.04 meters with a draught 8.3 meters. With its main engine power at 5,270 kilowatts, it could sail at a speed of 13 kn and has a dead weight tonnage of 10,880 tons.

"华宝"轮由日本太平造船厂于 1976 年 7 月建造竣工出厂。招商局 1988 年 4 月 19 日签约购进，香港明华船务有限公司管理经营。1998 年 8 月 14 日出售给新加坡买家，并在新加坡港交船。

Built by Japanese Shin Kurushima Dockyard Co., Ltd and completed in July, 1976, the ship was procured by China Merchants with a contract signed on April 19, 1988 and managed by Hong Kong Ming Wah Shipping Co., Ltd. On August 14, 1998, the ship was sold to a Singaporean buyer and delivered at Singapore Port.

⚓ 兴安岭 Xing An Ling

"兴安岭"轮英文船名 Xing An Ling，灵便型散货船，船长 170 米，船宽 28 米，吃水 9.30 米，载重吨 27709，主机功率 7820 千瓦，航速每小时 12.5 海里。

Xing An Ling was a handysize bulk carrier. Its length overall is 170 meters and the beam is 28 meters with a draught of 9.30 meters. With its main engine power at 7,820 kilowatts, it could sail at a speed of 12.5 kn and has a dead weight tonnage of 27,709 tons.

"兴安岭"轮是日本幸阳造船厂于 1974 年 2 月建造竣工出厂的。招商局于 1981 年 12 月 1 日购进接船，原名 Hungtse Career，更名为"江乐"轮，注册巴拿马港。1984 年 11 月 24 日改名为"兴安岭"轮，注册蛇口港。1984 年 12 月 23 日出售给广州海运局。

Built by Koyo Dockyard Co., Ltd of Japan and completed in February, 1974, Xing An Ling was procured by and delivered to China Merchants on December 1, 1981. With an original name as Hungtse Career, the ship was renamed to Jiang Le and registered at Panama Port. On November 24, 1984, the ship was renamed again to Xing An Ling and registered in Shekou Port. It was sold to Guangzhou Maritime Transport Bureau on December 23, 1984.

新华龙 Xin Hua Long

"新华龙"轮英文船名 Xin Hua Long，多用途船，船长 135 米，船宽 20 米，吃水 8 米，载重吨 12918，主机功率 6000 千瓦，航速每小时 13.5 海里。

Xin Hua Long is a multi-purpose vessel. Its length overall is 135 meters and the beam is 20 meters with a draught of 8 meters. With its main engine power at 6,000 kilowatts, it could sail at a speed of 13.5 kn and has a dead weight tonnage of 12,918 tons.

新华龙 Xin Hua Long

"新华龙"轮是东德沃尔格斯特造船厂 1978 年 4 月建造完工出厂的。招商局 1982 年 2 月 22 日购进在香港接船。香港明华船务有限公司经营管理。1983 年 1 月 8 日出售给买家，在黄埔港交船。

Built by Walgast Shipbuilding Factory in East Germany and completed in April, 1978, Xin Hua Long was procured by China Merchants and delivered in Hong Kong on February 22, 1982. It was managed by Hong Kong Ming Wah Shipping Co., Ltd, and then sold on January 8, 1983 and delivered at Huangpu Port.

新华门 Xin Hua Men

"新华门"轮英文船名 Xin Hua Men，多用途船，船长 135 米，船宽 20 米，吃水 8 米，载重吨 13010，主机功率 6000 千瓦，航速每小时 13.5 海里。

Xin Hua Men is a multi-purpose vessel. Its length overall is 135 meters and the beam is 20 meters with a draught of 8 meters. With its main engine power at 6,000 kilowatts, it could sail at a speed of 13.5 kn and has a dead weight tonnage of 13,010 tons.

新华门 Xin Hua Men

"新华门"轮于 1978 年 6 月由东德沃

尔格斯特造船厂建造出厂。1982年3月10日招商局购进此轮,在马耳他接船。香港明华船务有限公司经营管理。1982年11月26日出售给买家并在黄埔港交船。

Built by Walgast Shipbuilding Factory in East Germany and completed in June, 1978, Xin Hua Men was procured by China Merchants and delivered in Malta on March 10, 1982. It was managed by Hong Kong Ming Wah Shipping Co., Ltd, and then sold on November 26, 1982 and delivered at Huangpu Port.

高德　Crusader

"高德"轮英文船名Crusader,灵便型散货船,船长187.73米,船宽28.4米,吃水10.77米,载重吨38110,主机功率7388千瓦,航速每小时13海里。

Crusader is a handysize bulk carrier. Its length overall is 187.73 meters and the beam is 28.4 meters with a draught 10.77 meters. With its main engine power at 7,388 kilowatts, it could sail at a speed of 13 kn and has a dead weight tonnage of 38,110 tons.

"高德"轮由日本石川岛造船厂建造,1982年7月1日香港明华船务有限公司派人接船,主要营运于加勒比至北欧航线,运输铝矿粉。1994年6月29日在巴拿马港出售给美国PLM投资公司。

Built by Ishikawajima Shipbuilding Factory of Japan, the carrier was delivered to Hong Kong Ming Wah Shipping Co., Ltd on July 1, 1982, mainly used to transport aluminum ore powder between the Caribbean and North Europe. On June 29, 1994, the ship was sold to the United States PLM Investment Company and delivered at the Port of Panama.

高德　Crusader

利德　Leader

⚓ 利德　Leader

"利德"轮英文船名 Leader，灵便型散货船，船长 187.73 米，船宽 28.4 米，吃水 10.77 米，载重吨 38110，主机功率 7388 千瓦，航速每小时 13 海里。

Leader is a handysize bulk carrier. Its length overall is 187.73 meters and the beam is 28.4 meters with a draught of 10.77 meters. With its main engine power at 7,388 kilowatts, it could sail at a speed of 13 kn and has a dead weight tonnage of 38,110 tons.

"利德"轮由日本石川岛造船厂建造，1983 年 3 月 1 日香港明华船务有限公司派船员接船，主要营运于加勒比至北欧航线，运输铝矿粉。1994 年 8 月 17 日在荷兰鹿特丹港出售给美国 PLM 投资公司。

Built by Ishikawajima Shipbuilding Factory of Japan, the carrier was delivered to Hong Kong Ming Wah Shipping Co., Ltd on March 1, 1983, mainly used to transport aluminum ore powder between the Caribbean and North Europe. On August 17, 1994, the ship was sold to the United States PLM Investment Company and delivered at the Port of Rotterdam of the Netherlands.

明玉　Ming Jade

⚓ 明玉　Ming Jade

"明玉"轮英文船名 Ming Jade，灵便型散货船，船长 179.61 米，船宽 28.45 米，吃水 10.7 米，载重吨 38056，主机功率 7836 千瓦，航速每小时 13 海里。

Ming Jade is a handysize bulk carrier. Its length overall is 179.61 meters and the beam is 28.45 meters with a draught of 10.7 meters. With its main engine power at 7,836 kilowatts, it could sail at a speed of 13 kn and has a dead weight tonnage of 38,056 tons.

"明玉"轮于 1983 年 3 月从日本大阪造船厂竣工出厂，香港明华船务有限公司接船，营运于全球航线。1992 年 2 月 19 日出售给希腊买家，于上海港交船。

Built by an Osaka Shipyard in Japan, the carrier was delivered to Hong Kong Ming Wah Shipping Co., Ltd after completed in March 1983 and had been sailing on international shipping lanes. On February 19, 1992, the bulker was sold to a Greece owner and delivered at the Port of Shanghai.

明华 Ming Hua

"明华"轮,豪华游轮,船长 168 米,船宽 21 米,载重吨 14000。

Ming Hua is a luxury cruiser. Its length overall is 168 meters and the beam is 21 meters with a dead weight tonnage of 14,000 tons.

"明华"轮原名 Anceevilla,法国维纳泽尔大西洋船厂建造的豪华邮轮,1962 年 8 月 7 日,法国总统戴高乐为该轮的下水剪彩,并将其作为他的专用船。

Originally known as Anceevilla, the ship was built by Chantiers de l'Atlantique, a French shipyard in Saint-Na zaire. On August 7, 1962, the French President Charles de Gaulle cut the ribbon for the launching of the cruiser and used it as his private ship.

1973 年 4 月 7 日,中国购下 Anceevilla,在马耳他接收,将其更名为"明华"。此后,"明华"轮投入中国至坦桑尼亚航线。1978 年 6 月,中华人民共和国国务院委派"明华"轮前往越南接中国侨民回国。1979 年 5 月,廖承志副委员长率领中日友好代表团乘"明华"轮访问日本。1983 年 8 月 27 日,"明华"轮抵达深圳蛇口,由广州远洋运输公司移交给招商局。招商局将"明华"轮改造成我国第一座以海洋为主题的船体酒店,由海上世界股份有限公司经营管理。1984 年 1 月 26 日,邓小平及夫人、王震及夫人、杨尚昆及夫人一行来"明华"轮视察,邓小平为"明华"轮题词:"海上世界"。

明华 Ming Hua

邓小平为"明华"轮题词
Deng Xiaoping wrote "The Sea World" for Ming Hua Ship

On April 7, 1973, the ship was sold and delivered to China in Malta, and then renamed as Ming Hua. Thereafter, it had mainly sailed between China and

Tanzania. In June 1978, the ship was sent by the State Council of the People's Republic of China to pick up some overseas Chinese in Vietnam back to China. In May 1979, the Sino-Japanese Friendship Delegation led by Mr. Liao Chengzhi, the Vice-Chairman of the Standing Committee of the National People's Congress, took the ship to visit Japan. On August 27, 1983, it was transferred from Guangzhou Ocean Shipping Co., Ltd to China Merchants in Shekou of Shenzhen. China Merchants converted it into China's first ocean-style boat hotel, which has been operated by Shenzhen Shekou Sea World Hotel Management Co., Ltd. On January 1, 1984, Mr. Deng Xiaoping, Mr. Wang Zhen, Mr. Yang Shangkun and their wives paid a visit to the ship. Mr. Deng handwrote an inscription for it: "Sea World".

多年以来,"海上世界""明华"轮酒店以独特的风格为中外游客提供了热情友好的接待服务,成为深圳市旅游文化的靓丽风景线。

Over the years, the "Sea World" cruise hotel has become a tourism and cultural landmark of Shenzhen, attracting numerous domestic and overseas visitors with its exotic style and warm hospitality.

明谊 Calumet

"明谊"轮,英文船名 Calumet,灵便型散货船,船长 163.09 米,船宽 23.8 米,吃水 9.4 米,载重吨 22536,主机功率 7388 千瓦,航速每小时 12.5 海里。

Calumet is a handysize bulk carrier. Its length overall is 163.09 meters and the beam is 23.8 meters with a draught of 9.4 meters. With its main engine power at 7,388 kilowatts, it could sail at a speed of 12.5 kn and has a dead weight tonnage of 22,536 tons.

明谊 Calumet

"明谊"轮由日本幸阳造船厂建造,1971 年 11 月出厂。招商局 1988 年 6 月 17 日签约购进,在直布罗陀港接船。香港明华船务有限公司负责管理经营。1993 年 9 月 15 日在上海宝山锚地交船,出售给汕头广澳海湾发展公司。

Built by Japan Koyo Dockyard Co., Ltd and completed in November, 1971, the carrier was bought by China Merchants on June 17, 1988 and delivered at the Port of Gibraltar. Since then it had been operated by

Hong Kong Ming Wah Shipping Company Co., Ltd. On September 15, 1993, the ship was sold to Shantou Special Economic Zone Guang'ao Port Development Company and delivered in the anchorage off Baoshan, Shanghai.

⚓ 明辉 Pacific Brilliance

"明辉"轮英文船名 Pacific Brilliance，大灵便型散货船，船长 229.29 米，吃水 13.5 米，船宽 32.94 米，载重吨 63894，主机功率 11343 千瓦，航速每小时 15 海里。

Pacific Brilliance is a handymax bulk carrier. Its length overall is 229.29 meters and the beam is 32.94 meters with a draught of 13.5 meters. With its main engine power at 11,343 kilowatts, it could sail at a speed of 15 kn and has a dead weight tonnage of 63,894 tons.

"明辉"轮由日本常石造船厂建造，1981 年 5 月出厂。原名 Pacific Pride，挂香港船旗。招商局 1988 年 6 月 20 日购进，于上海港接船，香港明华船务有限公司管理经营，更改为现名，注册利比里亚船籍。1990 年 4 月 6 日出售给希腊买家，在香港交船。

Built by Japan Tsuneishi Shipbuilding Co., Ltd and completed in May, 1981, the carrier was originally named as Pacific Pride and hung the flag of Hong Kong. After being bought by and delivered at Shanghai Port to China Merchants on June 20, 1988, it was changed to the current name with Libya as its flag state and had been operated by Hong Kong Ming Wah Shipping Co., Ltd. On April 6, 1990, the ship was sold to a Greece owner and delivered in Hong Kong.

明辉 Pacific Brilliance

明贝　Conch

⚓ 明贝　Conch

"明贝"轮，英文船名 Conch，灵便型散货船，船长 163 米，船宽 23 米，吃水 9.4 米，载重吨 11542，主机功率 7388 千瓦，航速每小时 12.5 海里。

Conch is a handysize bulk carrier. Its length overall is 163 meters and the beam is 23 meters with a draught of 9.4 meters. With its main engine power at 7,388 kilowatts, it could sail at a speed of 12.5 kn and has a dead weight tonnage of 11,542 tons.

"明贝"轮由日本幸阳造船厂制造，1971 年 5 月出厂。原名 Paschalis，船旗国塞浦路斯，船籍港利马索尔。招商局 1988 年 8 月 3 日购进该轮，于意大利港接船，更改为现名。香港明华船务有限公司管理经营。1991 年 11 月 1 日出售给韩国买家并交船。

Built by Japan Koyo Dockyard Co., Ltd and completed in May, 1971, the carrier was originally known as Paschalis and registered in Limassol Port of Cyprus. After being bought by and delivered at an Italian port to China Merchants on August 3, 1988, it was changed to its current name and had been operated by Hong Kong Ming Wah Shipping Co., Ltd. On November 1, 1991, the ship was sold and delivered to a Republic of Korea buyer.

⚓ 明智 Pacific Wisdom

"明智"轮，英文船名 Pacific Wisdom，巴拿马型散货船，船长 224.5 米，吃水 13.5 米，船宽 32.21 米，载重吨 63988，主机功率 11184 千瓦，航速每小时 15.1 海里。

Pacific Wisdom is a Panamax bulk carrier. Its length overall is 224.5 meters and the beam is 32.21 meters with a draught of 13.5 meters. With its main engine power at 11,184 kilowatts, it could sail at a speed of 15.1 kn and has a dead weight tonnage of 63,988 tons.

"明智"轮由日本舞鹤造船厂于 1981 年 3 月建造完工出厂。原名 Pacific Prestige。招商局 1988 年 9 月 1 日购入，在天津新港接船，改为现名。香港明华船务有限公司负责管理经营。1989 年 1 月 4 日出售给希腊买家，在美国港口交船。

Built by Japan Maizuru Shipyard and completed in March, 1981, the ship was originally named as Pacific Prestige. After being bought by and delivered at the Xingang Port of Tianjin to China Merchants on September 1, 1988, it was changed to its current name and had been operated by Hong Kong Ming Wah Shipping Co., Ltd. On January 4, 1989, the ship was sold to a Greece buyer and delivered at an American port.

⚓ 明锋 Pacific Pioneer

"明锋"轮，英文船名 Pacific Pioneer，巴拿马型散货船，船长 225.93 米，船宽 32.81 米，吃水 13.5 米，载重吨 63894，主机功率 11176 千瓦，航速每小时 15.1 海里。

Pacific Pioneer is a Panamax bulk carrier. Its length overall is 225.93 meters and the beam is 32.81 meters with a draught of 13.5 meters. With its main engine power at 11,176 kilowatts, it could sail at a speed of 15.1 kn and has a dead weight tonnage of 63,894 tons.

"明锋"轮由日本日立造船厂于 1982 年 6 月建造竣工出厂。原名 Pacific Prominence。招商局 1988 年 10 月 7 日购进，在秦皇岛港接船，更改为现名，由香港明华船务有限公司管理经营。1989 年 2 月 22 日出售给希腊买家，在日本港交船。

Built by Japan Hitachi Zosen Corporation and completed in June, 1982, the ship was originally named as Pacific Prominence. After being bought by and delivered at the Qinhuangdao Port to China Merchants on October 7, 1988, it was changed to its current name and had been operated by Hong Kong Ming Wah Shipping Co., Ltd. On February 22, 1989, the ship was sold to a Greece buyer and delivered at a Japanese port.

明富 Pacific Source

"明富"轮,英文船名 Pacific Source,大灵便型散货船,船长 185.84 米,船宽 30.4 米,吃水 11.32 米,载重吨 43479,主机功率 7119 千瓦,航速每小时 13.5 海里。

Pacific Source is a handymax bulk carrier. Its length overall is 185.84 meters and the beam is 30.4 meters with a draught of 11.32 meters. With its main engine power at 7,119 kilowatts, it could sail at a speed of 13.5 kn and has a dead weight tonnage of 43,479 tons.

明富 Pacific Source

该船由日本常石造船厂建造,1985 年 7 月出厂,1988 年 11 月 28 日签约购进,香港明华船务有限公司经营管理。1993 年 7 月 17 日出售给美国 PLM 投资公司,在印度尼西亚 Banjar-Masin 港交船。

Built by Japan Tsuneishi Shipbuilding Co., Ltd and completed in July 1985, the carrier was bought by China Merchants on November 28, 1988 and had thereafter been operated by Hong Kong Ming Wah Shipping Co., Ltd. On July 17, 1993, the ship was sold to the U.S. PLM Investment Company and delivered at the Port of Banjar-Masin in Indonesia.

明珠 Ming Zhu

"明珠"轮英文船名 Ming Zhu,灵便型散货船,船长 177.79 米,吃水 12 米,船宽 27.65 米,载重吨 41052,主机功率 10448 千瓦,航速每小时 13 海里。

Ming Zhu is a handysize bulk carrier. Its length overall is 177.79 meters and the beam is 27.65 meters with a draught of 12 meters. With its main engine power at 10,448 kilowatts, it could sail at a speed of 13 kn and has a dead weight tonnage of 41,052 tons.

该船由日本大阪造船厂建造,1976 年 1 月出厂,"明珠"轮原名 Petra,船旗国希腊,船籍港比雷埃夫斯。1989 年 3 月 21 日购进,改挂中国船旗,船籍港深圳。后又改为巴拿马船旗。香港明华船务有限公司经营管理。1992 年 1 月 30 日出售给土耳其买家,在沙特阿拉伯港交船。

Built by an Osaka shipyard of Japan and completed in January 1976, the ship was originally named as

Petra and registered in the Piraeus Port of Greek. After being bought by China Merchants on March 21, 1989, it began to hang Chinese national flag with Shenzhen Port as its port of registry and had been operated by Hong Kong Ming Wah Shipping Co., Ltd. Later its flag was changed into Panama. On January 30, 1992, the carrier was sold to a Turkish buyer and got delivered at a port of Saudi Arabia.

明锋　Pacific Pioneer

"明锋"轮，英文船名 Pacific Pioneer，大灵便型散货船，船长 180 米，船宽 30.5 米，吃水 11.23 米，载重吨 41971，主机功率 5373 千瓦，航速每小时 14 海里。

Pacific Pioneer is a handymax bulk carrier. Its length overall is 180 meters and the beam is 30.5 meters with a draught of 11.23 meters. With its main engine power at 5,373 kilowatts, it could sail at a speed of 14 kn and has a dead weight tonnage of 41,971 tons.

该船由日本大岛造船厂建造，1992 年 1 月 13 日出厂，该轮与 1988 年 10 月 7 日入局的一艘船名字重复。该轮由香港明华船务有限公司管理经营，穿行于国际航线上，运输干散货。

Built by Japan Oshima Shipbuilding Co., Ltd and completed on January 13, 1992, the carrier has been operated by Hong Kong Ming Wah Shipping Co., Ltd, transporting dry bulk cargo on international shipping lanes. It has the same English name with another ship China Merchants bought on October 7, 1988.

明锋　Pacific Pioneer

明智　Pacific Wisdom

⚓ 明智　Pacific Wisdom

"明智"轮，英文船名 Pacific Wisdom，大灵便型散货船，船长 180 米，船宽 30.5 米，吃水 11.23 米，载重吨 42010，主机功率 5373 千瓦，航速每小时 14 海里。

Pacific Wisdom is a handysize bulk carrier. Its length overall is 180 meters and the beam is 30.5 meters with a draught of 11.23 meters. With its main engine power at 5,373 kilowatts, it could sail at a speed of 14 kn and has a dead weight tonnage of 42,010 tons.

该船由日本大岛造船厂建造，1992 年 5 月 20 日出厂，"明智"轮由香港明华船务有限公司管理，航行于全球运输干散货。该轮与 1988 年 9 月 1 日入局的一艘散货船名字重复。

Built by Japan Oshima Shipbuilding Co., Ltd and completed on May 20, 1992, the carrier has been operated by Hong Kong Ming Wah Shipping Co., Ltd, transporting dry bulk cargo around the globe. Its English name is the same with another bulk carrier bought by China Merchants on September 1, 1988.

⚓ 明勤　Pacific Endeavor

"明勤"轮英文船名 Pacific Endeavor，大灵便型散货船，船长 184.99 米，船宽 30.5 米，吃水 11.25 米，载重吨 43366，主机功率 6060 千瓦，航速每小时 15.5 海里。

Pacific Endeavor is a handymax bulk carrier. Its length overall is 184.99 meters and the beam is 30.5 meters with a draught of 11.25 meters. With its main engine power at 6,060 kilowatts, it could sail at a speed of 15.5 kn and has a dead weight tonnage of 43,366 tons.

"明勤"轮由日本大岛造船厂建造，1992 年 9 月 18 日出厂。香港明华船务有限公司管理经营，从事散货运输，穿行于国际航线。1998 年度被船舶管理公司评为先进船舶。

Built by Japan Oshima Shipbuilding Co., Ltd and completed on September 18, 1992, the carrier has been operated by Hong Kong Ming Wah Shipping Co., Ltd, transporting bulk cargo on international shipping lanes. It was awarded as "Outstanding Vessel" by the operator in 1998.

明奋　Pacific Vigorous

⚓ 明奋　Pacific Vigorous

"明奋"轮英文船名 Pacific Vigorous，大灵便型散货船，船长 184.99 米，船宽 30.5 米，吃水 11.25 米，载重吨 43354，主机功率 6060 千瓦，航速每小时 15.5 海里。

Pacific Vigorous is a handymax bulk carrier. Its length overall is 184.99 meters and the beam is 30.5 meters with a draught of 11.25 meters. With its main engine power at 6,060 kilowatts, it could sail at a speed of 15.5 kn and has a dead weight tonnage of 43,354 tons.

"明奋"由日本大岛造船厂建造，1993 年 2 月 9 日出厂，"明奋"轮主要在国际航线上运输干散货，由香港明华船务有限公司管理经营。2004 年度和 2005 年度被船舶管理公司评为先进船舶。

Built by Japan Oshima Shipbuilding Co.,Ltd and completed on February 9, 1993, the carrier has been operated by Hong Kong Ming Wah Shipping Co., Ltd, mainly transporting dry bulk cargo around the world. It was awarded by the operator as "Outstanding Vessel" successively in 2004 and 2005.

明业 Pacific Career

"明业"轮英文船名 Pacific Career，大灵便型散货船，船长 184.99 米，船宽 30.5 米，吃水 11.25 米，载重吨 43415，主机功率 6060 千瓦，航速每小时 15.5 海里。

Pacific Career is a handymax bulk carrier. Its length overall is 184.99 meters and the beam is 30.5 meters with a draught of 11.25 meters. With its main engine power at 6,060 kilowatts, it could sail at a speed of 15.5 kn and has a dead weight tonnage of 43,415 tons.

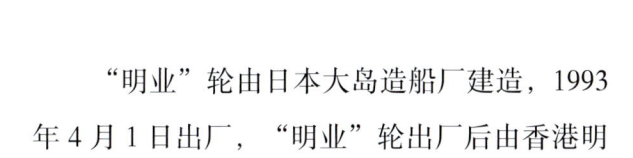

"明业"轮过亚丁湾，驾驶员正在进行防海盗瞭望。
Pacific Career in the Gulf of Aden, the pilot on high alert to pirates

"明业"轮由日本大岛造船厂建造，1993年4月1日出厂，"明业"轮出厂后由香港明华船务有限公司经营管理。该轮 2002 年度被船舶管理公司评为先进船舶。

Built by Japan Oshima Shipbuilding Co., Ltd, the carrier has been operated by Hong Kong Ming Wah Shipping Co., Ltd since completed on April 1, 1993. In 2002, it was awarded by the operator as "Outstanding Vessel".

明神 Pacific Embolden

"明神"轮英文船名 Pacific Embolden，大灵便型散货船，船长 184.99 米，船宽 30.5 米，吃水 11.25 米，载重吨 43396，主机功率 6060 千瓦，航速每小时 14 海里。

Pacific Embolden is a handymax bulk carrier. Its length overall is 184.99 meters and the beam is 30.5 meters with a draught of 11.25 meters. With its main engine power at 6,060 kilowatts, it could sail at a speed of 14 kn and has a dead weight tonnage of 43,396 tons.

"明神"轮由日本大岛造船厂建造，1993 年 5 月 14 日出厂，该轮由香港明华船务有限公司负责经营管理，航行于全球港口，运输干散货。

Built by Japan Oshima Shipbuilding Co., Ltd and completed on May 14, 1993, the ship has been operated by Hong Kong Ming Wah Shipping Co., Ltd, transporting dry bulk cargo around the world.

明神 Pacific Embolden

明兴 Pacific Prospect

⚓ 明兴 Pacific Prospect

"明兴"轮英文船名 Pacific Prospect，巴拿马型散货船，船长 225 米，船宽 32.26 米，吃水 13.87 米，载重吨 73630，主机功率 8261 千瓦，航速每小时 14.5 海里。

Pacific Prospect is a Panamax bulk carrier. Its length overall is 225 meters and the beam is 32.26 meters with a draught of 13.87 meters. With its main engine power at 8,261 kilowatts, it could sail at a speed of 14.5 kn and has a dead weight tonnage of 73,630 tons.

"明兴"轮由日本大岛造船厂建造，1993 年 7 月 1 日出厂。"明兴"轮运营于国际航线，运输干散货。香港明华船务有限公司实施管理经营。该轮 2004 年度被船舶管理公司评为先进船舶。

Built by Japan Oshima Shipbuilding Co.,Ltd and completed on July 1, 1993, the carrier has been operated by Hong Kong Ming Wah Shipping Co., Ltd, transporting dry bulk cargo around the globe. It was awarded by the operator as "Outstanding Vessel" in 2004.

明爱　Pacific Paradise

明爱　Pacific Paradise

"明爱"轮英文船名 Pacific Paradise，巴拿马型散货船，船长 225 米，船宽 32.26 米，吃水 13.87 米，载重吨 73645，主机功率 8261 千瓦，航速每小时 14.5 海里。

Pacific Paradise is a Panamax bulk carrier. Its length overall is 225 meters and the beam is 32.26 meters with a draught of 13.87 meters. With its main engine power at 8,261 kilowatts, it could sail at a speed of 14.5 kn and has dead weight tonnage of 73,645 tons.

"明爱"轮由日本大岛造船厂建造，1993 年 9 月 1 日出厂。"明爱"轮出厂后隶属于香港明华船务有限公司管理经营，航行于全球各港运输干散货。2003 年度和 2004 年度被船舶管理公司评为先进船舶。

Built by Japan Oshima Shipbuilding Co., Ltd, the carrier has been operated by Hong Kong Ming Wah Shipping Co., Ltd. since completed on September 1, 1993, transporting dry bulk cargo around the world. It was awarded by the operator as "Outstanding Vessel" successively in 2003 and 2004.

明繁 Pacific Acadian

"明繁"轮英文船名Pacific Acadian，大灵便型散货船，船长189.99米，船宽32.2米，吃水11.73米，载重吨49052，主机功率6851千瓦，航速每小时15.5海里。

Pacific Acadian is a handymax bulk carrier. Its length overall is 189.99 meters and the beam is 32.2 meters with a draught of 11.73 meters. With its main engine power at 6,851 kilowatts, it could sail at a speed of 15.5 kn and has a dead weight tonnage of 49,052 tons.

"明繁"轮船员庆祝"公司日"
The Crew of Pacific Acadian celebrating the "Company Day"

"明繁"轮由日本大岛造船厂建造，1995年9月29日出厂。"明繁"轮营运于国际航线，运输干散货，由香港明华船务有限公司管理经营。2002年度被船舶管理公司评为先进船舶。2013年度被招商局能源运输股份有限公司评为先进船舶。

Built by Japan Oshima Shipbuilding Co.,Ltd and completed on September 29, 1995, the carrier has been operated by Hong Kong Ming Wah Shipping Co., Ltd., transporting dry bulk cargo around the world. It was awarded as "Outstanding Vessel" respectively by the operator in 2002 and by China Merchants Energy Shipping Co., Ltd. in 2013.

明繁 Pacific Acadian

明荣 Pacific Dolphin

"明荣"轮英文船名 Pacific Dolphin，大灵便型散货船，船长 189.99 米，船宽 32.2 米，吃水 11.73 米，载重吨 49047，主机功率 6851 千瓦，航速每小时 15.5 海里。

Pacific Dolphin is a handymax bulk carrier. Its length overall is 189.99 meters and the beam is 32.2 meters with a draught of 11.73 meters. With its main engine power at 6,851 kilowatts, it could sail at a speed of 15.5 kn and has a dead weight tonnage of 49,047 tons.

"明荣"轮由日本大岛造船厂建造，1996 年 4 月 23 日出厂，"明荣"轮由香港明华船务有限公司经营管理，穿行于国际航线运输干散货。1999 年度、2000 年度、2001 年度连续三年被船舶管理公司评为先进船舶，受到表彰。

Built by Japan Oshima Shipbuilding Co., Ltd and completed on April 23, 1996, the carrier has been operated by Hong Kong Ming Wah Shipping Co., Ltd., transporting dry bulk cargo around the world. It was awarded by the operator as "Outstanding Vessel" for three successive years in 1999, 2000 and 2001.

明荣 Pacific Dolphin

明昌　Pacific Emerald

⚓ 明昌　Pacific Emerald

"明昌"轮英文船名 Pacific Emerald，大灵便型散货船，船长 189.99 米，船宽 32.2 米，吃水 11.73 米，载重吨 49016，主机功率 6851 千瓦，航速每小时 15.5 海里。

Pacific Emerald is a handymax bulk carrier. Its length overall is 189.99 meters and the beam is 32.2 meters with a draught of 11.73 meters. With its main engine power at 6,851 kilowatts, it could sail at a speed of 15.5 kn and has a dead weight tonnage of 49,016 tons.

"明昌"轮由日本大岛造船厂建造，1996 年 6 月 28 日出厂。由香港明华船务有限公司管理经营，运输干散货于国际航线上。

Built by Japan Oshima Shipbuilding Co., Ltd and completed on June 28, 1996, the carrier has been operated by Hong Kong Ming Wah Shipping Co., Ltd., transporting dry bulk cargo on international shipping lanes.

"明昌"轮船员庆祝"公司日"
The crew from Pacific Emerald celebrating the "Company Day"

明盛 Pacific Mercury

⚓ 明盛 Pacific Mercury

"明盛"轮英文船名 Pacific Mercury，大灵便型散货船，船长 189.99 米，船宽 32.2 米，吃水 11.73 米，载重吨 49016，主机功率 6851 千瓦，航速每小时 15.5 海里。

Pacific Mercury is a handymax bulk carrier. Its length overall is 189.99 meters and the beam is 32.2 meters with a draught of 11.73 meters. With its main engine power at 6,851 kilowatts, it could sail at a speed of 15.5 kn and has a dead weight tonnage of 49,016 tons.

"明盛"轮庆祝"公司日"开展拔河活动
Tug of War held on Pacific Mercury to celebrate the "Company Day"

"明盛"轮由日本大岛造船厂建造，1996 年 7 月 31 日出厂，该轮由香港明华船务有限公司管理经营，在国际航线上运输干散货。2001 年度被船舶管理公司评为先进船舶。

Built by Japan Oshima Shipbuilding Co., Ltd and completed on July 31, 1996, the carrier has been operated by Hong Kong Ming Wah Shipping Co., Ltd., transporting dry bulk cargo on international shipping lanes. It was awarded by the operator as "Outstanding Vessel" in 2001.

明达 Pacific Scorpio

"明达"轮英文船名 Pacific Scorpio，大灵便型散货船，船长 189.99 米，船宽 32.2 米，吃水 11.73 米，载重吨 49052，主机功率 6851 千瓦，航速每小时 15.5 海里。

Pacific Scorpio is a handymax bulk carrier. Its length overall is 189.99 meters and the beam is 32.2 meters with a draught of 11.73 meters. With its main engine power at 6,851 kilowatts, it could sail at a speed of 15.5 kn and has a dead weight tonnage of 49,052 tons.

"明达"轮驾驶员正在进行模拟器培训
The Pilot of Pacific Scorpio on simulator training

"明达"轮由日本大岛造船厂建造，1997 年 1 月 9 日出厂，该轮属于国际航线营运干散货的船舶，由香港明华船务有限公司管理经营。2012 年度被招商局能源运输股份有限公司评为先进船舶。

Built by Japan Oshima Shipbuilding Co.,Ltd and completed on January 9, 1997, the carrier has been operated by Hong Kong Ming Wah Shipping Co., Ltd., transporting dry bulk cargo around the world. It was awarded by China Merchants Energy Shipping Co., Ltd. as "Outstanding Vessel" in 2012.

明达 Pacific Scorpio

⚓ 明发　Pacific Primate

"明发"轮英文船名 Pacific Primate，大灵便型散货船，船长 189.99 米，船宽 32.2 米，吃水 11.73 米，载重吨 49016，主机功率 6851 千瓦，航速每小时 15.5 海里。

Pacific Primate is a handymax bulk carrier. Its length overall is 189.99 meters and the beam is 32.2 meters with a draught of 11.73 meters. With its main engine power at 6,851 kilowatts, it could sail at a speed of 15.5 kn and has a dead weight tonnage of 49,016 tons.

明发　Pacific Primate

"明发"轮由日本大岛造船厂建造，1997 年 1 月 28 日出厂，该轮从事远洋干散货运输，香港明华船务有限公司管理经营。

Built by Japan Oshima Shipbuilding Co., Ltd and completed on January 28, 1997, the carrier has been operated by Hong Kong Ming Wah Shipping Co., Ltd., transporting dry bulk cargo on the ocean.

⚓ 凯誉　New Renown

"凯誉"轮英文船名 New Renown，超大型油轮（VLCC），船长 325.36 米，吃水 20.63 米，船宽 49.04 米，载重吨 240830，主机功率 23880 千瓦，航速每小时 15.9 海里。

New Renown is a Very Large Crude Carrier (VLCC). Its length overall is 325.36 meters and the beam is 49.04 meters with a draught of 20.63 meters. With its main engine

凯誉　New Renown

power at 23,880 kilowatts, it could sail at a speed of 15.9 kn and has a dead weight tonnage of 240,830 tons.

"凯誉"轮是德国德意志造船厂 1976 年 2 月建造完工出厂的。原名 Energy Renown。招商局 1988 年 8 月 4 日购进，海宏轮船（香港）有限公司负责管理经营。2003 年 6 月 16 日在新会港锚地出售交船。

Built by Germany Deutsche Shipyard Werke and completed in February 1976, the carrier was originally named as Energy Renown. It was bought by China Merchants on August 4, 1988 and had thereafter been operated by Associated Maritime Company (Hong Kong) Limited. On June 16, 2003, the ship was sold and delivered to another owner in an anchorage off the Xinhui Port.

⚓ 凯达　New Explorer

"凯达"轮，英文船名 New Explorer，超大型油轮（VLCC），船长 373.52 米，船宽 64 米，吃水 22.93 米，载重吨 390038，主机功率 33600 千瓦，航速每小时 15.1 海里。

New Explorer is a Very Large Crude Carrier (VLCC). Its length overall is 373.52 meters and the beam is 64 meters with a draught of 22.93 meters. With its main engine power at 33,600 kilowatts, it could sail at a speed of 15.1 kn and has a dead weight tonnage of 390,038 tons.

凯达　New Explorer

"凯达"轮由日本常石造船厂建造，1976年7月出厂。原名 Energy Explorer。招商局 1988年8月26日购进，海宏轮船（香港）有限公司负责经营管理。

Built by Japan Tsuneishi Shipbuilding Co., Ltd and completed in July 1976, the carrier was originally named as Energy Explorer. It was bought by China Merchants on August 26, 1988 and had thereafter been operated by Associated Maritime Company (Hong Kong) Limited.

"凯达"轮是我国国有企业拥有的第一艘超大型油轮，航行于国际航线运输原油。后来，"凯达"轮租给印度尼西亚 Pertamina 公司作为储油轮。1999年5月10日出售给德国买家，在新加坡交船。

The carrier was the first VLCC owned by a Chinese state-owned company, and had been transporting crude oil on international lines. Later, it was rent to Indonesia's Pertamina to be used for crude storage, and then sold and delivered to a German buyer in Singapore on May 10, 1999.

⚓ 凯荣　New Prosperity

"凯荣"，英文船名 New Prosperity，超大型油轮，船长333.99米，船宽55.05米，吃水20.44米，载重吨271967，主机功率26900千瓦，航速每小时14海里。

New Prosperity is a Very Large Crude Carrier (VLCC). Its length overall is 333.99 meters and the beam is 55.05 meters with a draught of 20.44 meters. With its main engine power at 26,900 kilowatts, it could sail at a speed of 14 kn and has a dead weight tonnage of 271,967 tons.

该船由西班牙造船厂建造，1981年3月出厂，1989年10月26日购进接船。原名 Golar Liz，后来改现名。海宏轮船（香港）有限公司经营管理。1999年7月24日出售给欧洲买家并交船。

Built by a Spanish shipyard and completed in March 1981, the carrier was originally named as Golar Liz. It changed to its current name after being bought by China Merchants on October 26, 1989, and had been operated by Associated Maritime Company (Hong Kong) Limited. On July 24, 1999, the ship was sold and delivered to an European buyer.

凯荣　New Prosperity

凯舟　New Argosy

⚓ 凯舟　New Argosy

"凯舟"轮英文船名 New Argosy，阿芙拉型油轮，船长 243.8 米，船宽 40 米，吃水 13.12 米，载重吨 88782，主机功率 10450 千瓦，航速每小时 14 海里。

New Argosy is an Aframax oil tanker. Its length overall is 243.8 meters and the beam is 40 meters with a draught of 13.12 meters. With its main engine power at 10,450 kilowatts, it could sail at a speed of 14 kn and has a dead weight tonnage of 88,782 tons.

该船由日本川崎造船厂建造，1987 年 3 月出厂，该轮原名 Atlantic Argosy，1990 年 3 月 8 日购进，改为现船名。"凯舟"轮此张照片为澳大利亚人所摄，悉尼邮政部门将其制成明信片发行。2009 年 12 月 30 日出售，在新加坡交船。

Built by Japan Kawasaki Dockyard and completed in March 1987, the tanker was originally named as Atlantic Argosy. It was bought by China Merchants on March 8, 1990 and then changed to the current name. Its photography above was taken by an Australian and had been made into a postcard by the Sydney postal office. The ship was sold and delivered to another buyer in Singapore on December 30, 2009.

凯仪 New Ace

"凯仪"轮,英文船名 New Ace,阿芙拉型油轮,船长 243.8 米,船宽 40.03 米,吃水 13.12 米,载重吨 88878,主机功率 10450 千瓦,航速每小时 14 海里。

New Ace is an Aframax oil tanker. Its length overall is 243.8 meters and the beam is 40.03 meters with a draught of 13.12 meters. With its main engine power at 10,450 kilowatts, it could sail at a speed of 14 kn and has a dead weight tonnage of 88,878 tons.

凯仪 New Ace

该船由日本幸阳造船厂建造,1987 年 3 月出厂,该轮原名 Atlantic Ace,1990 年 3 月 20 日购进,改为现名。2010 年 2 月 8 日出售交船。

Built by Japan Koyo Dockyard Co., Ltd and completed in March 1987, the tanker was originally named as Atlantic Ace. It was bought by China Merchants on March 20, 1990 and then changed to the current name. The ship was sold on February 8, 2010.

凯珠 New Amber

"凯珠"轮英文船名 New Amber,阿芙拉型油轮,船长 243.84 米,船宽 40 米,吃水 13.12 米,载重吨 89558,主机功率 10450 千瓦,航速每小时 14 海里。

New Amber is an Aframax oil tanker. Its length overall is 243.84 meters and

凯珠 New Amber

the beam is 40 meters with a draught of 13.12 meters. With its main engine power at 10,450 kilowatts, it could sail at a speed of 14 kn and has a dead weight tonnage of 89,558 tons.

该船由日本川崎造船厂建造，1987年1月20日出厂，该轮原名Sidelia，1990年3月22日购进，改为现名。由海宏轮船（香港）有限公司经营管理。2008年3月14日出售交船。

Built by Japan Kawasaki Dockyard and completed on January 20, 1987, the tanker was originally named as Sidelia. It was changed to its current name after being bought by China Merchants on March 22, 1990, and had been operated by Associated Maritime Company (Hong Kong) Limited. On March 14, 2008, the ship was sold and delivered to another buyer.

⚓ 凯志 New Ambition

"凯志"轮，英文船名New Ambition，阿芙拉型油轮，船长243.8米，船宽40米，吃水13.12米，载重吨88761，主机功率10500千瓦，航速每小时14海里。

New Ambition is an Aframax oil tanker. Its length overall is 243.8 meters and the beam is 40 meters with a draught of 13.12 meters. With its main engine power at 10,500 kilowatts, it could sail at a speed of 14 kn and has a dead weight tonnage of 88,761 tons.

该船由日本幸阳造船厂建造，1987年3月25日出厂，该轮原名Ambition，1990年3月27日购进，改为现名。由海宏轮船（香港）有限公司管理经营。2009年9月3日出售交船。

Built by Japan Koyo Dockyard Co., Ltd and completed on March 25, 1987, the tanker was originally known as Ambition. It was changed to the current name after being bought by China Merchants on March 27, 1990, and had been operated by Associated Maritime Company (Hong Kong) Limited. On September 3, 2009, the ship was sold and delivered to another buyer.

• 凯志 New Ambition

⚓ 凯安 New Assurance

"凯安"轮英文船名 New Assurance，阿芙拉型油轮，船长 243.84 米，船宽 40 米，吃水 13.12 米，载重吨 89618，主机功率 10450 千瓦，航速每小时 14 海里。

New Assurance is an Aframax oil tanker. Its length overall is 243.84 meters and the beam is 40 meters with a draught of 13.12 meters. With its main engine power at 10,450 kilowatts, it could sail at a speed of 14 kn and has a dead weight tonnage of 89,618 tons.

凯安 New Assurance

该船由日本川崎造船厂建造，1987 年 2 月出厂，该轮原名 Atlantic Assurance，1990 年 4 月 13 日购进，改为现名。由海宏轮船（香港）有限公司经营管理。2008 年 5 月 15 日出售交船。

Built by Japan Kawasaki Dockyard and completed in February 1987, the tanker was originally known as Atlantic Assurance. It was changed to the current name after being bought by China Merchants on April 13, 1990, and had been operated by Associated Maritime Company (Hong Kong) Limited. On May 15, 2008, the ship was sold and delivered to another buyer.

⚓ 凯恩 Gadia Ayu

"凯恩"轮英文船名 Gadis Ayu，灵便型油轮，船长 175.43 米，船宽 30 米，吃水 11.17 米，载重吨 37623，主机功率 7690 千瓦，航速每小时 14.5 海里。

Gadia Ayu is a handysize tanker. Its length overall is 175.43 meters and the beam is 30 meters with a draught of 11.17 meters. With its main engine power at 7,690 kilowatts, it could sail at a speed of 14.5 kn and has a dead weight tonnage of 37,623 tons.

该船由日本山口造船厂建造，1987 年 6 月出厂，该轮曾用名 Atlantic Charisma。1990 年 5 月 1 日购进。2000 年 3 月 17 日售出交船。

Built by Yamaguchi Dockyard of Japan and completed in June 1987, the tanker was originally named as Atlantic Charisma. It was bought by China Merchants on May 1, 1990, and was sold and delivered on March 17, 2000.

⚓ 凯业 New Venture

"凯业"轮，英文船名 New Venture，超大型油轮，船长328米，船宽57米，吃水21.63米，载重吨285699，主机功率16388千瓦，航速每小时14海里。

New Venture is a Very Large Crude Carrier (VLCC). Its length overall is 328 meters and the beam is 57 meters with a draught of 21.63 meters. With its main engine power at 16,388 kitowatts, it could sail at a speed of 14 kn and has a dead weight tonnage of 285,699 tons.

该船由日本日立造船厂建造，1992年1月8日出厂，由海宏轮船（香港）有限公司经营管理，航行于全球航线运输原油。2009年10月4日在山海关船厂完成了单壳改双壳的工程。2014年2月17日在广东江门港出售并交船。

Built by Hitachi Zosen Corporation of Japan and completed on August 1, 1992, the carrier was managed by Associated Maritime Company (Hong Kong) Limited, and used to sail international sea routes for crude oil transportation. It was changed into double-hulled tanker in Shanhaiguan Shipbuilding Heavy Industry Co., Ltd on October 4, 2009, and was sold and delivered at Jiangmen port in Guangdong on February 17, 2014.

凯福 New Fortuner

"凯福"轮英文船名 New Fortuner，苏伊士型油轮，船长 277 米，船宽 44.4 米，吃水 16.9 米，载重吨 146591，主机功率 11164 千瓦，航速每小时 14 海里。

New Fortuner is a Suezmax tanker. Its length overall is 277 meters and the beam is 44.4 meters with a draught of 16.9 meters. With its main engine power at 11,164 kilowatts, it could sail at a speed of 14 kn and has a dead weight tonnage of 146,591 tons.

凯福 New Fortune

该船由日本川崎造船厂建造，1992 年 1 月 10 日出厂，投入营运后一直由海宏轮船（香港）有限公司管理。2009 年 1 月 10 日在招商局蛇口友联船厂完成了单壳改双壳的工程。2013 年 9 月 27 日，在广东新会港出售交船。

Built by Kawasaki Dockyard in Japan on January 10, 1992, the tanker was managed by Associated Maritime Company (Hong Kong) Limited for operation. On January 10, 2009, it was changed into a double-hulled tanker, and was sold and delivered at Xinhui port in Guangdong on September 27, 2013.

凯勇 New Valor

"凯勇"轮，英文船名 New Valor，超大型油轮，船长 328.04 米，船宽 57 米，吃水 21.63 米，载重吨 284631，主机功率 15380 千瓦，航速每小时 14 海里。

New Valor is a Very Large Crude Carrier (VLCC). Its length overall is 328.04 meters and the beam is 57 meters with a draught of

凯勇 New Valor

21.63 meters. With its main engine power at 15,380 kilowatts, it could sail at a speed of 14 kn and has a dead weight tonnage of 284,631 tons.

该船由日本日立造船厂建造，1992年6月30日出厂，由海宏轮船（香港）有限公司管理，航行于国际航线运输原油。2008年1月1日在山海关船厂完成了单壳改双壳的工程。2012年度被招商局能源运输股份有限公司评为先进船舶。

Built by Hitachi Zosen Corporation and completed on June 30, 1992, the carrier was managed by Associated Maritime Company (Hong Kong) Limited and used to sail on international sea routes for crude oil transportation. It was changed into a double-hulled tanker in Shanhaiguan Shipbuilding Heavy Industry Co., Ltd. on January 1, 2008, and was rewarded as "Outstanding Vessel" by China Merchants Energy Shipping Co., Ltd. in 2012.

凯旋 New Victory

"凯旋"轮英文船名 New Victory，超大型油轮，船长328.05米，船宽57米，吃水21.63米，舱容333835立方米，载重吨285733，主机功率16388千瓦，航速每小时14海里。

New Victory is a Very Large Crude Carrier (VLCC). Its length overall is 328.05 meters and the beam is 57 meters with a draught of 21.63 meters. It measures a capacity of 333,835 cubic meters and a dead weight tonnage of 285,733 tons. With its main engine power at 16,388 kilowatts, it could sail at a speed of 14 kn.

"凯旋"轮由日本日立造船厂建造，1993年3月30日出厂，出厂后由海宏轮船（香港）有限公司管理营运。2008年12月25日在山海关船厂完成了单壳改双壳的工程。2013年10月11日出售，在大连港交船。

Built by Hitachi Zosen Corporation of Japan and completed on March 30, 1993, it was managed by Associated Maritime Company (Hong Kong) Limited. It was changed into double-hulled tanker in Shanhaiguan Shipbuilding Heavy Industry Co., Ltd on December 25, 2008, and sold and delivered at Dalian port on October 11, 2013.

凯旋 New Victory

⚓ 凯力 New Vitality

"凯力"轮英文船名 New Vitality，超大型油轮，船长 330.25 米，船宽 56 米，吃水 21.52 米，舱容 334001 立方米，载重吨 284569，主机功率 20933 千瓦，航速每小时 15.2 海里。

New Vitality is a Very Large Crude Carrier (VLCC). Its length overall is 330.25 meters and the beam is 56 meters with a draught of 21.52 meters. It measures a capacity of 334,001 cubic meters with a dead weight tonnage of 284,569 tons. With its main engine power at 20,933 kilowatts, it could sail at a speed of 15.2 kn.

"凯力"轮由日本佐世保造船厂建造，1993 年 7 月 2 日出厂，航行于国际航线运输原油。由海宏轮船（香港）有限公司经营管理。2009 年 4 月 19 日在招商局蛇口友联船厂完成了单壳改双壳的工程。2014 年 4 月 2 日在广东新会港出售交船。

Built by Sasebo Heavy Industries Co.,Ltd on July 2, 1993, the carrier was used to sail on international routes to transport crude oil and was managed by Associated Maritime Company (Hong Kong) Limited. On April 19, 2009, it was changed into a double-hulled tanker in Yiulian Dockyard (Shekou) Co. Ltd, and sold and delivered at Xinhui Port in Guangdong on April 2, 2014.

凯力 New Vitality

凯和　New Amity

⚓ 凯和　New Amity

"凯和"轮英文船名 New Amity，阿芙拉型油轮，船长 241 米，船宽 42 米，吃水 14.92 米，舱容 119588 立方米，载重吨 106120，主机功率 10597 千瓦，航速每小时 14.5 海里。

New Amity is an Aframax carrier. Its length overall is 241 meters and the beam is 42 meters with a draught of 14.92 meters. It measures a capacity of 119,588 cubic meters and a dead weight tonnage of 106,120 tons. With its main engine power at 10,597 kilowatts, it could sail at a speed of 14.5 kn.

"凯和"轮由日本伊万里造船厂建造，1998 年 7 月 9 日出厂。该轮由海宏轮船（香港）有限公司经营管理，航行于国际航线运输原油。2013 年被招商局能源运输股份有限公司评为先进船舶。

Built by Namura Shipbuilding Co., Ltd of Japan and completed on July 9, 1998, the carrier was managed by Associated Maritime Company (Hong Kong) Limited and used to sail on international routes for crude oil transportation. It was granted as "Outstanding Vessel" by China Merchants Energy Shipping Co., Ltd. in 2013.

凯盟 New Alliance

"凯盟"轮英文船名 New Alliance，阿芙拉型油轮，船长 240.99 米，船宽 42 米，吃水 14.92 米，舱容 119588 立方米，载重吨 106118，主机功率 10597 千瓦，航速每小时 14.5 海里。

New Alliance is an Aframax oil tanker. Its length overall is 240.99 meters and the beam is 42 meters with a draught of 14.92 meters. It measures a capacity 119,588 cubic meters and a dead weight tonnage of 106,118 tons. With its main engine power at 10,597 kilowatts, it could sail at a speed of 14.5 kn.

凯盟 New Alliance

"凯盟"轮由日本伊万里造船厂建造，1998 年 8 月 7 日出厂。"凯盟"轮由海宏轮船（香港）有限公司负责管理经营，航行于国际航线运输原油。

Built by Namura Shipbuilding Co.,Ltd of Japan and completed on August 7, 1998, the tanker was managed by Associated Maritime Company (Hong Kong) Limited and used to sail on international routes for crude oil transportation.

惠砂 Weser Ore

"惠砂"轮，英文船名 Weser Ore，超大型散货船，船长 336 米，船宽 52 米，吃水 22 米，载重吨 274326，主机功率 29850 千瓦，航速每小时 16.5 海里。

Weser Ore is a Very Large Ore Carrier (VLOC). Its length overall is 336 meters and the beam is 52 meters with a draught of 22 meters. With its main engine power at 29,850 kilowatts, it could sail at a speed of 16.5 kn and has a dead weight tonnage of 274,326 tons.

惠砂 Weser Ore

"惠砂"轮由南斯拉夫乌利亚尼克造船厂建造，1974年10月竣工出厂。招商局1988年8月12日从香港董氏集团购进。

Built by Uljanik Shipyard in Yugoslavia and completed in October 1974, the carrier was purchased by China Merchants from Tung Shi International (HK) Co., Ltd. on August 12, 1988.

"惠砂"轮是我国第一艘最大的散货船，刷新了我国散货航运的历史。1999年10月3日，"惠砂"轮在巴西Tubarao港装载矿砂出港时，引水员在船领航，船舶驾驶员操作不当，偏离航道中央线搁浅。经勘验，保险公司宣告船舶全损。

As the first VLOC in China, the carrier broke the record in China's bulk transportation history. On October 3, 1999, it was stranded when loaded with ore sand to depart from Tubarao port due to an ill operation of the pilot. After investigation, the insurance company declared that the carrier was fully damaged.

⚓ 泰源　Thai Resource

"泰源"，英文船名Thai Resource，超大型油轮，船长343.49米，船宽51.82米，吃水20.46米，载重吨262222，主机功率23880千瓦，航速每小时14海里。

Thai Resource is a Very Large Crude Carrier (VLCC). Its length overall is 343.49 meters and the beam is 51.82 meters with a draught of 20.46 meters. With its main engine power at 23,880 kilowatts, it could sail at a cruising speed of 14 kn and has a dead weight tonnage of 262,222 tons.

该船由英国亨特造船厂建造，1976年11月出厂，1989年10月25日购入接船。原名New Resource，由海宏轮船（香港）有限公司管理经营。1994年10月18日改为现名。1997

泰源　Thai Resource

年至 2005 年租给印度尼西亚石油公司做储油船。2005 年 8 月 1 日出售给当地买家并交船。

Built by Swan Hunter Shipbuilders Ltd. in Britain and completed in November 1976, the carrier was purchased by China Merchants on October 25, 1989. Originally named as New Resource, it was managed by Associated Maritime Company (Hong Kong) Limited and changed into its current name on October 18, 1994. From 1997 to 2005, it was leased to an oil company in Indonesia as a storage tanker, and then was sold and delivered to a local buyer in Indonesia on August 1, 2005.

Atlantic Amity

"Atlantic Amity" 轮，阿芙拉型油轮，船长 235.52 米，船宽 40 米，吃水 13.12 米，载重吨 89696，主机功率 10450 千瓦，航速每小时 14 海里。

Atlantic Amity is an Aframax oil tanker. Its length overall is 235.52 meters and the beam is 40 meters with a draught of 13.12 meters. With its main engine power at 10,450 kilowatts, it could sail at a speed of 14 kn and has a dead weight tonnage of 89,696 tons.

该轮由日本川崎造船厂建造，1985 年 4 月出厂。招商局 1988 年 9 月 16 日购进，由海宏轮船（香港）有限公司经营管理。1990 年 5 月 24 日出售给苏联买家并交船。

Built by Kawasaki Dockyard of Japan and completed in April 1985, the tanker was purchased by China Merchants on September 16, 1988, and managed by Associated Maritime Company (Hong Kong) Limited. It was sold and delivered to a buyer in former Soviet Union on May 24, 1990.

Oriental Bravery

Oriental Bravery 轮，苏伊士型油轮，船长 252.28 米，船宽 43 米，主机功率 13433 千瓦，载重吨 104015，吃水 15.49 米，航速每小时 15 海里。

Oriental Bravery is a Suezmax oil tanker. Its length overall is 252.28 meters and the beam is 43 meters with a draught of 15.49 meters. With its main engine power at 13,433 kilowatts, it could sail at a speed of 15 kn and has a dead weight tonnage of 104,015 tons.

该轮为日本太平造船厂建造，1979 年 10 月出厂。招商局 1988 年 9 月 29 日购进，由海宏轮船（香港）有

Oriental Bravery

限公司管理经营。1989 年 9 月 6 日出售交船。

Built by Shin Kurushima Dockyard Co., Ltd of Japan and completed in October 1979, the tanker was purchased by China Merchants on September 29, 1988, and managed by Associated Maritime Company (Hong Kong) Limited. It was sold and delivered on September 6, 1989.

Stellaris

⚓ Stellaris

Stellaris，阿芙拉型油轮，船长 235.5 米，船宽 40 米，吃水 13.1 米，载重吨 89636，主机功率 10304 千瓦，航速每小时 14.5 海里。

Stellaris is an Aframax oil tanker. Its length overall is 235.5 meters and the beam is 40 meters with a draught of 13.1 meters. With its main engine power at 10,304 kilowatts, it could sail at a speed of 14.5 kn and has a dead weight tonnage of 89,636 tons.

该轮由日本大阪造船厂于 1985 年 1 月建造完工出厂。招商局 1988 年 10 月 25 日购进，由海宏轮船（香港）有限公司管理经营。1990 年 1 月 10 日出售给买家并交船。

Built by Osaka Shipyard in Japan and completed in January 1985, the tanker was purchased by China Merchants on October 25, 1988 and managed by Associated Maritime Company (Hong Kong) Limited. It was sold and delivered to another buyer on January 10, 1990.

Sarda

⚓ Sarda

Sarda 轮，阿芙拉型油轮，船长 235.52 米，船宽 40 米，吃水 13.12 米，载重吨 89636，主机功率 10304 千瓦，航速每小时 14 海里。

Sarda is an Aframax oil tanker. Its length overall is 235.52 meters and the beam is 40 meters with a draught of 13.12 meters. With its main engine power at 10,304 kilowatts, it could sail at a speed of 14 kn and has a dead weight tonnage of 89,636 tons.

该船由日本大阪造船厂建造，1985 年 5 月出厂，1988 年 11 月 29 日购进，由海宏轮船（香港）有限公司经营管理。1990 年 4 月 25 日出售给买家 Lisnave 并交船。

Built by Osaka Shipyard of Japan and completed in May 1985, the tanker was purchased by China Merchants November 29, 1988, and managed by Associated Maritime Company (Hong Kong) Limited. It was sold and delivered to Lisnave on April 25, 1990.

Sentis

Sentis 轮，阿芙拉型油轮，船长 235 米，船宽 40 米，吃水 13.1 米，载重吨 89570，主机功率 10450 千瓦，航速每小时 14.4 海里。

Sentis is an Aframax oil tanker. Its length overall is 235 meters and the beam is 40 meters with a draught of 13.1 meters. With its main engine power at 10,450 kilowatts, it could sail at a speed of 14.4 kn and has a dead weight tonnage of 89,570 tons.

该船由日本川崎造船厂建造，1985 年 10 月出厂，1988 年 11 月 30 日购进，由海宏轮船（香港）有限公司经营管理。航行于国际航线运输原油。1990 年 4 月 9 日出售给 Lisbon 买家。

Built by Kawasaki Dockyard of Japan and completed in October 1985, the tanker was purchased by China Merchants on November 30, 1988, and managed by Associated Maritime Company (Hong Kong) Limited. It was assigned to sail on international routes for oil transportation, and was sold to a buyer in Lisbon on April 9, 1990.

Energy Growth

Energy Growth 轮，超大型油轮，船长 319.92 米，船宽 53.04 米，吃水 19.66 米，载重吨 233961，主机功率 26865 千瓦，航速每小时 14 海里。

Energy Growth is a Very Large Crude Carrier (VLCC). Its length overall is 319.92 meters and the beam is 53.04 meters with a draught of 19.66 meters. With its main engine power at 26,865 kilowatts, it could sail at a speed of 14 kn and has a dead weight tonnage of 233,961 tons.

该船由日本川崎造船厂建造，1974 年 10 月 8 日出厂，1988 年 12 月 15 日购进，由海宏轮船（香港）有限公司管理经营。航行于全球航线运输原油。1989 年 12 月 28 日出售交船。

Built by Kawasaki Dockyard of Japan and completed on October 8, 1974, the carrier was purchased by China Merchants on December

Energy Growth

15, 1988, and managed by Associated Maritime Company (Hong Kong) Limited. It was assigned to sail on international routes for oil transportation, and was sold and delivered on December 28, 1989.

⚓ Araguaney

Araguaney 轮，灵便型油轮，船长 132 米，船宽 32 米，吃水 11.2 米，载重吨 45396，主机功率 8380 千瓦，航速每小时 14 海里。

Araguaney is a handysize carrier. Its length overall is 132 meters and the beam is 32 meters with a draught of 11.2 meters. With its main engine power at 8,380 kilowatts, it could sail at a cruising speed of 14 kn and has a dead weight tonnage of 45,396 tons.

Araguaney

该船由南斯拉夫造船厂建造，1982 年 9 月出厂，1989 年 2 月 10 日购进，海宏轮船（香港）有限公司经营管理。1990 年 7 月 5 日售给 Curacao 买家并交船。

Built by Yugoslavia Shipyard and completed in September 1982, the carrier was bought by China Merchants on February 10, 1989, and was managed by Associated Maritime Company (Hong Kong) Limited. On July 5, 1990, it was sold and delivered to a buyer in Curacao.

⚓ Carolines

Carolines 轮，灵便型散货船，船长 119.88 米，船宽 20.5 米，吃水 7.54 米，载重吨 10010，主机功率 4627 千瓦，航速每小时 13.5 海里。

Carolines is a handysize bulk carrier. Its length overall is 119.88 meters and the beam is 20.5 meters with a draught of 7.54 meters. With its main engine power at 4,627 kilowatts, it could sail at a speed of 13.5 kn and has a dead weight tonnage of 10,010 tons.

Carolines 轮由日本神户造船厂建造，1974 年 10 月出厂。1987 年 4 月 21 日招商局购进，由香港明华船务有限公司负责经营管理。1996 年 1 月 10 日出售交船。

Built by Kobe Shipyard of Japan and completed in October 1974, the carrier was purchased by China

Merchants on April 21, 1987, and managed by Hong Kong Ming Wah Shipping Co, Ltd. It was sold and delivered on January 10, 1996.

⚓ Marina Cathya

Marina Cathya 轮为多用途船，船长 131.8 米，船宽 19 米，吃水 8.3 米，载重吨 11200，主机功率 5100 千瓦，航速每小时 13 海里。

Marina Cathya is a multi-purpose carrier. Its length overall is 131.8 meters and the beam is 19 meters with a draught of 8.3 meters. With its main engine power at 5,100 kilowatts, it could sail at a cruising speed of 13 kn and has a dead weight tonnage of 11,200 tons.

Marina Cathya 轮由日本太平造船厂于 1976 年 2 月建造完工出厂。招商局 1987 年 10 月 15 日购进，由香港明华船务有限公司管理经营。该轮原名 Cacia，挂巴拿马船旗。1995 年 7 月改为现名，注册新加坡船籍。1998 年 1 月 20 日出售给新加坡买家并交船。

Built by Shin Kurushima Dockyard Co., Ltd of Japan and completed in February 1976, the carrier was purchased by China Merchants on October 15, 1987 and managed by Hong Kong Ming Wah Shipping Co, Ltd. Originally named as Cacia and registered under the Panamanian flag, it was renamed into Marina Cathya and registered as a Singaporean carrier in July 1995. The carrier was sold and delivered to a buyer in Singapore on January 20, 1998.

Maina Cahya

⚓ Atlantic Concord

Atlantic Concord 轮，灵便型油轮，船长 167.43 米，船宽 30 米，吃水 11.15 米，载重吨 37583，主机功率 7680 千瓦，航速每小时 14.5 海里。

Atlantic Concord is a handysize oil tanker. Its length overall is 167.43 meters and the beam is 30 meters with a draught of 11.15 meters. With its main engine power at 7,680 kilowatts, it could sail at a speed of 14.5 kn and has a dead weight tonnage of 37,583 tons.

该船由日本山口造船厂建造，1987 年 9 月出厂，1990 年 2 月 27 日购进。1990 年 4 月 10 日出售给科威特买家并交船。

Built by Yamaguchi Shipyard of Japan and completed in September 1987, the carrier was purchased by China Merchants on February 27, 1990, and sold and delivered to a buyer in Kuwait on April 10, 1990.

⚓ Atlantic Conquest

Atlantic Conquest 轮，灵便型油轮，船长 167.43 米，船宽 30 米，吃水 11.1 米，载重吨 37574，主机功率 7680 千瓦，航速每小时 14.5 海里。

Atlantic Conquest is a handysize oil tanker. Its length overall is 167.43 meters and the beam is 30 meters with a draught of 11.1 meters. With its main engine power at 7,680 kilowatts, it could sail at a speed of 14.5 kn and has a dead weight tonnage of 37,574 tons.

该船由日本山口造船厂建造，1987 年 8 月出厂，1990 年 4 月 12 日购进，1990 年 4 月 25 日出售给科威特买家并交船。

Built by Yamaguchi Shipyard of Japan and completed in August 1987, the carrier was purchased by China Merchants on April 12, 1990, and sold and delivered to a buyer in Kuwait on April 25, 1990.

⚓ Creation

Creation 轮，灵便型油轮，船长 167.43 米，船宽 30 米，吃水 11.1 米，载重吨 37615，主机功率 7680 千瓦，航速每小时 14.3 海里。

Creation is a handysize oil tanker. Its length overall is 167.43 meters and the beam is 30 meters with a draught of 11.1 meters. With its main engine power at 7,680 kilowatts, it could sail at a speed of 14.3 kn and has a dead weight tonnage of 37,615 tons.

该船由日本山口造船厂建造，1987 年 11 月出厂，1990 年 5 月 2 日购入，1991 年 7 月 2 日售出交船。

Built by Yamaguchi Shipyard of Japan and completed in November 1987, the carrier was purchased by China Merchants on May 2, 1990, and sold and delivered on July 2, 1991.

⚓ Mutank Vision

Mutank Vision 轮，灵便型油轮，船长 184.45 米，船宽 28 米，吃水 11.03 米，舱容 37735 立方米，载重吨 36981，主机功率 8731 千瓦，航速每小时 15.3 海里。

Mutank Vision is a handysize oil tanker. Its length overall is 184.45 meters and the beam is 28 meters with a draught of 11.03 meters. It measures a capacity of 37,735 cubic meters and a dead weight tonnage of 36,981 tons. With its main engine power at 8,731 kilowatts, it could sail at a speed of 15.3 kn.

Mutank Vision 轮由日本山口造船厂建造，1976 年 7 月出厂，1996 年 7 月 15 日购进接船，由海宏轮船（香港）有限公司经营管理。2000 年 3 月 20 日出售给新加坡买家并交船。

Built by Yamaguchi Shipyard of Japan and completed in July 1976, the carrier was purchased by China Merchants on July 15, 1996, and sold and delivered to a buyer in Singapore on March 20, 2000.

⚓ 飞龙 Fei Long

"飞龙"轮英文船名 Fei Long，杂货船，船长 125 米，船宽 18 米，吃水 7.8 米，载重吨 7950，主机功率 4800 千瓦，航速每小时 12.5 海里。

Fei Long is a general cargo vessel. Its length overall is 125 meters and the beam is 18 meters with a draught of 7.8 meters. With its main engine power at 4,800 kilowatts, it could sail at a speed of 12.5 kn and has a dead weight tonnage of 7,950 tons.

"飞龙"轮由日本佐世保造船厂建造，1971 年 10 月出厂。招商局 1985 年 11 月 8 日购进，于香港接船。由香港明华船务有限公司负责管理经营。1988 年 8 月 11 日出售给韩国买家并交船。

Built by Sasebo Heavy Industries Co., Ltd of Japan and completed in October 1971, the carrier was purchased by China Merchants on November 8, 1985, and managed by Hong Kong Ming Wah Shipping Co, Ltd. On August 11, 1988, it was sold and delivered to a buyer in Republic of Korea.

⚓ 海龙 Ocean Glory

"海龙"轮英文船名 Ocean Glory，灵便型散货船，船长 164.3 米，船宽 22.86 米，吃水 8.8 米，载重吨 17350，主机功率 8358 千瓦，航速每小时 12.5 海里。

Ocean Glory is a handysize carrier. Its length overall is 164.3 meters and the beam is 22.86 meters with a draught of 8.8 meters. With its main engine power at 8,358 kilowatts, it could sail at a speed of 12.5 kn and has a dead weight tonnage of 17,350 tons.

"海龙"轮原名 Green Win，由上海中华造船厂建造，1981 年 3 月出厂。1992 年 8 月 3 日签约购进，由香港明华船务有限公司负责管理，1994 年 10 月出售交船。

Originally named as Green Win, it was built by Shanghai Zhonghua Shipyard and completed in March 1981. The carrier was purchased by China Merchants on August 3, 1992, and managed by Hong Kong Ming Wah Shipping Co, Ltd. In October 1994, it was sold and delivered.

安龙　An Long

⚓ 安龙 An Long

"安龙"轮英文船名 An Long，液化石油气船，船长 67.9 米，船宽 11 米，吃水 4.2 米，载重吨 1245.6，主机功率 1176 千瓦，航速每小时 10 海里。

An Long is an LPG tanker. Its length overall is 67.9 meters and the beam is 11 meters with a draught of 4.2 meters. With its main engine power at 1,176 kilowatts, it could sail at a speed of 10 kn and has a dead weight tonnage of 1,245.6 tons.

"安龙"轮由日本三洋造船厂建造,1974年8月出厂。招商局1988年3月购进,由深圳华南液化气船务有限公司管理经营。2002年2月退役报废。

Built by Sanyo Shipyard of Japan and completed in August 1974, the carrier was purchased by China Merchants in March, 1988, and managed by Shenzhen Southern China L.P.G. Shipping Co., Ltd. In February 2002, it was retired and scrapped.

"安龙"轮是我国购进的第一艘液化石油气船。1988年3月24日首航返回蛇口,开创了中国历史上石油液化气航运的先河,书写了中国能源运输的新篇章。

An Long is the first LPG tanker that China has ever bought. On March 24, 1988, it returned to Shekou after its maiden voyage, creating the history of China's liquefied gas shipment and ushering in a new chapter in China's energy transport.

⚓ 泰龙 Tai Long

"泰龙"轮英文船名Tai Long,液化石油气船,船长68.35米,船宽11.2米,吃水4.3米,载重吨1102.11,主机功率1544千瓦,航速每小时10.5海里。

Tai Long is an LPG tanker. Its length overall is 68.35 meters and the beam is 11.2 meters with a draught of 4.3 meters. With its main engine power at 1,544 kilowatts, it could sail at a cruising speed of 10.5 kn and has a dead weight tonnage of 1,102.11 tons.

该船由日本三岛造船厂建造,1977年12月出厂。1989年6月30日购进投入营运。由深圳华南液化气船务有限公司管理经营,2008年12月退役报废。

泰龙 Tai Long

Built by Mishima Shipyard of Japan and completed in December 1977, the carrier was purchased by China Merchants on June 30, 1989, and managed by Shenzhen Southern China L.P.G. Shipping Co., Ltd. In December 2008, it was retired and scrapped.

祥龙 Xiang Long

⚓ 祥龙 Xiang Long

"祥龙"轮英文船名 Xiang Long，液化石油气船，船长 93.78 米，船宽 15 米，吃水 5.04 米，舱容 3202 立方米，载重吨 2253，主机功率 2352 千瓦，航速每小时 11.5 海里。

Xiang Long is an LPG tanker. Its length overall is 93.78 meters and the beam is 15 meters with a draught of 5.04 meters. It measures a capacity of 3,202 cubic meters and a dead weight tonnage of 2,253 tons. With its main engine power at 2,352 kilowatts, it could sail at a speed of 11.5 kn.

"祥龙"轮由日本德岛造船厂建造，1973 年 2 月出厂，1992 年 8 月 28 日购入营运。由深圳华南液化气船务有限公司管理经营。2003 年 12 月退役报废。

Built by Tokushima Shipyard of Japan and completed in February 1973, the tanker was purchased by China Merchants on August 28, 1992, and managed by Shenzhen Southern China L.P.G. Shipping Co., Ltd. In December 2003, it was retired and scrapped.

⚓ 新龙 Xin Long

"新龙"轮英文船名 Xin Long，液化石油气船，船长 61.2 米，船宽 10 米，吃水 3.95 米，舱容 1180 立方米，载重吨 766，主机功率 1177 千瓦，航速每小时 10 海里。

Xin Long is an LPG tanker. Its length overall is 61.2 meters and the beam is 10 meters with a draught of 3.95 meters. It measures a capacity of 1,180 cubic meters and a dead weight tonnage of 766 tons. With its main engine power at 1,177 kilowatts, it could sail at a speed of 10 kn.

"新龙"轮由日本白滨造船厂建造，1979 年 8 月 19 日出厂。"新龙"轮曾用名"青龙"，1994 年 9 月 3 日购进，由深圳华南液化气船务有限公司经营管理，2009 年 10 月退役报废。

Built by Shirahama Shipyard of Japan and completed on August 19, 1979, the tanker was originally named as Qing Long, purchased by China Merchants on September 3, 1994, and managed by Shenzhen Southern China L.P.G. Shipping Co., Ltd. In October 2009, it was retired and scrapped.

新龙 Xin Long

彰龙　Zhang Long

"彰龙"轮英文船名 Zhang Long，液化石油气船，船长 65.28 米，船宽 11.4 米，吃水 4.31 米，舱容 1555 立方米，载重吨 1135，主机功率 1312 千瓦，航速每小时 12 海里。

Zhang Long is an LPG tanker. Its length overall is 65.28 meters and the beam is 11.4 meters with a draught of 4.31 meters. It measures a capacity of 1,555 cubic meters and a dead weight tonnage of 1,135 tons. With its main engine power at 1,312 kilowatts, it could sail at a speed of 12 kn.

"彰龙"轮由日本造船厂建造，1979 年 11 月 1 日出厂。该轮由深圳华南液化气船务有限公司经营管理，1998 年 3 月 21 日购进投入营运，2010 年 9 月退役报废。

Built by a Japanese shipyard and completed on November 1, 1979, the tanker was managed by Shenzhen Southern China L.P.G. Shipping Co., Ltd, and put into operation on March 21, 1998. It was retired and scrapped in September 2010.

彰龙　Zhang Long

豪威　Good Rider

⚓ 豪威　Good Rider

"豪威"轮英文船名 Good Rider，多用途船，船长 99.57 米，船宽 19.54 米，吃水 5.91 米，载重吨 5521，主机功率 2374 千瓦，航速每小时 13.7 海里。

Good Rider is a multi-purpose carrier. Its length overall is 99.57 meters and the beam is 19.54 meters with a draught of 5.91 meters. With its main engine power at 2,374 kilowatts, it could sail at a speed of 13.7 kn and has a dead weight tonnage of 5,521 ton.

"豪威"轮由南斯拉夫造船厂建造，1985 年 5 月出厂，1993 年 3 月 16 日购入，由香港朝联货柜运输有限公司经营管理，1995 年 6 月 23 日划归香港明华船务有限公司。2002 年 7 月 30 日出售交船。

Built by Yugoslav Shipyard and completed in May 1985, the carrier was purchased by China Merchants on March 16, 1993. Originally managed by Chiu Lun Container Transportation Co. Ltd, it was later managed by Hong Kong Ming Wah Shipping Co, Ltd on June 23, 1995. It was sold and delivered on July 30, 2002.

豪胜　Good Success

豪胜　Good Success

"豪胜"轮英文船名Good Success，多用途船，船长99.57米，船宽19.5米，吃水5.91米，载重吨5521，主机功率2374千瓦，航速每小时13.7海里。

Good Success is a multi-purpose carrier. Its length overall is 99.57 meters and the beam is 19.5 meters with a draught of 5.91 meters. With its main engine power at 2,374 kilowatts, it could sail at a speed of 13.7 kn and has a dead weight tonnage of 5,521 tons.

"豪胜"轮由南斯拉夫造船厂建造，1985年4月出厂，1993年3月20日购入，由香港朝联货柜运输有限公司经营管理，1995年6月23日划归香港明华船务有限公司。2002年6月25日出售交船。

Built by Yugoslav Shipyard and completed in April 1985, the carrier was purchased by China Merchants on March 20, 1993. Originally managed by Chiu Lun Container Transportation Co. Ltd, it was later managed by Hong Kong Ming Wah Shipping Co, Ltd on June 23,1995. On June 25, 2002, it was sold and delivered.

豪勇　Good Fighter

"豪勇"轮英文船名Good Fighter，多用途船，船长99.57米，船宽19.5米，吃水5.9米，载重吨5521，主机功率2374千瓦，航速每小时13.5海里。

Good Fighter is a multi-purpose carrier. Its length overall is 99.57 meters and the beam is 19.5 meters with a draught of 5.9 meters. With its main engine power at 2,374 kilowatts, it could sail at a speed of 13.5 kn and has a dead weight tonnage of 5,521 tons.

"豪勇"轮由南斯拉夫造船厂建造，1984 年 2 月出厂，1993 年 4 月 21 日购入，由香港朝联货柜运输有限公司负责经营管理，1995 年 1 月售出交船。

Built by Yugoslav Shipyard and completed in February 1984, the carrier was purchased by China Merchants on April 21, 1993. Managed by Chiu Lun Container Transportation Co. Ltd, it was sold and delivered in January 1995.

⚓ 豪泰　Good Most

"豪泰"轮英文船名 Good Most，多用途船，船长 132.7 米，船宽 19.86 米，吃水 6.88 米，载重吨 7365，主机功率 5194 千瓦，航速每小时 13.7 海里。

Good Most is a multi-purpose carrier. Its length overall is 132.7 meters and the beam is 19.86 meters with a draught of 6.88 meters. With its main engine power at 5,194 kilowatts, it could sail at a speed of 13.7 kn and has a dead weight tonnage of 7,365 tons.

"豪泰"轮由西班牙造船厂建造，1994 年 3 月 9 日出厂，最初由香港朝联货柜运输有限公司经营管理，1995 年 6 月 23 日划归香港明华船务有限公司，1998 年 6 月 22 日出售交船给希腊买家。

豪泰　Good Most

Built by Spanish Shipyard and completed on March 9, 1994, the carrier was originally managed by Chiu Lun Container Transportation Co. Ltd. It was later managed by Hong Kong Ming Wah Shipping Co, Ltd on June 23, 1995, and sold and delivered to a buyer in Greece on June 22, 1998.

豪畅 Good Fast

"豪畅"英文船名 Good Fast，多用途船，船长 132.7 米，船宽 19.86 米，吃水 6.88 米，载重吨 7365，主机功率 5194 千瓦，航速每小时 13.7 海里。

Good Fast is a multi-purpose carrier. Its length overall is 132.7 meters and the beam is 19.86 meters with a draught of 6.88 meters. With its main engine power at 5,194 kilowatts, it could sail at a speed of 13.7 kn and has a dead weight tonnage of 7,365 tons.

"豪畅"轮由西班牙造船厂建造，1994 年 6 月 17 日出厂，该轮出厂后由香港朝联货柜运输有限公司经营管理，1995 年 6 月 23 日划归香港明华船务有限公司。1998 年 5 月 11 日出售交船。

Built by Spanish Shipyard and completed on June 17, 1994, the carrier was originally managed by Chiu Lun Container Transportation Co. Ltd. It was later managed by Hong Kong Ming Wah Shipping Co, Ltd on June 23, 1995, and sold and delivered on May 11, 1998.

豪畅 Good Fast

豪乐　Good Luck

⚓ 豪乐　Good Luck

"豪乐"轮英文船名 Good Luck，集装箱船，船长 120.57 米，船宽 19.6 米，吃水 6.14 米，载重吨 7390，主机功率 3348 千瓦，航速每小时 13.8 海里。

Good Luck is a container carrier. Its length overall is 120.57 meters and the beam is 19.6 meters with a draught of 6.14 meters. With its main engine power at 3,348 kilowatts, it could sail at a speed of 13.8 kn and has a dead weight tonnage of 7,390 tons.

"豪乐"轮由中国马尾造船厂建造，1994 年 8 月 25 日出厂。由香港朝联货柜运输有限公司经营管理，1995 年 6 月 23 日划归香港明华船务有限公司，从事中国沿海和东南亚集装箱航运。2004 年 2 月 28 日在香港出售交船。

Built by Fujian Mawei Shipyard and completed on August 25, 1994, the carrier was originally managed by Chiu Lun Container Transportation Co. Ltd. and later managed by Hong Kong Ming Wah Shipping Co, Ltd. on June 23, 1995, used for container shipping in the coastal areas of China and Southeast Asia. On February 28, 2004, it was sold and delivered in Hongkong.

⚓ 豪达 Good Explorer

"豪达"轮英文船名 Good Explorer，多用途船，船长 132.7 米，船宽 19.86 米，吃水 6.88 米，载重吨 7365，主机功率 5194 千瓦，航速每小时 13.7 海里。

Good Explorer is a multi-purpose carrier. Its length overall is 132.7 meters and the beam is 19.86 meters with a draught of 6.88 meters. With its main engine power at 5,194 kilowatts, it could sail at a speed of 13.7 kn and has a dead weight tonnage of 7,365 tons

"豪达"轮由西班牙造船厂建造，1994 年 5 月 3 日出厂。该轮于 1994 年 11 月 23 日购入，由香港朝联货柜运输有限公司负责管理，1995 年 2 月 3 日售出交船。

Built by Spanish Shipyard and completed on May 3, 1994, the carrier was purchased by China Merchants on November 23, 1994, and managed by Chiu Lun Container Transportation Co. Ltd. On February 3, 1995, it was sold and delivered.

⚓ 豪顺 Good Easy

"豪顺"轮英文船名 Good Easy，多用途船，船长 132.7 米，船宽 19.86 米，吃水 6.88 米，载重吨 7365，主机功率 5194 千瓦，航速每小时 13.7 海里。

Good Easy is a multi-purpose carrier. Its length overall is 132.7 meters and the beam is 19.86 meters with a draught of 6.88 meters. With its main engine power at 5,194 kilowatts, it could sail at a speed of 13.7 kn and has a dead weight tonnage of 7,365 tons,

"豪顺"轮由西班牙造船厂建造，1994 年 12 月 2 日出厂。由香港朝联货柜运输有限公司经营管理，1995 年 6 月 23 日划归香港明华船务有限公司，1998 年 5 月 5 日售出交船。

Built by Spanish Shipyard and completed on December 2, 1994, the carrier was purchased by China Merchants and managed by Chiu Lun Container Transportation Co. Ltd. It was allocated to Hong Kong Ming Wah Shipping Co, Ltd. on June 23, 1995, sold and delivered on May 5, 1998.

豪顺 Good Easy

豪安 Good Well

"豪安"轮英文船名 Good Well，集装箱船，船长 120.57 米，船宽 19.6 米，吃水 6.14 米，载重吨 7390，主机功率 3355 千瓦，航速每小时 13.8 海里。

Good Well is a container carrier. Its length overall is 120.57 meters and the beam is 19.6 meters with a draught of 6.14 meters. With its main engine power at 3,355 kilowatts, it could sail at a speed of 13.8 kn and has a dead weight tonnage of 7,390 tons.

"豪安"轮由中国马尾造船厂建造，1995 年 1 月 18 日出厂。出厂后主要从事中国沿海航线和东南亚航线的集装箱运输，由香港朝联货柜运输有限公司经营管理。1995 年 6 月 23 日划归香港明华船务有限公司。2004 年 2 月 26 日出售，在香港交船。

豪安 Good Well

Built by Fujian Mawei Shipyard and completed on January 18, 1995, the carrier was originally managed by Chiu Lun Container Transportation Co. Ltd. and used for container shipping in the coastal areas of China and Southeast Asia. It was later managed by Hong Kong Ming Wah Shipping Co, Ltd. on June 23, 1995, and was sold and delivered in Hongkong on February 26, 2004.

迅隆壹号 Xun Long Yi Hao

"迅隆壹号"轮英文船名 Xun Long Yi Hao，高速客船，船长 35 米，船宽 9.6 米，吃水 1.5 米，载重吨 505，主机功率 2940 千瓦，航速每小时 30 海里。

Xun Long Yi Hao is a high-speed passenger vessel. Its length overall is 35 meters and the beam is 9.6 meters with a draught of 1.5 meters. With its main engine power at 2, 940 kilowatts, it could sail at a speed of 30 kn and has a dead weight tonnage of 505 tons.

迅隆壹号　Xun Long Yi Hao

"迅隆壹号"轮由挪威造船厂建造，1995年7月25日出厂，该轮作为中挪两国的合作项目，建造期间，时任中共中央政治局常委、国务院副总理李岚清出访挪威时，曾莅临船厂登轮视察。"迅隆壹号"轮由袁庚题写船名。1995年10月1日，该轮投入蛇口至香港的水上客运航线。1997年被交通部授予"全国文明客船"荣誉称号。2008年4月被广东省总工会授予"工人先锋号"先进班组称号。2012年被国家海事局授予"安全诚信船舶"。

Built by Norway Shipyard and completed on July 25, 1995, Xun Long Yi Hao was a cooperative project between China and Norway. During its construction, Mr. Li Lanqing, the member of the Standing Committee of the Political Bureau of the Central Committee and the Vice Premier of the People's Republic of China boarded the ship during his visit to Norway. Xun Long Yi Hao, the name of the ship was inscribed by Mr. Yuan Geng[1]. On October 1, 1995, the ship was put into operations for the passenger route between Shekou and Hong Kong. After that, it was awarded with the honor of "National Civilized Passenger Vessel" by the Ministry of Transport in 1997, "Workers Pioneer Vessel" by the Federation of Trade Union of Guangdong Province in April 2008, and "Safe and Credit Standing Vessel" by Maritime Safety Administration of the People's Republic of China in 2012.

1　Yuan Geng: Born in 1917, was the pioneer in China's reform and opening up. He established Shekou Industry District in Shenzhen.

迅隆贰号 Xun Lun Er Hao

"迅隆贰号"英文船名 Xun Long Er Hao，高速客船，船长 38 米，船宽 11.2 米，吃水 1.8 米，载重吨 531，主机功率 3152 千瓦，航速每小时 34 海里。

Xun Long Er Hao is a high-speed passenger vessel. Its length overall is 38 meters and the beam is 11.2 meters with a draught of 1.8 meters. With its main engine power at 3, 152 kilowatts, it could sail at a speed of 34 kn and has a dead weight tonnage of 531 tons.

"迅隆贰号"由挪威造船厂建造，1998 年 7 月 30 日出厂，该轮于 1998 年 10 月 1 日投入蛇口至香港的客运航线。由深圳迅隆船务有限公司管理营运。该轮 2004 年被交通部评为"部级文明客船"。2005 年以来，连续被国家海事局授予"安全诚信船舶"。

Built by Norway Shipyard and completed on July 30, 1998, the ship was managed by Xunlong Shipping Co., Ltd and put into operations for the passenger route between Shekou and Hong Kong on October 1, 1998. It was awarded with the honor of Civilized Passenger Vessel of Guangdong Province by the Ministry of Transport in 2004 and "Safe and Credit Standing Vessel" by Maritime Safety Administration of the People's Republic of China since 2005.

迅隆贰号　Xun Lun Er Hao

第三节　跨越世纪 振兴崛起（2001年至今）

SECTION THREE
Rapid Rise in the New Century (2001 till Now)

进入新世纪以来，招商局的航运业务不断创新，勇拓新局。在航运业发展的道路上，招商局正昂首向前，迎接新一轮的迅速崛起。

China Merchants has been exploring shipping business since the beginning of the new century. On the way of the development, China Merchants stands ready to embrace another rapid rise.

2004年12月，招商局能源运输股份有限公司成立，并于2006年12月成功在上海证券交易所上市。截至2012年底，招商轮船拥有船舶48艘，运力达718万载重吨。其中有油轮21艘，总载重吨为472万吨；散货船21艘，船队由12艘大灵便型散货船和2艘巴拿马型散货船及7艘好望角型散货船组成，共196万载重吨。此外，招商局还与中远集团合资组建了中国第一支LNG运输船队（招商轮船占股50%），目前已经有6艘LNG船投入广东、福建、上海等地进口LNG项目的海上运输，并在积极推进新的LNG运输项目。

China Merchants Energy Shipping Co., Ltd. was established in December 2004. In December 2006, it got listed on the Shanghai Stock Exchange. By the end of 2012, China Merchants' fleet has been comprised of 48 vessels, with a shipping capacity of 7.18 million tons. Among them, there are 21 oil tankers with a total dead weight tonnage of 4.72 million tons. The bulk carrier fleet, consisting of 12 handymax bulk carriers, 2 Panamax bulk carriers and 7 Capesize bulk carriers, contributes to a total dead weight tonnage of 1.96 million tons. In addition, in partnership with China Ocean Shipping (Group) Company (COSCO), China Merchants formed the first LNG fleet in China (China Merchants Shipping taking up 50% of shares). Currently, 6 vessels of the LNG fleet are engaged in importing LNG projects to terminals of Guangdong, Fujian and Shanghai, and are still exploring new LNG transportation projects.

新世纪招商局航运将以远洋油轮运输业务为核心，积极开拓液化天然气运输业务，将公司所属船队打造为国内领先的大型能源运输船队，并向拥有核心竞争力的国际一流航运企业迈进。

Into the new century, China Merchants will focus its core shipping business on developing ocean oil tankers, and actively explore LNG transportation business. All these endeavors are aimed at making its fleet to be the leading energy shipping fleet in China, strengthening the core competitiveness and making China Merchants the first-class in international shipping field.

⚓ 凯鸿　New Century

"凯鸿"轮英文船名 New Century，超大型油轮，船长 329.99 米，船宽 60 米，吃水 21.52 米，舱容 333416 立方米，载重吨 299031，主机功率 22910 千瓦，航速每小时 16 海里。

New Century is a Very Large Crude Carrier (VLCC). Its length overall is 329.99 meters and the beam is 60 meters with a draught of 21.52 meters. It measures a capacity of 333,416 cubic meters and a dead weight tonnage of 299,031 tons. With its main engine power at 22,910 kilowatts, New Century could sail at a speed of 16 kn.

凯鸿　New Century

"凯鸿"轮首航全体船员合影　The Crew of New Century

　　"凯鸿"轮由日本有明造船厂建造，2004年4月28日出厂，航行于国际航线上运输原油，由海宏轮船（香港）有限公司负责管理营运。

　　New Century, built by Japan Universal Shipbuilding Corporation, was launched on April 28, 2004. It is engaged in international crude oil shipping, and managed by Associated Maritime Company (Hong Kong) Limited.

⚓ 凯誉 New Spirit

　　"凯誉"轮英文船名 New Spirit，超大型油轮，船长329.99米，船宽60米，吃水21.52米，舱容333416立方米，载重吨298972，主机功率22910千瓦，航速每小时16海里。

　　New Spirit is a Very Large Crude Carrier (VLCC). Its length overall is 329.99 meters and the beam is 60 meters with a draught of 21.52 meters. It measures a capacity of 333,416

凯誉　New Spirit

cubic meters and a dead weight tonnage of 298,972 tons. With its main engine power at 22,910 kilowatts, New Spirit could sail at a speed of 16 kn.

"凯誉"轮于2005年7月26日由日本有明造船厂建造竣工出厂，航行于国际航线运输原油，由海宏轮船（香港）有限公司负责管理经营。此"凯誉"轮与另一艘"凯誉"轮（New Renown）的中文船名相同，英文船名不同。

Built by Japan Universal Shipbuilding Corporation, New Spirit was launched on July 26, 2005. It is engaged in international crude oil shipping, and managed by Associated Maritime Company (Hong Kong) Limited. This vessel shares the same Chinese name of Kaiyu with the other ship New Renown.

凯进 New Advance

"凯进"轮英文船名New Advance，阿芙拉型油轮，船长239米，船宽42米，吃水14.88米，舱容119884立方米，载重吨105544，主机功率10955千瓦，航速每小时14.6海里。

New Advance is an Aframax oil tanker. Its length overall is 239 meters and the beam is 42 meters with a draught of 14.88 meters. It measures a capacity of 119,884 cubic meters and a dead weight tonnage of 105,544 tons. With its main engine power at 10,955 kilowatts, New Advance could sail at a speed of 14.6 kn.

凯进 New Advance

"凯进"轮接新船的高级船员
New senior crew members to New Advance

"凯进"轮接新船的普通船员
New crew members to New Advance

　　"凯进"轮于2007年12月10日由日本横须贺造船厂建造竣工出厂，由海宏轮船（香港）有限公司管理经营，从事原油运输，航行于国际航线。

　　Built by Japan Yokosuka Shipyard, New Advance was completed on December 10, 2007. It is managed by Associated Maritime Company (Hong Kong) Limited, and engaged in international crude oil shipping.

凯智 New Ability

"凯智"轮英文船名 New Ability，阿芙拉型油轮，船长 228.60 米，船宽 42 米，吃水 14.81 米，舱容 119588 立方米，载重吨 105381，主机功率 11285 千瓦，航速每小时 14.5 海里。

New Ability is an Aframax oil tanker. Its length overall is 228.60 meters and the beam is 42 meters with a draught of 14.81 meters. It measures a capacity of 119,588 cubic meters and a dead weight tonnage of 105,381 tons. With its main engine power at 11,285 kilowatts, New Ability could sail at a speed of 14.5 kn.

"凯智"轮于 2008 年 1 月 22 日由日本横须贺造船厂建造竣工出厂，出厂后一直由海宏轮船（香港）有限公司管理经营，主要从事原油远洋运输工作。

Built by Japan Yokosuka Shipyard, New Ability was completed on January 22, 2008. It is managed by Associated Maritime Company (Hong Kong) Limited, and engaged in crude oil shipping.

凯敏 New Activity

"凯敏"英文船名 New Activity，阿芙拉型油轮，船长 228.6 米，船宽 42 米，吃水 14.81 米，舱容 114719 立方米，载重吨 105342，主机功率 11285 千瓦，航速每小时 14.5 海里。

New Activity is an Aframax oil tanker. Its length overall is 228.6 meters and the beam is 42 meters with a draught of 14.81 meters. It measures a capacity of 114,719 cubic meters and a dead weight tonnage of 105,342 tons. With its main engine power at 11,285 kilowatts, New Activity could sail at a speed of 14.5 kn.

凯敏 New Activity

"凯敏"轮于 2008 年 3 月 4 日由日本横须贺造船厂建造竣工出厂，航行于国际航线，主要运输原油，由海宏轮船（香港）有限公司管理经营。

Built by Japan Yokosuka Shipyard, New Activity was completed on March 4, 2008. It is managed by Associated Maritime Company (Hong Kong) Limited, and engaged in international crude oil shipping.

凯达 New Accord

"凯达"轮英文船名 New Accord，阿芙拉型油轮，船长 244.6 米，船宽 42 米，吃水 15.52 米，舱容 122048 立方米，载重吨 109804，主机功率 13164 千瓦，航速每小时 15.50 海里。

New Accord is an Aframax oil tanker. Its length overall is 244.6 meters and the beam is 42 meters with a draught of 15.52 meters. It measures a capacity of 122,048 cubic meters and a dead weight tonnage of 109,804 tons. With its main engine power at

凯达 New Accord

13,164 kilowatts, New Accord could sail at a speed of 15.5 kn.

"凯达"轮于 2009 年 1 月 3 日由大连造船厂建造竣工出厂，出厂后由海宏轮船（香港）有限公司管理经营，航行于国际航线运输原油。该"凯达"轮与 1999 年 5 月 10 日出售的另一艘"凯达"轮（New Explorer）的中文名字相同。

Built by Dalian Shipbuilding Industry Co. Ltd., New Accord was completed on January 3, 2009. It is managed by Associated Maritime Company (Hong Kong) Limited, and engaged in international crude oil shipping .The vessel shares the same Chinese name of Kai Da with New Explorer, which was sold on May 10, 1999.

凯兴 New Prospect

"凯兴"轮英文船名 New Prospect，超大型油轮，船长 330 米，船宽 60 米，吃水 21.52 米，舱容 333364 立方米，载重吨 297934，主机功率 22910 千瓦，航速每小时 16 海里。

New Prospect is a Very Large Crude Carrier (VLCC). Its length overall is 330 meters and the beam is 60 meters with a draught of 21.52 meters. It measures a capacity of 333,364 cubic meters and a dead weight tonnage of 297,934 tons. With its main engine power at 22,910 kilowatts, New Prospect could sail at a speed of 16 kn.

"凯兴"轮于 2009 年 4 月 15 日由日本有明造船厂建造竣工出厂，航行于国际航线运输原油，由海宏轮船（香港）有限公司负责经营管理。2009 年，"凯兴"轮被交通部评为"全国交通运输行业精神文明建设示范窗口"。2013 年，"凯兴"轮船长钟文新被人力资源和社会保障部及国有资产监督管理委员会授予"中央企业劳动模范"的光荣称号。2012 年度和 2013 年度该轮被招商局能源运输股份有限公司评为"先进船舶"。

Built by Japan Universal Shipbuilding Corporation, New Prospect was completed on April 15, 2009. It is managed by Associated Maritime Company (Hong Kong)

凯兴 New Prospect

Limited, and engaged in international crude oil shipping. In 2009, New Prospect was awarded as a "National Model for Spiritual Building in the Transportation Sector" by the Ministry of Transport. In 2013, Mr. Zhong Wenxin, the Capitain of the vessel, was honored as a "Model Worker" by the Ministry of Human Resources and Social Security and State-owned Assets Supervision and Administration of the State Council. The vessel was rated as "Outstanding Vessel" by China Merchants Energy Shipping Co., Ltd. in 2012 and 2013 consecutively.

凯成　New Creation

"凯成"轮英文船名 New Creation，超大型油轮，船长 330 米，船宽 60 米，吃水 21.52 米，舱容 333305 立方米，载重吨 297259，主机功率 23270 千瓦，航速每小时 15.8 海里。

New Creation is a Very Large Crude Carrier (VLCC). Its length overall is 330 meters and the beam is 60 meters with a draught of 21.52 meters. It measures a capacity of 333,305 cubic meters and a dead weight tonnage of 297,259 tons. With its main engine power at 23, 270 kilowatts, New Creation could sail at a speed of 15.8 kn.

"凯成"轮于 2009 年 4 月 28 日由大连造船厂建造竣工出厂，原名"凯立"轮，由海宏轮船（香港）有限公司管理经营，航行于国际航线运输原油。

Built by Dalian Shipbuilding Industry Co. Ltd., New Creation was completed on April 28, 2009. It was renamed from "Kai Li" to "Kai Cheng" in Chinese. Under the management of Associated Maritime Company (Hong Kong) Limited, the vessel is engaged in international crude oil shipping.

凯成　New Creation

凯爱　New Paradise

凯爱　New Paradise

"凯爱"轮英文船名 New Paradise，超大型油轮，船长330米，船宽60米，吃水21.52米，舱容333364立方米，载重吨297863，主机功率22910千瓦，航速每小时16海里。

New Paradise is a Very Large Crude Carrier (VLCC). Its length overall is 330 meters and the beam is 60 meters with a draught of 21.52 meters. It measures a capacity of 333,364 cubic meters and a dead weight tonnage of 297,863 tons. With its main engine power at 22, 910 kilowatts, New Paradise could sail at a speed of 16 kn.

"凯爱"轮由海宏轮船（香港）有限公司管理经营，航行于国际航线运输原油。2011年2月，轮机长张栋川由于环保节能工作表现突出，被交通部授予"车、船、路、港千家企业低碳交通运输专项行动先进个人"荣誉称号。

New Paradise is managed by Associated Maritime Company (Hong Kong) Limited, and engaged in international crude oil shipping. In February 2011, Mr. Zhang Dongchuan, the Chief Engineer of the vessel, was awarded "Outstanding Person for Low-carbon Action in 1000 Companies in the Transportation Sector" because of his remarkable achievement in environment protection and energy saving.

⚓ 凯源 New Resource

"凯源"轮英文船名New Resource，超大型油轮，船长330米，船宽60米，吃水21.52米，舱容333305立方米，载重吨297101，主机功率23270千瓦，航速每小时15.8海里。

New Resource is a Very Large Crude Carrier (VLCC). Its length overall is 330 meters and the beam is 60 meters with a draught of 21.52 meters. It measures a capacity of 333,305 cubic meters and a dead weight tonnage of 297,101 tons. With its main engine power at 23, 270 kilowatts, New Resource could sail at a speed of 15.8 kn.

凯源 New Resource

"凯源"轮于2010年1月14日由大连造船厂建造竣工出厂，由海宏轮船（香港）有限公司管理经营，在国际航线上运输原油。该轮与另一艘油轮中英文名字重复，另一艘油轮于1994年10月18日更名"泰源"轮（Thai Resource）。

Built by Dalian Shipbuilding Industry Co., Ltd. New Resource was completed on January 14, 2010. It is managed by Associated Maritime Company (Hong Kong) Limited, and engaged in international crude oil shipping. New Resource carries the same Chinese and English name of another vessel, which was renamed as Tai Yuan (Thai Resource) on October 18, 1994.

⚓ 凯胜 New Success

"凯胜"轮英文船名New Success，超大型油轮，船长330米，船宽60米，吃水21.52米，载重吨297027，主机功率23270千瓦，航速每小时15.8海里。

New Success is a Very Large Crude Carrier (VLCC). Its length overall is 330 meters and the beam is 60 meters with a draught of 21.52 meters. With its main engine power at 23, 270 kilowatts, New Success could sail at a speed of

凯胜 New Success

15.8 kn and has a dead weight tonnage of 297,027 tons.

"凯胜"轮于 2010 年 7 月 13 日由大连造船厂建造竣工出厂，由海宏轮船（香港）有限公司管理经营，航行于国际航线运输原油。

Built by Dalian Shipbuilding Industry Co., Ltd., New Success was completed on July 13, 2010. It is managed by Associated Maritime Company (Hong Kong) Limited, and engaged in international crude oil shipping.

凯德 New Award

"凯德"轮英文船名 New Award，阿芙拉型油轮，船长 244.6 米，船宽 42 米，吃水 15.52 米，载重吨 109804，主机功率 13164 千瓦，航速每小时 15.5 海里。

New Award is an Aframax oil tanker. Its length overall is 244.6 meters and the beam is 42 meters with a draught of 15.52 meters. With its main engine power of 13,164 kilowatts, New Award could sail at a speed of 15.5 kn and has a dead weight tonnage of 109,804 tons.

凯德 New Award

"凯德"轮于 2010 年 9 月 3 日由大连造船厂建造竣工出厂，由海宏轮船（香港）有限公司管理经营，航行于国际航线运输原油。

Built by Dalian Shipbuilding Industry Co., Ltd., New Award was completed on September 3, 2010. It is managed by Associated Maritime Company (Hong Kong) Limited, and engaged in international crude oil shipping.

凯丰 New Vanguard

"凯丰"轮英文船名 New Vanguard，超大型油轮，船长 330 米，船宽 60 米，吃水 21.52 米，载重吨 297115，主机功率 23270 千瓦，航速每小时 15.8 海里。

New Vanguard is a Very Large Crude Carrier (VLCC). Its length overall is 330 meters and the beam is

60 meters with a draught of 21.52 meters. With its main engine power at 23,270 kilowatts, New Vanguard could sail at a speed of 15.8 kn and has a dead weight tonnage of 297,115 tons.

"凯丰"轮于 2011 年 3 月 30 日由大连造船厂建造竣工出厂，航行于国际航线运输原油，由海宏轮船（香港）有限公司管理经营。

凯丰　New Vanguard

Built by Dalian Shipbuilding Industry Co., Ltd., New Vanguard was completed on March 30, 2011. It is managed by Associated Maritime Company (Hong Kong) Limited, and engaged in international crude oil shipping.

⚓ 凯景　New Vista

"凯景"轮英文船名 New Vista，超大型油轮，船长 330 米，船宽 60 米，吃水 21.52 米，载重吨 297253，主机功率 23270 千瓦，航速每小时 15.8 海里。

New Vista is a Very Large Crude Carrier (VLCC). Its length overall is 330 meters and the beam is 60 meters with a draught of 21.52 meters. With its main engine power at 23,270 kilowatts, New Vista could sail at a speed of 15.8 kn and has a dead weight tonnage of 297,253 tons.

凯景　New Vista

"凯景"轮于 2011 年 7 月 19 日由大连造船厂建造竣工出厂，由海宏轮船（香港）有限公司管理经营，在国际航线上运输原油。

Built by Dalian Shipbuilding Industry Co., Ltd., New Vista was completed on July 19, 2011. It is managed by Associated Maritime Company (Hong Kong) Limited, and engaged in international crude oil shipping.

⚓ 明源 Pacific Resource

"明源"轮英文船名 Pacific Resource，好望角型散货船，船长 294.8 米，船宽 46 米，吃水 18.12 米，载重吨 180090，主机功率 16097 千瓦，航速每小时 15.5 海里。

Pacific Resource is a Capesize bulk carrier. Its length overall is 294.8 meters and the beam is 46 meters with a draught of 18.12 meters. With its main engine power at 16,097 kilowatts, Pacific Resource could sail at a speed of 15.5 kn and has a dead weight tonnage of 180,090 tons.

明源 Pacific Resource

"明源"轮于 2010 年 1 月 14 日由大连造船厂建造竣工出厂，航行于国际航线运输干散货，由香港明华船务有限公司管理经营。

Built by Dalian Shipbuilding Industry Co., Ltd., Pacific Resource was completed on January 14, 2010. It is engaged in international dry bulk shipping, and managed by Hong Kong Ming Wah Shipping Co., Ltd.

⚓ 明立 Pacific Creation

"明立"轮英文船名 Pacific Creation，好望角型散货船，船长 295 米，船宽 46 米，吃水 18.12 米，载重吨 180050，主机功率 16097 千瓦，航速每小时 15.5 海里。

Pacific Creation is a Capesize bulk carrier. Its length overall is 295 meters and the beam is 46 meters with a draught of 18.12 meters. With its main engine power at 16,097 kilowatts, Pacific Creation could sail at a speed of 15.5 kn and has a dead weight tonnage of 180,050 tons.

"明立"轮于 2010 年 8 月 30 日由青岛北海造船厂建造竣工出厂，航行于全球运输干散货，由香港明华船务有限公司管理经营。

明立　Pacific Creation

Built by Qingdao Beihai Shipbuilding Heavy Industry Co., Ltd., Pacific Creation was completed on August 30, 2010. It is engaged in international dry bulk shipping, and managed by Hong Kong Ming Wah Shipping Co., Ltd.

⚓ 明鸿　Pacific Century

"明鸿"轮英文船名 Pacific Century，好望角型散货船，船长 295 米，船宽 46 米，吃水 18.12 米，载重吨 180467，主机功率 16097 千瓦，航速每小时 15.5 海里。

Pacific Century is a Capesize bulk carrier. Its length overall is 295 meters and the beam is 46 meters with a draught of 18.12 meters. With its main engine power at 16,097 kilowatts, Pacific Century could sail at a speed of 15.5 kn and has a dead weight tonnage of 180,467 tons.

"明鸿"轮于 2011 年 1 月 18 日由大连造船厂建造竣工出厂，航行于全球航线运输干散货，由香港明华船务有限公司管理经营。

Built by Dalian Shipbuilding Industry Co., Ltd., Pacific Century was completed on January 18, 2011. It is engaged in international dry bulk shipping, and managed by Hong Kong Ming Wah Shipping Co., Ltd.

明鸿　Pacific Century

明顺　Pacific Success

"明顺"轮英文船名 Pacific Success，好望角型散货船，船长 294.99 米，船宽 45.99 米，吃水 18.12 米，载重吨 180407，主机功率 16097 千瓦，航速每小时 15.5 海里。

Pacific Success is a Capesize bulk carrier. Its length overall is 294.99 meters and the beam is 45.99 meters with a draught of 18.12 meters. With its main engine power at 16,097 kilowatts, Pacific Success could sail at a speed of 15.5 kn and has a dead weight tonnage of 180,407 tons.

"明顺"轮于 2011 年 4 月 21 日由大连造船厂建造竣工出厂，在国际航线上运输干散货，由香港明华船务有限公司经营管理。2012 年度被招商局能源运输股份有限公司评为"先进船舶"。

Built by Dalian Shipbuilding Industry Co., Ltd., Pacific Success was completed on April 21, 2011. It is engaged in international dry bulk shipping, and managed by Hong Kong Ming Wah Shipping Co., Ltd. In 2012, the vessel was awarded as "Outstanding Vessel" by China Merchants Energy Shipping Co., Ltd.

明顺　Pacific Success

明誉 Pacific Spirit

"明誉"轮英文船名 Pacific Spirit，好望角型散货船，船长 295 米，船宽 46 米，吃水 18.12 米，载重吨 180399，主机功率 16097 千瓦，航速每小时 15.5 海里。

Pacific Spirit is a Capesize bulk carrier. Its length overall is 295 meters and the beam is 46 meters with a draught of 18.12 meters. With its main engine power at 16,097 kilowatts , Pacific Spirit could sail at a speed of 15.5 kn and has a dead weight tonnage of 180, 399 tons.

明誉 Pacific Spirit

"明誉"轮于 2011 年 5 月 30 日由大连造船厂建造竣工出厂，作为国际商船，出厂后一直在国际航线上运输干散货，由香港明华船务有限公司负责管理经营。

Built by Dalian Shipbuilding Industry Co., Ltd., Pacific Spirit was completed on May 30, 2011. It is engaged for international dry bulk shipping, and managed by Hong Kong Ming Wah Shipping Co., Ltd.

明景 Pacific Vista

"明景"轮英文船名 Pacific Vista，好望角型散货船，船长 295 米，船宽 46 米，吃水 18.12 米，载重吨 180000，主机功率 16097 千瓦，航速每小时 15.5 海里。

Pacific Vista is a Capesize bulk carrier. Its length overall is 295 meters and the beam is 46 meters with a draught of 18.12 meters. With its main engine power at 16,097 kilowatts, Pacific Vista could sail at a speed of 15.5 kn and has a dead weight tonnage of 180,000 tons.

"明景"轮于 2012 年 6 月 15 日由大连造船厂建造竣工出厂，由香港明华船务有限公司管理经营，在国际航线上运输干散货。2013 年

明景 Pacific Vista

度被招商局能源运输股份有限公司评为"先进船舶"。

Built by Dalian Shipbuilding Industry Co., Ltd., Pacific Vista was completed on June 15, 2012. It is engaged in international dry bulk shipping, and managed by Hong Kong Ming Wah Shipping Co., Ltd. In 2013, the vessel was awarded as "Outstanding Vessel" by China Merchants Energy Shipping Co., Ltd.

⚓ 明舟　Pacific Argosy

"明舟"轮英文船名 Pacific Argosy，好望角型散货船，船长 295 米，船宽 46 米，吃水 18.12 米，载重吨 180000，主机功率 16097 千瓦，航速每小时 15.5 海里。

Pacific Argosy is a Capesize bulk carrier. Its length overall is 295 meters and the beam is 46 meters with a draught of 18.12 meters. With its main engine power at 16,097 kilowatts, Pacific Argosy could sail at a speed of 15.5 kn and has a dead weight tonnage of 180,000 tons.

"明舟"轮于 2012 年 6 月 27 日由青岛北海造船厂建造竣工出厂，于国际航线运输干散货，隶属于香港明华船务有限公司。

Built by Qingdao Beihai Shipbuilding Heavy Industry Co., Ltd., Pacific Argosy was completed on June 27, 2012. It is engaged in international dry bulk shipping, and managed by Hong Kong Ming Wah Shipping Co., Ltd.

明舟　Pacific Argosy

招商六　Zhao Shang Liu

⚓ 招商六　Zhao Shang Liu

"招商六"轮英文船名 Zhao Shang Liu，石油液化气船，船长 69.5 米，船宽 13 米，吃水 4.5 米，舱容 1558 立方米，载重吨 850，主机功率 1837 千瓦，航速每小时 12 海里。

Zhao Shang Liu is an LPG tanker. Its length overall is 69.5 meters and the beam is 13 meters with a draught of 4.5 meters. It measures a capacity of 1,558 cubic meters and a dead weight tonnage of 850 tons. With its main engine power at 1,837 kilowatts, Zhao Shang Liu could sail at a speed of 12 kn.

"招商六"轮由日本岸上造船厂建造，1979 年 6 月 1 日出厂，曾用名"招港二号"，2005 年 5 月 31 日从海南招港海运有限公司转入深圳华南液化气船务有限公司管理营运，2010 年 5 月退役报废。

Built by Kishigami Shipbuilding Company in Japan, Zhao Shang Liu was launched on June 1, 1979, and previously named "Zhao Gang Er Hao". On May 31, 2005, its management was transferred by Hainan Zhaogang Shipping Co., Ltd. to Shenzhen Southern China LNG Shipping Co., Ltd. It was retired and scrapped in May 2010.

⚓ 大鹏昊　Dapeng Sun

"大鹏昊"轮英文船名 Dapeng Sun，大薄膜型液化天然气船，船长 292 米，船宽 43.35 米，吃水 11.43 米，舱容 145028 立方米，载重吨 83050，主机功率 27700 千瓦，航速每小时 19.5 海里。

Dapeng Sun is a large membrane LNG tanker. Its length overall is 292 meters and the beam is 43.35 meters with a draught of 11.43 meters. It measures a capacity of 145,028 cubic meters and a dead weight tonnage of 83,050 tons. With its main engine power at 27,700 kilowatts, Dapeng Sun could sail at a speed of 19.5 kn.

"大鹏昊"轮于 2008 年 4 月 3 日由上海沪东中华造船厂建造竣工出厂，由中国液化天然气运输（控股）有限公司管理经营，运输液化天然气，服务于澳大利亚丹皮尔港至广东深圳航线。"大鹏昊"轮是中国自行建造的第一艘大型薄膜型液化天然气船，也是中国第一支液化天然气运输船队的第一艘船。"大鹏昊"轮开创了中国液化天然气海上贸易运输的新局面，创造了我国液化天然气运输历史上的若干个第一，填补了中国能源运输方面诸多的空白。

Built by Hudong-Zhonghua Shipbuilding (Group) Co., Ltd., Dapeng Sun was launched on April 3, 2008. It is managed by China LNG Shipping (Holdings) Limited, and engaged in shipping between Australia's Dampier Port and Shenzhen of Guangdong Province in China. Being the first self-made membrane LNG tanker in China, Dapeng Sun is also the first vessel of LNG fleet in China. It ushers in a new era for LNG shipping, and has made several breakthroughs in the history of LNG transportation and energy shipping in China.

⚓ 大鹏月　Dapeng Moon

"大鹏月"轮英文船名 Dapeng Moon，大薄膜型液化天然气船，船长 292.3 米，船宽 43.35 米，吃水 11.43 米，舱容 145028 立方米，载重吨 82645，主机功率 27700 千瓦，航速每小时 19.5 海里。

Dapeng Moon is a large membrane LNG tanker. Its length overall is 292.3 meters and the beam is 43.35 meters with a draught of 11.43 meters. It measures a capacity of 145,028 cubic meters and a dead weight tonnage of 82,645 tons. With its main engine power at 27,700 kilowatts, Dapeng Moon could sail at a speed of 19.5 kn.

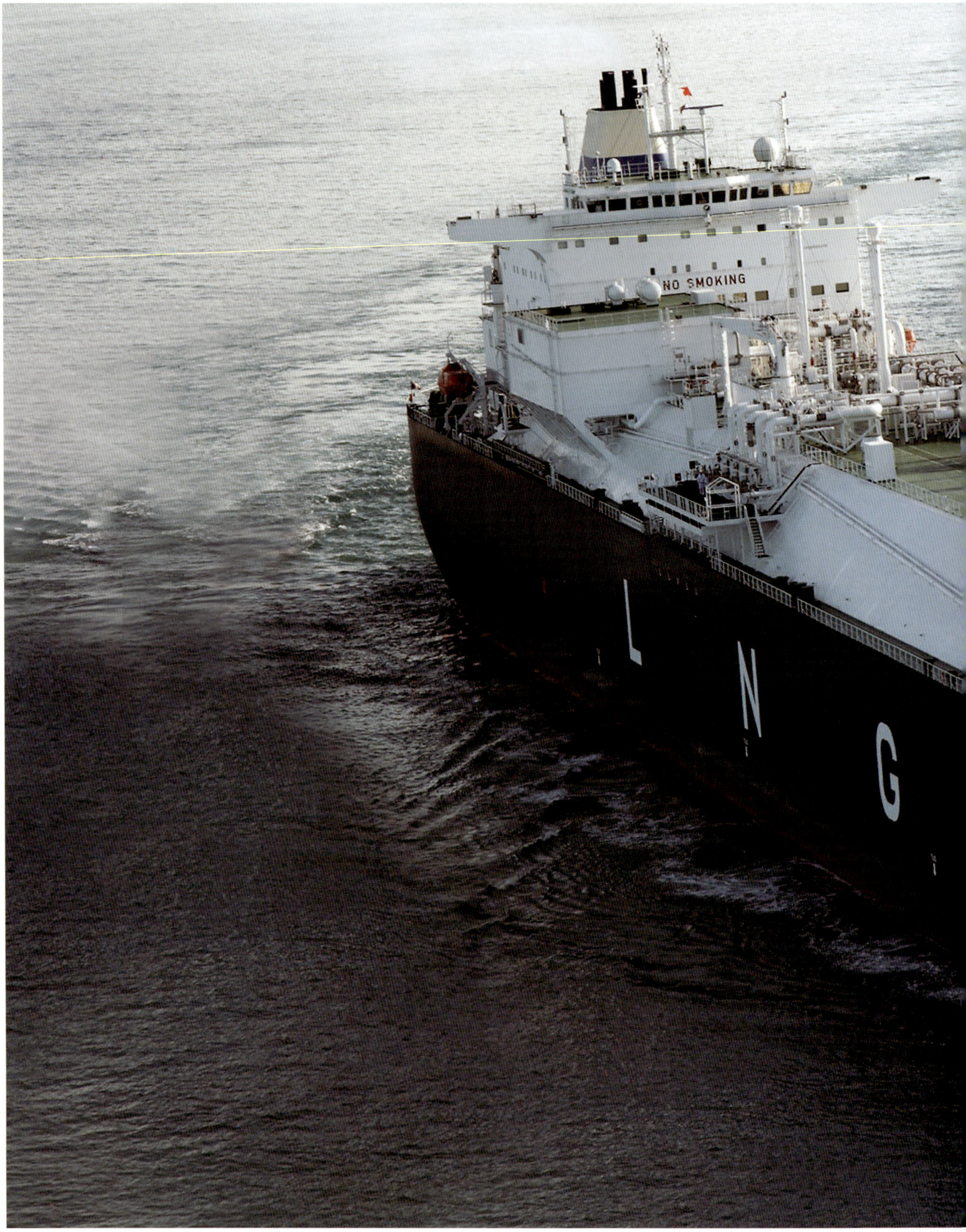
NO SMOKING
L N G

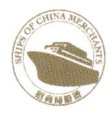

大鹏昊　Dapeng Sun

大鹏月　Dapeng Moon

"大鹏月"轮于 2008 年 7 月 10 日由上海沪东中华造船厂建造竣工出厂，是我国自行建造的第二艘大薄膜型液化天然气船，由中国液化天然气运输（控股）有限公司管理经营，运输液化天然气，服务于澳大利亚丹皮尔港至广东深圳的航线。

Built by Hudong-Zhonghua Shipbuilding (Group) Co., Ltd., Dapeng Moon was launched on July 10, 2008 as the second LNG tanker made by China. Under the operation of China LNG Shipping (Holdings) Limited, Dapeng Moon is engaged in LNG transportation between Dampier Port of Australia and Shenzhen of Guangdong Province in China.

⚓ 大鹏星　Dapeng Star

"大鹏星"轮英文船名 Dapeng Star，大薄膜型液化天然气船，船长 292 米，船宽 43.35 米，吃水 11.5 米，舱容 145338 立方米，载重吨 82428，主机功率 27700 千瓦，航速每小时 19.5 海里。

Dapeng Star is a large membrane LNG tanker. Its length overall is 292 meters and the beam is 43.35 meters with a draught of 11.5 meters. It measures a capacity of 145,338 cubic meters and a dead weight tonnage of 82,428 tons. With its main engine power at 27,700 kilowatts, Dapeng Star could sail at a speed of 19.5 kn.

"大鹏星"轮于2009年12月10日由上海沪东中华造船厂建造竣工出厂，运输液化天然气，服务于澳大利亚丹皮尔港至广东深圳航线，隶属于中国液化天然气运输（控股）有限公司。

Built by Hudong-Zhonghua Shipbuilding (Group) Co., Ltd., Dapeng Star was launched on December 10, 2009. It is engaged in LNG shipping service between Dampier Port of Australia and Shenzhen of Guangdong Province in China under the management of China LNG Shipping (Holdings) Limited.

大鹏星　Dapeng Star

⚓ 闽榕　Min Rong

"闽榕"轮英文船名 Min Rong，大薄膜型液化天然气船，船长292米，船宽43.35米，吃水11.43米，舱容145028立方米，载重吨82359，主机功率27700千瓦，航速每小时19.5海里。

闽榕　Min Rong

Min Rong is a large membrane LNG tanker. Its length overall is 292 meters and the beam is 43.35 meters with a draught of 11.43 meters. It measures a capacity of 145,028 cubic meters and a dead weight tonnage of 82,359 tons. With its main engine power at 27,700 kilowatts, Min Rong could sail at a speed of 19.5 kn.

"闽榕"轮于 2009 年 2 月 24 日由上海沪东中华造船厂建造竣工出厂，航行于印度尼西亚东固至福建秀屿航线，由中国液化天然气运输（控股）有限公司管理经营。

Built by Hudong-Zhonghua Shipbuilding (Group) Co., Ltd., Min Rong was launched on February 24, 2009. It is engaged in transportation service between Tangguh of Indonesia and Xiuyu of Fujian Province in China under the management of China LNG Shipping (Holdings) Limited.

闽鹭　Min Lu

"闽鹭"轮英文船名 Min Lu，大薄膜型液化天然气船，船长 292 米，船宽 43.35 米，吃水 11.43 米，舱容 145386 立方米，载重吨 82598，主机功率 27700 千瓦，航速每小时 19.5 海里。

Min Lu is a large membrane LNG tanker. Its length overall is 292 meters and the beam is 43.35 meters with a draught of 11.43 meters. It measures a capacity of 145,386 cubic meters and a dead weight tonnage of 82,598 tons. With its main engine power at 27,700 kilowatts, Min Lu could sail at a speed of 19.5 kn.

闽鹭　Min Lu

华南 1　Hua Nan 1

"闽鹭"轮于 2009 年 8 月 13 日由上海沪东中华造船厂建造竣工出厂，由中国液化天然气运输（控股）有限公司管理经营，运输液化天然气，服务于印度尼西亚东固至福建秀屿航线。

Built by Hudong-Zhonghua Shipbuilding (Group) Co., Ltd., Min Lu was launched on August 13, 2009. It is engaged in LNG shipping service between Tangguh of Indonesia and Xiuyu of Fujian Province in China. It is managed by China LNG Shipping (Holdings) Limited.

⚓ 华南 1　Hua Nan 1

"华南 1" 英文船名 Hua Nan 1，液化石油气船，船长 99.99 米，船宽 15.2 米，吃水 5.3 米，载重吨 2521，主机功率 2574 千瓦，航速每小时 13.5 海里。

Hua Nan 1 is an LPG tanker. Its length overall is 99.99 meters and the beam is 15.2 meters with a draught of 5.3 meters. With its main engine power at 2,574 kilowatts, Hua Nan 1 could sail at a speed of 13.5 kn and has a dead weight tonnage of 2,521 tons.

"华南 1" 于 2011 年 7 月 7 日由台州市五洲船业有限公司建造竣工出厂，2011 年 7 月 27 日顺利完成首航，从事东南亚和中国沿海液化气的运输。该轮由深圳华南液化气船务有限公司管理。

Built by Taizhou Wuzhou Shipbuilding Industry Co., Ltd., Hua Nan 1 was launched on July 7, 2011. After finishing its maiden voyage on July 27, 2011, it is engaged in service for LPG shipping between South-east Asia and coastal cities in China. It is managed by Shenzhen Southern China LNG Shipping Co., Ltd.

华南 2 Hua Nan 2

"华南 2"英文船名 Hua Nan 2，液化石油气船，船长 99.99 米，船宽 15.2 米，吃水 5.30 米，载重吨 2521，主机功率 2574 千瓦，航速每小时 13.5 海里。

Hua Nan 2 is an LPG tanker. Its length overall is 99.99 meters and the beam is 15.2 meters with a draught of 5.3 meters. With its main engine power at 2,574 kilowatts, Hua Nan 2 could sail at a speed of 13.5 kn and has a dead weight tonnage of 2,521 tons.

"华南 2"于 2011 年 11 月 2 日由台州市五洲船业有限公司建造竣工出厂，2011 年 11 月 18 日顺利完成首航，由深圳华南液化气船务有限公司管理经营，航行于东南亚和中国沿海。

Built by Taizhou Wuzhou Shipbuilding Industry Co., Ltd., Hua Nan 2 was launched on November 2, 2011. After finishing its maiden voyage on November 18, 2011, Hua Nan 2 is engaged in service for LPG shipping between South-east Asia and coastal cities in China. It is managed by Shenzhen Southern China LNG Shipping Co., Ltd.

华南 2　Hua Nan 2

华南 3　Hua Nan 3

⚓ 华南 3　Hua Nan 3

"华南 3"英文船名 Hua Nan 3，液化石油气船，船长 99.99 米，船宽 15.2 米，吃水 5.3 米，载重吨 2521，主机功率 2574 千瓦，航速每小时 13.5 海里。"华南 3"于 2011 年 11 月 28 日由台州市五洲船业有限公司建造竣工出厂，2011 年 12 月 18 日顺利完成首航，由深圳华南液化气船务有限公司管理经营。

Hua Nan 3 is an LPG tanker. Its length overall is 99.99 meters and the beam is 15.2 meters with a draught of 5.3 meters. With its main engine power at 2,574 kilowatts, Hua Nan 3 could sail at a speed of 13.5 kn and has a dead weight tonnage of 2,521 tons. Built by Taizhou Wuzhou Shipbuilding Industry Co., Ltd., Hua Nan 3 was launched on November 28, 2011. It finished its maiden voyage on December 18, 2011, and it managed by Shenzhen Southern China LNG Shipping Co., Ltd.

⚓ 申海　Shen Hai

"申海"轮英文船名 Shen Hai，大薄膜型液化天然气船，船长 292 米，船宽 43.35 米，吃水 11.45 米，载重吨 82598，主机功率 27700 千瓦，航速每小时 20.47 海里。

Shen Hai is a large membrane LNG tanker. Its length overall is 292 meters and the beam is 43.35 meters with a draught of 11.45 meters. With its main engine power at 27,700 kilowatts, Shen Hai could sail at a speed of 20.47 kn and has a dead weight tonnage of 82,598 tons.

"申海"轮于 2012 年 9 月 8 日由上海沪东中华造船厂建造出厂，中国液化天然气运输（控股）有限公司管理经营，航行于马来西亚宾土卢至上海洋山航线，为中国运输进口液化天然气。

Built by Hudong-Zhonghua Shipbuilding (Group) Co., Ltd., Shen Hai was launched on September 8, 2012. It is engaged in shipping imported LNG from Bintulu in Malaysia to Yangshan of Shanghai in China. It is managed by China LNG Shipping (Holdings) Limited.

"申海"轮新接船的高级船员和管理公司领导合影

New senior crew members of Shen Hai taking photo with the management team

申海　Shen Hai

招商一　Zhao Shang Yi

招商一　Zhao Shang Yi

"招商一"英文船名 Zhao Shang Yi，液化石油气船，船长 94.6 米，船宽 15.6 米，吃水 3.8 米，载重吨 1760，主机功率 1200 千瓦，航速每小时 12.5 海里。

Zhao Shang Yi is an LPG tanker. Its length overall is 94.6 meters and the beam is 15.6 meters with a draught of 3.8 meters. With its main engine power at 1,200 kilowatts, Zhao Shang Yi could sail at a speed of 12.5 kn and has a dead weight tonnage of 1,760 tons.

"招商一"于 2011 年 8 月 31 日由上海江南造船厂建造竣工出厂，出厂后一直从事东南亚、中国沿海及长江液化气的运输，2013 年由招商局长江液化气运输有限公司划归深圳华南液化气船务有限公司管理经营。

Built by Jiangnan Shipyard in Shanghai, Zhao Shang Yi was launched on August 31, 2011. It is in service for shipping LPG between South-east Asia and Chinese ports along the ocean and the Yangtze River. In 2013, China Merchants transferred its management from the Yangtze River LNG Shipping Co., Ltd. to Shenzhen Southern China LNG Shipping Co., Ltd.

台山　Tai Shan

⚓ 台山　Tai Shan

"台山"轮英文船名 Tai Shan，高速客船，船长 39.9 米，船宽 12.9 米，吃水 1.3 米，载重吨 560，主机功率 3840 千瓦，航速每小时 32 海里。

Tai Shan is a high-speed passenger vessel. Its length overall is 39.9 meters and the beam is 12.9 meters with a draught of 1.3 meters. With its main engine power at 3,840 kilowatts, Tai Shan could sail at a speed of 32 kn and has a dead weight tonnage of 560 tons.

"台山"轮由澳大利亚造船厂建造，1993 年 6 月 4 日出厂，该轮于 2002 年 8 月 5 日购进并投入蛇口至香港航线。由深圳迅隆船务有限公司管理营运。2011 年度和 2013 年度被国家海事局授予"安全诚信船舶"。

Built by Australian Shipyard, Tai Shan was launched on June 4, 1993 and was purchased by China Merchants on August 5, 2002, serving the passenger route between Shekou and Hong Kong. It is managed by Xunlong Shipping Co., Ltd. and was awarded "Safe and Credit Standing Vessel" by Maritime Safety Administration of the People's Republic of China.

⚓ 迅隆 3　Xun Long 3

"迅隆 3"英文船名 Xun Long 3，高速客船，船长 33 米，船宽 8.8 米，吃水 1 米，载重吨 438，主机功率 2100 千瓦，航速每小时 27.5 海里。

Xun Long 3 is a high-speed passenger vessel. Its length overall is 33 meters and the beam is 8.8 meters with a draught of 1 meters. With its main engine power at 2,100 kilowatts, Xun Long could sail at a speed of 27.5 kn and has a dead weight tonnage of 438 tons.

"迅隆 3"于 2007 年 9 月 20 日由广东宏深船舶工程有限公司建造竣工出厂，2007 年 10 月 29 日投入蛇口至港澳客运航线，由深圳迅隆船务有限公司管理经营。2011 年度和 2012 年度被国家海事局授予"安全诚信船舶"；2012 年 7 月荣获全国水运系统"安全优秀船舶"称号。

Built by Guangdong Hongshen Ship Technology Co., Ltd., Xun Long 3 was launched on September 20, 2007 and was put into use on October 29, 2007, serving the passenger routes between Shekou and Hong Kong/Macau. It is managed by Xunlong Shipping Co., Ltd. and was awarded "Safe and Credit Standing Vessel" by Maritime Safety Administration of the People's Republic of China in 2011 and 2012, and "Excellent and Safe Vessel" by National Water Transport System in July 2012.

⚓ 迅隆 4　Xun Long 4

"迅隆 4"英文船名 Xun Long 4，高速客船，船长 33 米，船宽 8.8 米，吃水 1 米，载重吨 438，主机功率 2100 千瓦，航速每小时 27.5 海里。

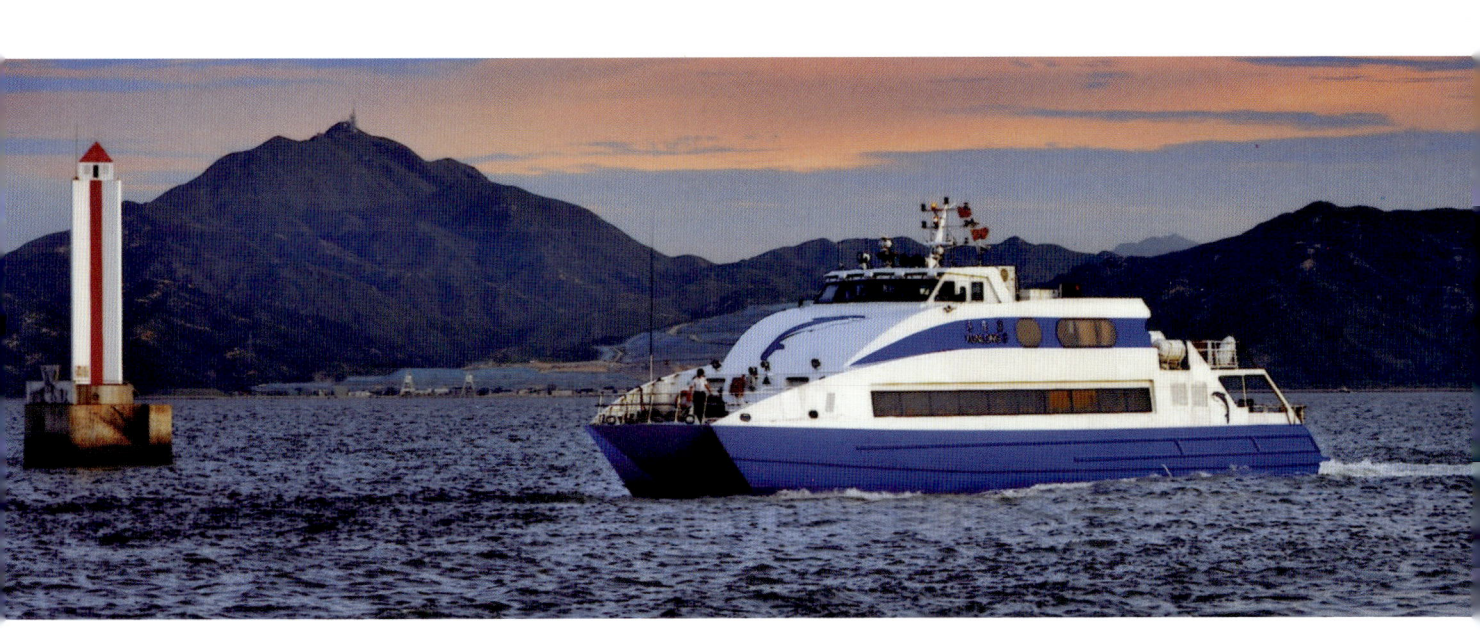

迅隆 3　Xun Long 3

迅隆 4　Xun Long 4

Xun Long 4 is a high-speed passenger vessel. Its length overall is 33 meters and the beam is 8.8 meters with a draught of 1 meters. With its main engine power at 2,100 kilowatts, Xun Long could sail at a speed of 27.5 kn and has a dead weight tonnage of 438 tons.

"迅隆 4" 于 2007 年 12 月 20 日由广东宏深船舶工程有限公司建造竣工出厂，2008 年 3 月投入蛇口至港澳客运航线。2011 年度和 2013 年度被国家海事局授予"安全诚信船舶"称号。

Built by Guangdong Hongshen Ship Technology Co., Ltd., Xun Long 4 was launched on December 20, 2007 and was put into use in March, 2008, serving the passenger routes between Shekou and Hong Kong/Macau. It was awarded "Safe and Credit Standing Vessel" by Maritime Safety Administration of the People's Republic of China in 2011 and 2013.

⚓ 迅隆 5　Xun Long 5

"迅隆 5" 英文船名 Xun Long 5，高速客船，船长 34 米，船宽 8.5 米，吃水 1.35 米，载重吨 282，主机功率 2100 千瓦，航速每小时 28 海里。

Xun Long 5 is a high-speed passenger vessel. Its length overall is 34 meters and the beam is 8.5 meters with a draught of 1.35 meters. With its main engine power at 2,100 kilowatts, Xun Long could sail at a speed of 28 kn and has a dead weight tonnage of 282 tons.

"迅隆 5" 于 2012 年 3 月 9 日由广州市英辉南方造船公司建造竣工出厂，2012 年 5 月投入深圳至港澳客运航线，由深圳迅隆船务有限公司管理经营。

Built by Afai Southern Shipyard (Panyu Guangzhou) Ltd., Xun Long 5 was launched on March 9, 2012 and was put into use in May 2012, serving the passenger routes between Shenzhen and Hong Kong/Macau. It is managed by Xunlong Shipping Co., Ltd.

迅隆 6　Xun Long 6

⚓ 迅隆 6　Xun Long 6

"迅隆 6" 英文船名 Xun Long 6，高速客船，船长 34 米，船宽 8.5 米，吃水 1.35 米，载重吨 282，主机功率 2100 千瓦，航速每小时 28 海里。

Xun Long 6 is a high-speed passenger vessel. Its length overall is 34 meters and the beam is 8.5 meters with a draught of 1.35 meters. With its main engine power at 2,100 kilowatts, Xun Long could sail at a speed of 28 kn and has a dead weight tonnage of 282 tons.

"迅隆 6" 于 2012 年 4 月 28 日由广州市英辉南方造船公司建造竣工出厂，2012 年 7 月投入深圳至港澳客运航线，由深圳迅隆船务有限公司管理经营。

Built by Afai Southern Shipyard (Panyu Guangzhou) Ltd., Xun Long 6 was launched on April 28, 2012 and was put into use in July 2012, serving the passenger routes between Shenzhen and Hong Kong/Macau. It is managed by Xunlong Shipping Co., Ltd.

附录
招商局船舶汇总表

APPENDIX
THE SUMMARY OF CHINA MERCHANTS' SHIPS

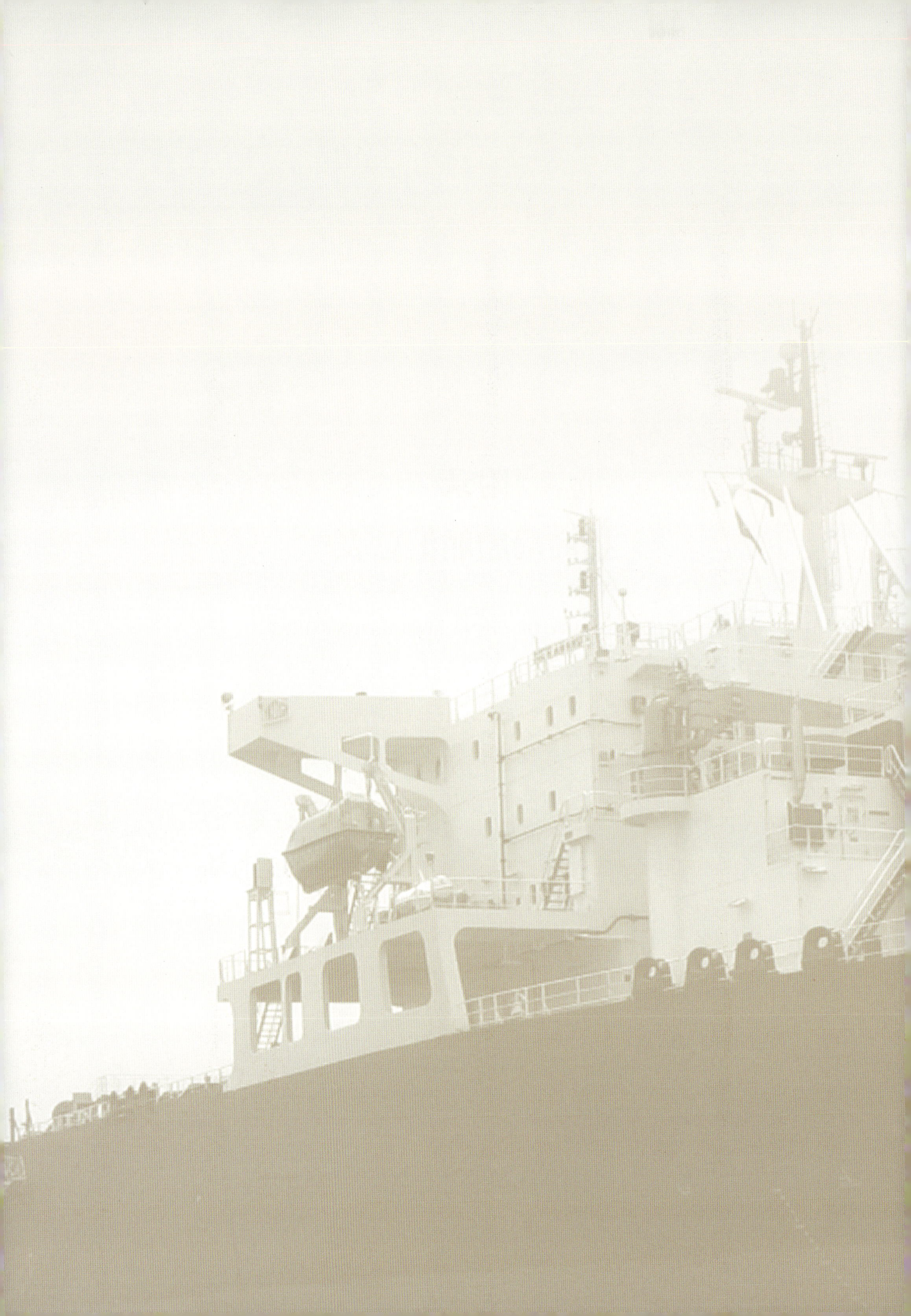

晚清时期
In the late Qing Dynasty

序号 No.	船名 Name	序号 No.	船名 Name	序号 No.	船名 Name
1	伊敦 Aden	16	江永 Jiang Yong	31	飞鲸 Fei Jing
2	永清 Yong Qing	17	永宁 Yong Ning	32	广大（富顺）Guang Da (Fu Shun)
3	利运 Li Yun	18	洞庭 Dong Ting	33	广利 Guang Li
4	福星 Fu Xing	19	海晏 Hai Yan	34	固陵 Gu Ling
5	和众 He Zhong	20	美富 Mei Fu	35	广济 Guang Ji
6	富有 Fu You	21	江天 Jiang Tian	36	新裕 Xin Yu
7	利航 Li Hang	22	江孚 Jiang Fu	37	爱仁 Ai Ren
8	日新 Ri Xin	23	江长 Jiang Chang	38	新济 Xin Ji
9	厚生 Hou Sheng	24	江裕 Jiang Yu	39	新丰 Xin Feng
10	保大 Bao Da	25	海定 Hai Ding	40	快利 Kuai Li
11	丰顺 Feng Shun	26	图南 Tu Nan	41	公平 Gong Ping
12	成大 Cheng Da	27	拱北 Gong Bei	42	安平 An Ping
13	伏波 Fu Bo	28	致远 Zhi Yuan	43	泰顺 Tai Shun
14	汉广 Han Guang	29	怀远 Huai Yuan	44	遇顺 Yu Shun
15	江宽 Jiang Kuan	30	普济 Pu Ji	45	新昌 Xin Chang

续表

序号 No.	船名 Name	序号 No.	船名 Name	序号 No.	船名 Name
46	新康 Xin Kang	61	江表 Jiang Biao	76	宝康（保康） Bao Kang
47	新铭（新捷） Xin Ming (Xin Jie)	62	镇东 Zhen Dong	77	海镜 Hai Jing
48	同华 Tong Hua	63	海琛 Hai Chen		
49	吉安 Ji An	64	益东 Yi Dong		
50	恒新 Heng Xin	65	镇西 Zhen Xi		
51	江新 Jiang Xin	66	新盛 Xin Sheng		
52	兴盛 Xing Sheng	67	协和 Xie He		
53	惠吉 Hui Ji	68	美宫 Mei Gong		
54	江平 Jiang Ping	69	海珊 Hai Shan		
55	新安 Xin An	70	江靖 Jiang Jing		
56	江华 Kiang Hwa	71	江汇 Jiang Hui		
57	江通 Jiang Tong	72	南浔 Nan Xun		
58	江源 Jiang Yuan	73	满洲 Man Zhou		
59	美利 Mei Li	74	大有 Da You		
60	康济 Kang Ji	75	汉阳 Han Yang		

民国时期
In the era of the Republic of China

序号 No.	船名 Name	序号 No.	船名 Name	序号 No.	船名 Name
1	嘉禾 Jia He	16	江汉 Kiang Han	31	津通 Jin Tong
2	江安 Jiang An	17	澄平 Cheng Ping	32	岷江 Min Jiang
3	江顺 Jiang Shun	18	利济 Li Ji	33	巴江 Ba Jiang
4	江庆 Jiang Qing	19	江兴 Jiang Xing	34	大业 Da Ye
5	新江天 Xin Jiang Tian	20	景德 Jing De	35	大运 Da Yun
6	新华 Xin Hua	21	镇昌 Zhen Chang	36	大载 Da Zai
7	江大 Jiang Da	22	恒吉 Heng Ji	37	飞舸 Fei Ge
8	江靖 Jiang Jing	23	恒通 Heng Tong	38	江襄 Jiang Xiang
9	海瑞 Hai Rui	24	安宁 An Ning	39	江济 Kiang Chi
10	海祥 Hai Xiang	25	骏发 Jun Fa	40	海天 Hai Tien
11	海元 Hai Yuan	26	利源 Li Yuan	41	海地 Hai Ti
12	海亨 Hai Heng	27	河宽 He Kuan	42	海玄 Hai Hsuan
13	海利 Hai Li	28	飞龙 Fei Long	43	海黄 Hai Huang
14	海贞 Hai Zhen	29	江建 Kiang Kien	44	海宇 Hai Yu
15	海云 Hai Yun	30	遇顺 Yu Shun	45	海宙 Hai Chiao

续表

序号 No.	船名 Name	序号 No.	船名 Name	序号 No.	船名 Name
46	海辰 Hai Chen	61	海粤 Hai Yueh	76	铁桥 Tieh Chiao
47	海宿 Hai Siu	62	海冀 Hai Chi	77	教仁 Chiao Jen
48	海列 Hai Lien	63	海鲁 Hai Lu	78	成功 Cheng Kung
49	海张 Hai Chang	64	海陇 Hai Lung	79	鸿章 Hung Chang
50	海苏 Hai Su	65	海辽 Hai Liao	80	郑和 Zheng He
51	海浙 Hai Chch	66	其美 Chi Mei	81	廷枢 Ting Shu
52	海皖 Hai Wan	67	黄兴 Huang Hsing	82	宣怀 Xuan Huai
53	海赣 Hai Kang	68	蔡锷 Tsai Er	83	继光 Ji Guang
54	海鄂 Hai Er	69	邓铿 Teng Keng	84	海穗 Hai Shui
55	海湘 Hai Xiang	70	执信 Chih Hsin	85	海甬 Hai Yun
56	海川 Hai Chuan	71	仲恺 Chung Kai	86	海杭 Hai Hang
57	海康 Hai Kang	72	延闿 Yen Kai	87	海汉 Hai Han
58	海滇 Hai Dean	73	培德 Pei Teh	88	海沪 Hai Hu
59	海黔 Hai Chien	74	汉民 Han Min	89	海津 Hai Tsin
60	海桂 Hai Kwei	75	林森 Lin Shen	90	海平 Hai Ping

续表

序号 No.	船名 Name	序号 No.	船名 Name	序号 No.	船名 Name
91	锡麟 Shih Lin	106	中 109 Zhong 109	121	华 206 Hua 206
92	秋瑾 Chiu Chin	107	中 110 Zhong 110	122	华 207 Hua 207
93	元培 Yuan Pei	108	中 112 Zhong 112	123	华 208 Hua 208
94	海亚 Hai Ya	109	中 113 Zhong 113	124	华 209 Hua 209
95	海美 Hai Me	110	中 117 Zhong 117	125	华 210 Hua 210
96	海欧 Hai Ou	111	中 118 Zhong 118	126	华 211 Hua 211
97	海澳 Hai Ao	112	中 111 Zhong 111	127	华 212 Hua 212
98	中 101 Zhong 101	113	中 114 Zhong 114	128	自忠 Zi Zhong
99	中 102 Zhong 102	114	中 115 Zhong 115	129	登禹 Deng Yu
100	中 103 Zhong 103	115	中 116 Zhong 116	130	麟阁 Lin Ge
101	中 104 Zhong 104	116	华 201 Hua 201	131	海菲 Hai Fei
102	中 105 Zhong 105	117	华 202 Hua 202	132	海厦 Hai Xia
103	中 106 Zhong 106	118	华 203 Hua 203	133	江新 Kiang Hsin
104	中 107 Zhong 107	119	华 204 Hua 204	134	江亚 Kiang Ya
105	中 108 Zhong 108	120	华 205 Hua 205	135	江静 Kiang Ging

续表

序号 No.	船名 Name	序号 No.	船名 Name	序号 No.	船名 Name
136	江泰 Kiang Tai	151	利110 Li 110	166	民315 Min 315
137	江宁 Kiang Ning	152	民301 Min 301	167	民316 Min 316
138	江平 Kiang Ping	153	民302 Min 302	168	民317 Min 317
139	江隆 Kiang Lung	154	民303 Min 303	169	民318 Min 318
140	江陵 Kiang Ling	155	民304 Min 304	170	和105 He 105
141	江和 Kiang Ho	156	民305 Min 305	171	和106 He 106
142	利101 Li 101	157	民306 Min 306	172	和107 He 107
143	利102 Li 102	158	民307 Min 307	173	和108 He 108
144	利103 Li 103	159	民308 Min 308	174	和109 He 109
145	利104 Li 104	160	民309 Min 309	175	和110 He 110
146	利105 Li 105	161	民310 Min 310	176	和101 He 101
147	利106 Li 106	162	民311 Min 311	177	和102 He 102
148	利107 Li 107	163	民312 Min 312	178	和103 He 103
149	利108 Li 108	164	民313 Min 313	179	和104 He 104
150	利109 Li 109	165	民314 Min 314	180	平801 Ping 801

续表

序号 No.	船名 Name	序号 No.	船名 Name	序号 No.	船名 Name
181	平 802 Ping 802	196	海新 Hai Xin	211	永洪 Yong Hong
182	平 803 Ping 803	197	增利 Zeng Li	212	永澄 Yong Cheng
183	平 804 Ping 804	198	登州 Deng Zhou	213	永泽 Yong Ze
184	平 805 Ping 805	199	青州 Qing Zhou	214	永清 Yong Qing
185	平 806 Ping 806	200	杭州 Hang Zhou	215	永涞 Yong Lai
186	胜 109 Sheng 109	201	苏州 Su Zhou	216	永洮 Yong Tao
187	胜 110 Sheng 110	202	常州 Chang Zhou	217	永潇 Yong Xiao
188	胜 111 Sheng 111	203	兰州 Lan Zhou	218	永湟 Yong Huang
189	胜 112 Sheng 112	204	中州 Zhong Zhou	219	永叙 Yong Xu
190	设 101 She 101	205	万富 Wan Fu	220	永淞 Yong Song
191	设 102 She 102	206	万国 Wan Guo	221	永潼 Yong Tong
192	复 101 Fu 101	207	万利 Wan Li	222	永涪 Yong Fu
193	复 102 Fu 102	208	万民 Wan Min	223	永汉 Yong Han
194	伯先 Bo Xian	209	永渝 Yong Yu	224	永滦 Yong Luan
195	海有 Hai You	210	永灏 Yong Hao	225	永泸 Yong Lu

续表

序号 No.	船名 Name	序号 No.	船名 Name	序号 No.	船名 Name
226	永沘 Yong Fei	241	国富 Guo Fu	256	飞赣 Fei Gan
227	永淮 Yong Huai	242	国达 Guo Da	257	飞康 Fei Kang
228	永湘 Yong Xiang	243	国盛 Guo Sheng	258	飞鄂 Fei E
229	永漳 Yong Zhang	244	飞沪 Fei Hu	259	飞桂 Fei Gui
230	永渭 Yong Wei	245	飞亨 Fei Heng	260	飞闽 Fei Min
231	永洛 Yong Luo	246	飞杭 Fei Hang	261	飞粤 Fei Yue
232	建甲 Jian Jia	247	飞艇 Fei Ting	262	飞加 Fei Jia
233	国强 Guo Qiang	248	飞彪 Fei Biao	263	飞钟 Fei Zhong
234	国伟 Guo Wei	249	飞厦 Fei Xia	264	飞旭 Fei Xu
235	国兴 Guo Xing	250	飞皖 Fei Wan	265	飞虹 Fei Hong
236	国本 Guo Ben	251	飞长 Fei Chang	266	国镇 Guo Zhen
237	国利 Guo Li	252	飞渊 Fei Yuan	267	飞钜 Fei Ju
238	国华 Guo Hua	253	飞侠 Fei Xia	268	飞镁 Fei Mei
239	国仲 Guo Zhong	254	飞宁 Fei Ning	269	飞钰 Fei Yu
240	国丰 Guo Feng	255	飞川 Fei Chuan	270	飞铃 Fei Ling

续表

序号 No.	船名 Name	序号 No.	船名 Name	序号 No.	船名 Name
271	飞镜 Fei Jing	286	飞龙 Fei Long	301	飞信 Fei Xin
272	飞锋 Fei Feng	287	飞鹰 Fei Ying	302	飞明 Fei Ming
273	国良 Guo Liang	288	飞星 Fei Xing	303	飞云 Fei Yun
274	国康 Guo Kang	289	飞骏 Fei Jun	304	飞狮 Fei Shi
275	国运 Guo Yun	290	飞天 Fei Tian	305	飞荣 Fei Rong
276	飞鸠 Fei Jiu	291	飞波 Fei Bo	306	飞中 Fei Zhong
277	飞州 Fei Zhou	292	飞新 Fei Xin	307	国光 Guo Guang
278	飞青 Fei Qing	293	飞涛 Fei Tao	308	国裕 Guo Yu
279	飞鹣 Fei Jian	294	飞元 Fei Yuan	309	飞盛 Fei Sheng
280	国沧 Guo Cang	295	飞胜 Fei Sheng	310	飞安 Fei An
281	飞雯 Fei Wen	296	飞快 Fei Kuai	311	飞雪 Fei Xue
282	飞豹 Fei Bao	297	飞淞 Fei Song	312	国怀 Guo Huai
283	国祥 Guo Xiang	298	飞大 Fei Da	313	飞流 Fei Liu
284	飞富 Fei Fu	299	飞顺 Fei Shun	314	飞开 Fei Kai
285	国宛 Guo Wuan	300	飞福 Fei Fu	315	飞源 Fei Yuan

续表

序号 No.	船名 Name	序号 No.	船名 Name	序号 No.	船名 Name
316	飞礼 Fei Li	331	国沽 Guo Gu	346	招商 5 Zhao Shang 5
317	飞虎 Fei Hu	332	国芦 Guo Lu	347	招商 11 Zhao Shang 11
318	飞鸵 Fei Tuo	333	国唐 Guo Tang	348	招商 12 Zhao Shang 12
319	飞国 Fei Guo	334	国通 Guo Tong	349	招商 20 Zhao Shang 20
320	飞邦 Fei Bang	335	国燕 Guo Yan	350	招商 21 Zhao Shang 21
321	飞永 Fei Yong	336	国朔 Guo Shuo	351	招商 25 Zhao Shang 25
322	飞兴 Fei Xing	337	国冀 Guo Ji	352	招商 26 Zhao Shang 26
323	飞台 Fei Tai	338	国栾 Guo Luan	353	招商 27 Zhao Shang 27
324	飞高 Fei Gao	339	国阳 Guo Yang	354	招商 29 Zhao Shang 29
325	国青 Guo Qing	340	国天 Guo Tian	355	招商 30 Zhao Shang 30
326	国洋 Guo Yang	341	国秦 Guo Qin	356	招商 31 Zhao Shang 31
327	国安 Guo An	342	飞鸿 Fei Hong	357	招商 32 Zhao Shang 32
328	国泰 Guo Tai	343	飞汉 Fei Han	358	招商 33 Zhao Shang 33
329	国山 Guo Shan	344	飞马 Fei Ma	359	招商 36 Zhao Shang 36
330	国津 Guo Jin	345	飞勤 Fei Qin	360	招商 37 Zhao Shang 37

续表

序号 No.	船名 Name	序号 No.	船名 Name	序号 No.	船名 Name
361	招商 38 / Zhao Shang 38	376	招商 333 / Zhao Shang 333	391	招商 461 / Zhao Shang 461
362	招商 39 / Zhao Shang 39	377	招商 346 / Zhao Shang 346	392	招商 468 / Zhao Shang 468
363	招商 40 / Zhao Shang 40	378	招商 367 / Zhao Shang 367	393	招商 64 / Zhao Shang 64
364	招商 41 / Zhao Shang 41	379	招商 44 / Zhao Shang 44	394	招商 367 / Zhao Shang 367
365	招商 46 / Zhao Shang 46	380	招商 304 / Zhao Shang 304	395	招商 368 / Zhao Shang 368
366	招商 47 / Zhao Shang 47	381	招商 49 / Zhao Shang 49	396	供水 4 号 / Gong Shui 4
367	招商 48 / Zhao Shang 48	382	招商 302 / Zhao Shang 302	397	供水 5 号 / Gong Shui 5
368	招商 102 / Zhao Shang 102	383	招商 363 / Zhao Shang 363	398	招商 448 / Zhao Shang 448
369	招商 103 / Zhao Shang 103	384	招商 366 / Zhao Shang 366	399	招商 450 / Zhao Shang 450
370	招商 104 / Zhao Shang 104	385	招商 384 / Zhao Shang 384	400	招商 436 / Zhao Shang 436
371	招商 105 / Zhao Shang 105	386	招商 385 / Zhao Shang 385	401	招商 437 / Zhao Shang 437
372	招商 107 / Zhao Shang 107	387	招商 393 / Zhao Shang 393	402	招商 22 / Zhao Shang 22
373	招商 110 / Zhao Shang 110	388	招商 396 / Zhao Shang 396	403	招商 34 / Zhao Shang 34
374	招商 113 / Zhao Shang 113	389	招商 462 / Zhao Shang 462	404	招商 35 / Zhao Shang 35
375	招商 460 / Zhao Shang 460	390	招商 67 / Zhao Shang 67	405	招商 108 / Zhao Shang 108

续表

序号 No.	船名 Name	序号 No.	船名 Name	序号 No.	船名 Name
406	招商 364 Zhao Shang 364	421	招商 50 Zhao Shang 50	436	招商 99 Zhao Shang 99
407	招商 466 Zhao Shang 466	422	招商 53 Zhao Shang 53	437	招商 100 Zhao Shang 100
408	招商 472 Zhao Shang 472	423	招商 55 Zhao Shang 55	438	招商 303 Zhao Shang 303
409	招商 316 Zhao Shang 316	424	招商 56 Zhao Shang 56	439	招商 306 Zhao Shang 306
410	招商 83 Zhao Shang 83	425	招商 57 Zhao Shang 57	440	招商 311 Zhao Shang 311
411	招商 383 Zhao Shang 383	426	招商 60 Zhao Shang 60	441	招商 315 Zhao Shang 315
412	招商 465 Zhao Shang 465	427	招商 91 Zhao Shang 91	442	招商 332 Zhao Shang 332
413	招商 6 Zhao Shang 6	428	招商 92 Zhao Shang 92	443	招商 451 Zhao Shang 451
414	招商 24 Zhao Shang 24	429	招商 93 Zhao Shang 93	444	招商 1 Zhao Shang 1
415	招商 43 Zhao Shang 43	430	招商 95 Zhao Shang 95	445	招商 3 Zhao Shang 3
416	招商 101 Zhao Shang 101	431	招商 96 Zhao Shang 96	446	招商 9 Zhao Shang 9
417	招商 106 Zhao Shang 106	432	招商 82 Zhao Shang 82	447	招商 10 Zhao Shang 10
418	供水 3 号 Gong Shui 3	433	招商 84 Zhao Shang 84	448	招商 14 Zhao Shang 14
419	招商 380 Zhao Shang 380	434	招商 87 Zhao Shang 87	449	招商 16 Zhao Shang 16
420	招商 45 Zhao Shang 45	435	招商 98 Zhao Shang 98	450	招商 17 Zhao Shang 17

续表

序号 No.	船名 Name	序号 No.	船名 Name	序号 No.	船名 Name
451	招商 407 Zhao Shang 407	466	招商 445 Zhao Shang 445	481	飞程 Fei Cheng
452	招商 408 Zhao Shang 408	467	招商 4 Zhao Shang 4	482	飞工 Fei Gong
453	招商 409 Zhao Shang 409	468	招商 94 Zhao Shang 94	483	供水 1 号 Gong Shui 1
454	招商 410 Zhao Shang 410	469	招商 387 Zhao Shang 387	484	起重 1 号 Qi Zhong 1
455	招商 413 Zhao Shang 413	470	招商 391 Zhao Shang 391	485	飞歙 Fei Xi
456	招商 414 Zhao Shang 414	471	招商 471 Zhao Shang 471	486	飞禾 Fei He
457	招商 415 Zhao Shang 415	472	招商 424 Zhao Shang 424	487	交 16 Jiao 16
458	招商 416 Zhao Shang 416	473	招商 426 Zhao Shang 426	488	交 17 Jiao 17
459	招商 422 Zhao Shang 422	474	招商 13 Zhao Shang 13	489	交 18 Jiao 18
460	招商 423 Zhao Shang 423	475	招商 440 Zhao Shang 440	490	飞府 Fei Fu
461	招商 427 Zhao Shang 427	476	招商 7 Zhao Shang 7	491	洪利 Hong Li
462	招商 428 Zhao Shang 428	477	招商 425 Zhao Shang 425	492	旭 Xu
463	招商 429 Zhao Shang 429	478	招商 473 Zhao Shang 473	493	招商 202 Zhao Shang 202
464	招商 443 Zhao Shang 443	479	招商 464 Zhao Shang 464	494	招商 204 Zhao Shang 204
465	招商 444 Zhao Shang 444	480	招商 469 Zhao Shang 469	495	招商 206 Zhao Shang 206

续表

序号 No.	船名 Name	序号 No.	船名 Name	序号 No.	船名 Name
496	招商208 Zhao Shang 208	511	招商261 Zhao Shang 261	526	招商284 Zhao Shang 284
497	招商213 Zhao Shang 213	512	招商262 Zhao Shang 262	527	招商285 Zhao Shang 285
498	招商214 Zhao Shang 214	513	235	528	招商222 Zhao Shang 222
499	招商215 Zhao Shang 215	514	237	529	招商263 Zhao Shang 263
500	招商218 Zhao Shang 218	515	招商242 Zhao Shang 242	530	招商264 Zhao Shang 264
501	招商219 Zhao Shang 219	516	招商243 Zhao Shang 243	531	招商265 Zhao Shang 265
502	招商217 Zhao Shang 217	517	招商247 Zhao Shang 247		
503	招商231 Zhao Shang 231	518	招商248 Zhao Shang 248		
504	招商232 Zhao Shang 232	519	招商256 Zhao Shang 256		
505	招商233 Zhao Shang 233	520	招商257 Zhao Shang 257		
506	招商234 Zhao Shang 234	521	招商258 Zhao Shang 258		
507	招商220 Zhao Shang 220	522	No.1		
508	招商221 Zhao Shang 221	523	No.2		
509	招商259 Zhao Shang 259	524	招商212 Zhao Shang 212		
510	招商260 Zhao Shang 260	525	招商283 Zhao Shang 283		

新中国成立后
After the foundation of the People's Republic of China

序号 No.	船名 Name	序号 No.	船名 Name	序号 No.	船名 Name
1	临江 Lin Jiang	16	华胜 Hua Sheng	31	明华 Ming Hua
2	顺江 Shun Jiang	17	华盈 Hua Ying	32	明谊 Calumet
3	江图 Jiang Tu	18	华琼 Hua Qiong	33	明辉 Pacific Brilliance
4	华阳 Hua Yang	19	华佳 Hua Jia	34	明贝 Conch
5	华富 Hua Fu	20	华川 Hua Chuan	35	明智 Pacific Wisdom
6	华兴 Hua Xing	21	华河 Hua He	36	明锋 Pacific Pioneer
7	华朋 Hua Peng	22	华泉 Hua Quan	37	明富 Pacific Source
8	华顺 Hua Shun	23	华利 Hua Li	38	明珠 Ming Zhu
9	华隆 Hua Long	24	华宝 Hua Bao	39	明锋 Pacific Pioneer
10	华发 Hua Fa	25	兴安岭 Xing An Ling	40	明智 Pacific Wisdom
11	华乐 Hua Le	26	新华龙 Xin Hua Long	41	明勤 Pacific Endeavor
12	华江 Hua Jiang	27	新华门 Xin Hua Men	42	明奋 Pacific Vigorous
13	华昌 Hua Chang	28	高德 Crusader	43	明业 Pacific Career
14	华强 Hua Qiang	29	利德 Leader	44	明神 Pacific Embolden
15	华都 Hua Du	30	明玉 Ming Jade	45	明兴 Pacific Prospect

续表

序号 No.	船名 Name	序号 No.	船名 Name	序号 No.	船名 Name
46	明爱 Pacific Paradise	61	凯恩 Gadia Ayu	76	Energy Growth
47	明繁 Pacific Acadian	62	凯业 New Venture	77	Araguaney
48	明荣 Pacific Dolphin	63	凯福 New Fortune	78	Carolines
49	明昌 Pacific Emerald	64	凯勇 New Valor	79	Marina Cathya
50	明盛 Pacific Mercury	65	凯旋 New Victory	80	Atlantic Concord
51	明达 Pacific Scorpio	66	凯力 New Vitality	81	Atlantic Conquest
52	明发 Pacific Primate	67	凯和 New Amity	82	Creation
53	凯誉 New Renown	68	凯盟 New Alliance	83	Mutank Vision
54	凯达 New Explorer	69	惠砂 Weser Ore	84	飞龙 Fei Long
55	凯荣 New Prosperity	70	泰源 Thai Resource	85	海龙 Ocean Glory
56	凯舟 New Argosy	71	Atlantic Amity	86	安龙 An Long
57	凯仪 New Ace	72	Oriental Bravery	87	泰龙 Tai Long
58	凯珠 New Amber	73	Stellaris	88	祥龙 Xiang Long
59	凯志 New Ambition	74	Sarda	89	新龙 Xin Long
60	凯安 New Assurance	75	Sentis	90	彰龙 Zhang Long

序号 No.	船名 Name	序号 No.	船名 Name	序号 No.	船名 Name
91	豪威 Good Rider	107	凯达 New Accord	123	招商六 Zhao Shang Liu
92	豪胜 Good Success	108	凯兴 New Prospect	124	大鹏昊 Dapeng Sun
93	豪勇 Good Fighter	109	凯成 New Creation	125	大鹏月 Dapeng Moon
94	豪泰 Good Most	110	凯爱 New Paradise	126	大鹏星 Dapeng Star
95	豪畅 Good Fast	111	凯源 New Resource	127	闽榕 Min Rong
96	豪乐 Good Luck	112	凯胜 New Success	128	闽鹭 Min Lu
97	豪达 Good Explorer	113	凯德 New Award	129	华南1 Hua Nan 1
98	豪顺 Good Easy	114	凯丰 New Vanguard	130	华南2 Hua Nan 2
99	豪安 Good Well	115	凯景 New Vista	131	华南3 Hua Nan 3
100	迅隆壹号 Xun Long Yi Hao	116	明源 Pacific Resource	132	申海 Shen Hai
101	迅隆贰号 Xun Lun Er Hao	117	明立 Pacific Creation	133	招商一 Zhao Shang Yi
102	凯鸿 New Century	118	明鸿 Pacific Century	134	台山 Tai Shan
103	凯誉 New Spirit	119	明顺 Pacific Success	135	迅隆3 Xun Long 3
104	凯进 New Advance	120	明誉 Pacific Spirit	136	迅隆4 Xun Long 4
105	凯智 New Ability	121	明景 Pacific Vista	137	迅隆5 Xun Long 5
106	凯敏 New Activity	122	明舟 Pacific Argosy	138	迅隆6 Xun Long 6

编印说明

STATEMENT

创立于1872年的招商局，组建了中国近代第一支商船队，开辟了中国第一条远洋航线，开启了中国航运业的新篇章。

　　船舶是航运业的标志，招商局的船舶承载了招商局的百年历程，见证了中国近现代航运业发展演变的轨迹。为了清晰系统地展现招商局船舶的发展状貌，让社会大众从一个侧面了解招商局140多年的历史变迁以及中国近现代航运史的发展，我们广搜资料，梳理史实，在汇集史料的基础上编印了《招商局船谱》一书。

　　本船谱以招商局档案为主要依据，参考了《交通史·航政编》、《国民政府清查整理招商局委员会报告书》、《国营招商局七十五周年纪念刊》等相关书籍。在编撰形式上，该船谱采用图文互照的例式，以船舶入局时间为主线加以编排，详细考证了720多艘船舶的资料，精选出近300幅珍贵船图，分别从"晚清时期"、"民国时期"、"新中国成立之后"三个时期进行梳理和论述，展现出一部完整的招商局船舶发展谱册。

　　在招商局集团领导的高度重视下，《招商局船谱》由集团办公厅、档案馆、招商轮船等机构分工协作，逐一考证，汇编而成。其中改革开放之后招商局船舶资料，得到招商局旗下的招商轮船、工业集团、迅隆船务、华南液化、漳州海达等单位的大力支持，对此谨表谢忱。

　　由于编者水平和时间有限，编写过程中难免有所疏忽，敬请读者指正。

招商局史研究会
二〇一四年十二月

Established in 1872, China Merchants built the first merchant fleet in modern China and explored the first ocean route of China, turning on a new chapter for China's shipping industry.

As ship is the sign of shipping industry, the ships of China Merchants have witnessed more than one hundred years' history of China Merchants and the evolution of shipping industry in modern China. In order to present the development of China Merchants' ships and the changes of China Merchants in over 140 years' history and the evolution of China's modern shipping industry, we searched and collected materials, clarified historical facts and events, and published *Ships of China Merchants* based on the data.

Ships of China Merchants takes files of China Merchants as major reference and also consults relevant books, such as *Traffic History·Shipping*, *Report on the Clarification of China Merchants by Nationalist Government Commission of the Republic of China* and *Memorial Volume for the 75th Anniversary of State-run China Merchants*, etc. With image and texts coordinating with each other, ships are presented in this book according to the time when the ships were brought into China Merchants. We have carefully verified information about over 720 ships and selected around 300 pictures of the ships in three periods, namely the periods in the Late Qing Dynasty, the Republic of China and the People's Republic of China, showing a full picture of ship development in China Merchants.

With the great attention from the leaders of China Merchants Group, *Ships of China Merchants* is verified and completed by the collaborative efforts of different departments, including the General Office of China Merchants Group, China Merchants Archives and China Merchants Energy Shipping . For the information about the ships bought by China Merchants after the reform and opening-up, we got great support from the following subsidiaries under China Merchants, including China Merchants Energy Shipping, China Merchants Industry Holdings, Xunlong Shipping, Southern China LGP Shipping and Haida Shipping, etc. We would like to express our gratitude to the above-mentioned enterprises for all the help provided.

Criticisms from the readers are welcome.

China Merchants Historical Research Institute

December 2014

图书在版编目(CIP)数据

招商局船谱 / 胡政主编. —北京：
社会科学文献出版社，2015.11
（招商局文库·文献丛刊）
ISBN 978-7-5097-7719-0

Ⅰ.①招… Ⅱ.①胡… Ⅲ.①轮船招商局–船舶–史料–中国
Ⅳ.①F552.9

中国版本图书馆CIP数据核字(2015)第147228号

招商局文库·文献丛刊
招商局船谱

主　　编 / 胡　政

出 版 人 / 谢寿光
项目统筹 / 宋荣欣
责任编辑 / 黄　丹　宋　超

出　　版 / 社会科学文献出版社·近代史编辑室(010)59367256
　　　　　 地址：北京市北三环中路甲29号院华龙大厦　邮编：100029
　　　　　 网址：www.ssap.com.cn
发　　行 / 市场营销中心 (010) 59367081　59367090
　　　　　 读者服务中心 (010) 59367028
印　　装 / 北京盛通印刷股份有限公司
规　　格 / 开　本：889mm×1194mm 1/16
　　　　　 印　张：19.5　字　数：240千字
版　　次 / 2015年11月第1版　2015年11月第1次印刷
书　　号 / ISBN 978-7-5097-7719-0
定　　价 / 298.00元

本书如有破损、缺页、装订错误，请与本社读者服务中心联系更换

▲ 版权所有　翻印必究